CH00407607

Yale Language Series

MARYSIA JOHNSON

Arizona State University

Department of English

Linguistics/TESL Program

A Philosophy of
Second Language Acquisition

Yale University Press

New Haven &

London

Copyright © 2004 by Yale University. All rights reserved. This book may not be reproduced, in whole or in part, including illustrations, in any form (beyond that copying permitted by Sections 107 and 108 of the U.S. Copyright Law and except by reviewers for the public press), without written permission from the publishers.

Publisher: Mary Jane Peluso
Editorial Assistant: Gretchen Rings
Manuscript Editor: Jane Zanichkowsky
Production Editor: Margaret Otzel
Marketing Manager: Tim Shea
Production Coordinator: Aldo Cupo

Set in Minion type by Keystone Typesetting, Inc.
Printed in the United States of America by Vail Ballou Press, Binghamton, New York.

Library of Congress Cataloging-in-Publication Data
Johnson, Marysia, 1958–
A philosophy of second language acquisition / Marysia Johnson.
    p. cm. — (Yale language series)
Includes bibliographical references and index.
ISBN 0-300-10026-4 (pbk. : alk. paper)
1. Second language acquisition. I. Title. II. Series.
P118.2.J645 2003
418′.001′9—dc21
2003053549

A catalogue record for this book is available from the British Library.

The paper in this book meets the guidelines for permanence and durability of the Committee on Production Guidelines for Book Longevity of the Council on Library Resources.

10   9   8   7   6   5   4   3   2   1

To my mother

Contents

Acknowledgments

I would like to thank my publisher, Mary Jane Peluso, for her support and guidance. I shall forever remain grateful for her generous spirit and wisdom.

I am deeply grateful to Fred Davidson and Jean Turner for their invaluable suggestions and comments on my manuscript and for their continuing support, encouragement, and friendship—for their dialogic inspiration.

Finally, I thank the anonymous reviewers of my book proposal and final manuscript for their comments and suggestions.

Introduction

The purpose of this book is twofold: First, it is to introduce the reader to Lev Vygotsky's sociocultural theory (SCT) and Mikhail Bakhtin's literary theory. These theories constitute the foundation for an *alternative* framework for theory, research, teaching, and testing in second language acquisition (SLA). Second, it is to discuss the existing cognitive bias in SLA theory and research.

In my opinion, the combined theories of Vygotsky and Bakhtin offer a powerful framework for the ever-expanding field of SLA. The power of this new framework lies in its capacity to unite divergent views of SLA that often present a source of frustration for students whose goal is to become teachers of English as a second language (ESL).

The abstractness and conflicting explanations of many important topics in SLA contribute to a sense of separation between those who "do" theorizing and those who "do" practicing. In addition, the largely quantitative nature of SLA research studies reinforces this sense of separateness between theoreticians and practitioners by sending a false signal that unless one's research study includes some sort of experiment and inferential statistics, one's contribution to understanding second language acquisition processes is insignificant and marginal, almost anecdotal. Therefore, most teachers view their positions as powerless, entirely controlled by theoreticians and researchers whose abstract models they often consider impractical and whose ideas they reluctantly follow.

In order to change these dynamics between researchers and practitioners, a major theoretical shift needs to take place in SLA theory. Some have already called for the empowerment of teachers (van Lier 1996; Clarke 1994), but these calls are mainly theoretical. Although we all may agree that teachers' empowerment is important and long overdue, there is a major gap between admitting it and actually implementing it in a real-life context.

I contend that the separation that currently exists between those involved in SLA theory-building and those who conduct classroom teaching and testing is due to the theoretical models to which most SLA researchers adhere: the cognitive and experimental scientific traditions, which SLA adopted from the other so-called hard sciences such as biology, chemistry, and above all cognitive psychology. As shown in Part One, the discussions and explanations of most important topics in SLA are heavily skewed in the direction of the cognitive scientific research tradition.

Closely associated with this prevailing tradition is the notion of a strict unidirectional flow of information (that is, knowledge) from theory to practice: First, new information is developed by theoreticians, and then some of this theoretical knowledge finds its way to practical settings, classrooms, or evaluation. In this paradigm, teachers are largely regarded as passive recipients of SLA research findings. Because of the nature of the theoretical models on which most of the SLA theory and research are based, teachers' feedback or collaboration is regarded as unnecessary or irrelevant.

One purpose of this book is to document the origin and evolution of this compartmentalization of the current way of developing and implementing SLA knowledge, which may be illustrated as shown in figure I.1. The dotted line in the first arrow indicates that not all of the acquired knowledge is passed along in a linear fashion from box 1 to box 2 and then to box 3. The figure shows that there is a hierarchy of power and control of knowledge in SLA and that within this hierarchical system each component is viewed as being independent of the others. There are rules and regulations that distinguish each component in this organization: the bigger the box, the greater the power and influence it represents with respect to the other components of the system.

In order to change this fixed order of interaction and codependency, a major shift in SLA is needed. I would like to propose a new model of interaction in which all participants have equal status, privileges, and rights. Figure I.2 represents this new dynamic.

If we are to achieve this interrelated and collaborative dynamic of develop-

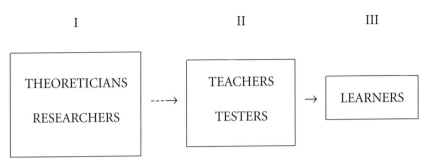

Figure I.1. The Current Model of Knowledge Transfer in SLA

ing and implementing SLA knowledge, there needs to be active involvement on the part of teachers, students, researchers, and theoreticians. Such a new collaborative system may only be achieved when the voices of teachers and students acquire the same status and prestige as the voices of researchers and theoreticians. This equality of voices, however, cannot be achieved within the existing cognitive and information-processing models of SLA. Without a new theoretical framework that empowers all the parties involved, all our discussions about teachers' and students' greater involvement in the process of SLA knowledge-building are futile because they would have to meet with the approval of the most powerful party in the system (see fig. I.1)—theoreticians and researchers.

Simply stated, my belief is that without a major theoretical shift, without a new, dramatically different model, there is no possibility of changing the relation between SLA theory and practice. I believe that this new framework, which is based on Vygotsky's sociocultural theory and Bakhtin's dialogized heteroglossia, will allow us to move from the era of "inequality" and "monarchy" to the new era of democracy and equal representation.

It is also my belief that this major shift in our understanding of how SLA research should be conducted will produce exciting and fruitful results. It will move our field in a new direction paved with countless possibilities and new challenges, which are, however, indispensable for the growth not only of the individual but also of the field as a whole.

The second purpose of the book is to bring to the forefront the shortcomings of current SLA models and theories, which adhere mainly to the cognitive and information-processing paradigms. These models are also predominately focused on linguistically based meaning-making, in which *social* aspects of meaning-making are disregarded.

Most of our current models of SLA are linear in nature; they go from input to intake to the developing system to output. They tend to subscribe to

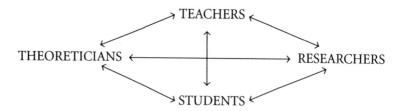

Fig. I.2. A New Model of SLA Knowledge-Building

Michael Reddy's (1979) conduit metaphor of knowledge transfer: the speaker encodes the message; the hearer decodes the sent message. In these models interaction is viewed mainly as the interaction among different language competencies that takes place in the individual's mind. These models also promote a false belief in the existence of a unidimensional reality governed by universal principles and rules. They promote a false sense of confidence and security among second-language (L2) learners, who are led to believe that once they acquire these universal rules, they will be able to fully and harmoniously function in the homogeneous reality of the target language.

Despite some researchers' efforts to acknowledge its importance, social context in existing SLA models is treated superficially and abstractly; it is accounted for by adding another box, another language competence, to the knowledge-based model.

Our current models of SLA make a clear distinction between linguistic competence (that is, knowledge of language) and linguistic performance (that is, the use of language competence in real-life contexts). They establish a strict line of demarcation between learners' mental and social processes. They focus on the investigation and explanation of universal mental processes of second language competence. Linguistic performance is relegated to the peripheries of inquiry.

I propose a new approach in which second language acquisition is viewed not in terms of competence but in terms of performance. The origin of SLA is located not in the human mind but in locally bound dialogical interactions conducted in a variety of sociocultural and institutional settings. This approach also focuses our attention on the investigation of dynamic and dialectical relationships between the interpersonal (social) plane and the intrapersonal (individual) plane. It examines dialectic transformations of one plane into another. The model advocates a shift in emphasis away from a preoccupation with language competence and toward the dialectical interaction between language competence and performance.

Although this approach is primarily based on Vygotsky's sociocultural theory and Bakhtin's dialogized heteroglossia, it also acknowledges the voices of other scholars such as Ragnar Rommetveit (1968, 1974, 1987, 1992), James Gibson (1979), Jürgen Habermas (1987), Ludwig Wittgenstein (1958, 1980), Jerome Bruner (1990, 1996), Leo van Lier (1996), Rom Harré and Grant Gillett (1994), and Pierre Bourdieu (1991), to name a few. These scholars express similar views regarding the role of society, culture, and institutions in the development of human cognition; they all subscribe to a dialogical and sociocultural view of human thought, language, and communication. The ideas of scholars working in many different scientific fields are closely related because they can be traced back to the work of the two great Russian scholars of the twentieth century: Lev Vygotsky (1896–1934) and Mikhail Bakhtin (1895–1975).

In sum, the book calls for embracing a new framework that is social and dialogical—a framework embedded in multidimensional, sociocultural, and institutional contexts. In order for this hyperdimensional social reality to work, many voices need to be acquired and accepted. These various voices are not universally but locally bounded. In this approach, the primary goal of SLA should be the investigation and explanation of the processes that lead to the acquisition of many local voices that reflect not imaginary and previously defined social contexts but real and local sociocultural contexts—social contexts that create speech and speech that creates social contexts. Such an approach to SLA theory, research, and practice is dialogically, not monologically, based (Rommetveit 1992).

The book is divided into two parts. Although several major current SLA theories and models are described and discussed in Part One, "Following the Cognitive Tradition," the purpose of this part of the book is not to introduce the reader to the fundamental principles of existing theories and models. There are many books whose main purpose is to achieve precisely this goal (for example, Gass and Selinker 2001; Cook 1993, 2001; Ellis 1985, 1990, 1994; Brown 2000; Larsen-Freeman and Long 1993; Sharwood Smith 1994). The main purpose of Part One is to illustrate the strong cognitive and experimental bias of current SLA models and theories and to advocate the application of a new framework that would remedy this bias.

Part One consists of five chapters. Chapter 1 provides an overview of three major scientific research traditions: behaviorism, cognitive-computational, and dialogical. Chapter 2 provides a historical overview of SLA as a scientific field. The purpose of this overview is to explain the origin of our field and to illustrate the general trend of its adherence to the rules and norms established in other scientific fields. That is, after behaviorism, SLA turned to cognitive psychology for guidance. The mentalist approach to SLA is illustrated by the application of Noam Chomsky's theories to SLA. The cognitive and linguistic origin of SLA theory and research is presented and discussed in Chapter 3. Chapter 4 discusses the impact of the information-processing paradigm on SLA theory and research. In Chapter 5 several communicative competence models are presented and discussed. The purpose of this chapter is to emphasize the cognitive view of interaction promoted in these models, in which the learner is solely responsible for his or her performance.

Although the notions of interaction and social context are introduced in these models, social contexts are described in terms of stable features defined a priori. The possibility that context can create language and that language can create context is not considered in these models. Social context is viewed abstractly—as a discrete component that can be identified, described, and measured prior to a speech event that may or may not take place in a social context. Interactional competence (Young 1999; He and Young 1998; Hall 1993, 1995) is also described and discussed in this chapter. Characteristics of interactional competence that stand in drastic contrast to communicative competence, such as locality of one's language competence and coconstruction (Jacoby and Ochs 1995), are addressed in this chapter as well. As with communicative competence, however, interactional competence focuses on the individual's competence rather than performance (that is, the use of language in a real-life context), which according to Vygotsky's theory represents an obligatory condition for human cognitive development. In my opinion, the theory of interactional competence can be easily subsumed within SCT, which offers a more powerful and overarching framework for SLA theory and practice than does interactional competence.

In order to introduce the reader to the new dialogical approach, I need to present a thorough introduction to Vygotsky's and Bakhtin's ideas. Part Two, "A Dialogical Approach to SLA," begins with such an introduction. Chapters 6 and 7 provide a comprehensive overview of Vygotsky's and Bakhtin's theories, respectively. Chapter 8 describes and discusses some of the major studies that examine the application of SCT to second language learning. In Chapter 9, I propose a new approach to SLA—a dialogically based approach—and I discuss some theoretical and practical implications of such an approach. The aim of this chapter is to provide theoretical and practical guidelines for developing, conducting, examining, and implementing research studies as well as teaching and testing practices within this new unified framework and to encourage and promote the implementation of the new relations among researchers, teachers, and students (see fig. I.2).

Because of the interdisciplinary nature of the topics and ideas presented, the book may be used as a textbook for second language acquisition courses as well as language teaching methods and testing courses.

PART I

Following the Cognitive Tradition

1

Three Major Scientific Research Traditions

In this chapter I describe three major scientific research traditions that greatly influenced theories and methods of SLA. For detailed discussions of these different traditions of scientific knowledge, the reader is encouraged to refer to the work of Rom Harré and Grant Gillett (1994), Ragnar Rommetveit (1968, 1974, 1987, 1992), Jerome Bruner (1996), Numa Markee (1994), Robert Ochsner (1979), Diane Larsen-Freeman and Michael Long (1993), and Kurt Danziger (1990).

From a historical point of view, these three scientific traditions can be ordered as follows:

1. Behaviorist
2. Cognitive-Computational
3. Dialogical

The last tradition has also been associated with the following names: discursive (Harré and Gillett 1994), hermeneutic (Young 1999; Markee 1994; Ochsner 1979), hermeneutic-dialectical (Rommetveit 1987), dialogically based social-cognitive (Rommetveit 1992), and cultural (Bruner 1996).

Although the three schools of thought are well established in other scientific fields, especially in psychology, the field of SLA, as we will see, strongly adheres to the second tradition—the cognitive. The third tradition, the dialogical, is rather unknown to the mainstream SLA community and is regarded as "unscientific" by SLA researchers. This book tries to remedy this situation by making a case for giving this third tradition a chance. It provides a thorough overview of the theories that laid the foundation for the third approach, so that the reader can appreciate the originality, flexibility, and appropriateness of the dialogic approach for SLA theory and practice.

Behaviorism

The first tradition, behaviorism, dominated the field of SLA until the end of the 1960s and found its most visible application in contrastive analysis and the audiolingual method (see Chapter 3 for details). In this tradition, the focus was on the learner's external environment. It was believed then that this external environment served as a stimulus for the processes of learning. Learning was regarded as a *habit formation,* the process of making a link between stimuli and responses. This link, viewed as being instrumental for learning, had to be reinforced, observed, corrected, and practiced. In the behavioristic tradition, the learner's mental processes were disregarded because they were not accessible to external observation. That is, they were viewed as too subjective, too "hidden," for observation, measurement, and verification. Under this old and by now disregarded paradigm, the mental processes that could not be externally evaluated were exempt from scientific investigations. The possibility of their existence was minimalized.

In the era of behaviorism, the subject's behavior was manipulated in order to elicit responses that were later interpreted by researchers according to their research questions and methods. Statistical relations were established between stimuli and responses. Stimuli were treated as independent variables selected, manipulated, and controlled by the researcher, and responses were treated as dependent variables.

Subjects were treated like objects in a laboratory experiment in which the researcher elicited and interpreted subjects' behaviors according to his or her own ideas and hypotheses. This was to be done within well-established scientific guidelines based on statistical logic and probability. Subjects' thought and feelings, their own interpretation of the behavior elicited during the experiment, were totally ignored because, as indicated above, they would be regarded as subjective and thus unscientific and unreliable. These types of data were mistrusted by researchers and considered irrelevant.

Although behaviorism has fallen into oblivion, its experimental method have survived. Both the behaviorist and the cognitive schools of thought are strongly embedded in the positivist (that is, empiricist) philosophy of sci ence, which favors quantitative methods. In order to fulfill the requirements of quantitative research methods, subjects in research studies, like objects in the hard sciences, are considered to represent "objects" under the control of researchers. Their behavior can be manipulated, controlled, and measured in such a way that it satisfies the requirements of the research question determined in advance by the researcher. In other words, subjects' behavior can be manipulated by the researcher's intention, by the nature of the tasks that subjects are asked to perform in an experiment. The individuality of subjects' intentions is disregarded. Subjects whose performance falls outside the established norms, whose behavior does not fit the group's behavior, are eliminated from the study. Their contribution to our understanding of how human cognition develops is marginalized.

The Cognitive-Computational Tradition

The second tradition, the cognitive, may be divided into two categories or versions: the older—hypothetico-deductive (Harré and Gillett 1994; Markee 1994)—and the new—information processing–computational (Harré and Gillett 1994; Bruner 1996). This tradition is strongly embedded in Cartesian philosophy, whose fundamental principle is summarized in its famous motto: "Cogito, ergo sum" (I think; therefore, I exist). According to René Descartes, the seventeenth-century scientist and philosopher, there is a separation between mind and body—a duality (Harré and Gillett 1994). That is, there exist two realities, two worlds: the material world (that is, the human body), accessible to human observation, and the mental world (that is, the human mind), which includes thoughts, emotions, and mental processes. This mental world is not accessible to external examination. The human body is responsible for outward behavior, and the human mind is responsible for inward behavior.

In Cartesian philosophy, the human mind is considered to be superior to the human body; as such it becomes the main focus of scientific investigations. Recall that behaviorism disregarded mental processes because they were not accessible to external examination. In the cognitive tradition this apparent inaccessibility was overcome by the application of the hypothetico-deductive method. As Harré and Gillett (1994) point out, the hypothetico-deductive method allowed researchers to overcome the inaccessibility of mental processes by assuming that a theory consists of "a group of hypotheses, from which, with the addition of some definitions and descriptions of the conditions under which an experimental test or observation was conducted, one drew a sentence expressing possible laws as logical consequences.

Then one tried to see whether the statements one had deduced were correct or incorrect. If one's deduction referred to a future event, it was a prediction; if to an event already known, the hypotheses and so on from which it had been deduced counted as an explanation of the event in question" (Harré and Gillett 1994, 10). An example of this method (also known as the logico-deductive method; Markee 1994) is Michael Long's (1983a) conversational adjustment hypothesis. Long's conclusion that linguistic and conversational adjustments promote second language acquisition is derived by the application of the hypothetico-deductive method and is illustrated in the following three steps:

> Put simply, if it could be shown that the linguistic/conversational *adjustments* promote *comprehension* of input, and also that *comprehensible input* promotes *acquisition*, then it could safely be deduced that the *adjustments* promote *acquisition*. If A signifies adjustments, B comprehension, and C acquisition, then the argument would simply be:
>
> A—B
> B—C
> A—C
>
> where "—" indicates a causal relationship.   (Long 1983a, 189)

Another illustration of the application of the hypothetico-deductive method to SLA is Noam Chomsky's theory of universal grammar (see Chapter 3 for more details), in which the existence and operation of universal principles and language-specific parameters are derived on the basis of this particular method.

Also, in the cognitive tradition, in contrast to the behavioristic, the subject's own interpretations of the elicited behavior and understanding of the investigated mental phenomena are taken into consideration. This is evident in the use of the so-called grammaticality judgment tasks frequently employed by the proponents of Chomsky's linguistic theory, for example. Subjects are asked to use their own intuition regarding the grammaticality or ungrammaticality of the sentences selected by the researcher. Such tasks are also used by SLA researchers working within Chomsky's theory of universal grammar to determine nonnative speakers' access to the language acquisition device (LAD) and to investigate natives' and nonnatives' intuitions about the grammaticality of target language sentences.

The newer version of the cognitive tradition—information processing—focuses on the mechanism responsible for the processing of information or knowledge. In this version, the metaphors of input, output, short-term memory, long-term memory, storage of information, intake, container, and computer are frequently evoked. The main assumption behind this computational branch of the cognitive tradition is the belief that mental processes are rule-governed. This assumption is evident in different versions of the theory of universal grammar such as Chomsky's transformational-generative grammar (Chomsky 1965; Radford 1988), the government and binding theory (Chomsky 1981a; Haegeman 1991), and the minimalist program (Chomsky 1995).

If human mental processes are rule-governed, the rules somehow need to be implemented. In order to run these rules, one needs a mechanism, a machine similar to a computer. Thus, the rule-governed mental processes require a hardware system—the human brain—and a software program—the human mind—where these rules are assimilated, processed, and stored. An example of the application of the computational (information-processing) version of the cognitive tradition to SLA is Bill VanPatten's input processing model (see Chapter 4 for more details).

Some researchers tend to combine the cognitive approach and experimental types of methodologies into one category, which they call the *nomothetic scientific* tradition (Ochsner 1979; Markee 1994), and contrast it with the *hermeneutic* scientific tradition. According to Ochsner (1979), "Nomothetic science (the prefix 'nomo' means lawful): This tradition goes back to Plato. As a research attitude it assumes that there is one ordered, discoverable reality which causally obeys the Laws of Nature. Social scientists in this tradition further assume that Laws of Human Nature exist" (53). *Hermeneutics* literally means "the art of interpretation"; nomothetic science is concerned with explaining and predicting, whereas hermeneutic science is concerned with understanding and interpreting natural phenomena. Quantitative experimental methods based on statistical logic and probability are primarily associated with the nomothetic scientific tradition, whereas qualitative methods are associated with the hermeneutic tradition, which assumes that multiple realities exist and that "human events must be interpreted teleologically; that is, according to their final ends" (Ochsner 1979, 54).

As Markee (1994) points out, SLA research subscribes primarily to the nomothetic tradition: the overwhelming majority of SLA studies are of the logico-deductive variety. They adhere to the following nomothetic principles:

One world:	There is one "lawful" reality.
One order:	To explain this reality we deduce causes from the Laws of Nature, including Laws of Human Nature.
One method:	There is one best research method, the controlled experiment. (Ochsner 1979, 65)

Like the nomothetic scientific tradition, the cognitive tradition advocates the search for generalizability, the power of statistical procedures, the uniformity of human mental processes, the universality of rule-governed mental behaviors, the existence of one reality for all human beings, the collective mind, an idealized human being placed in a homogeneous external reality speaking with one voice, and a giant and complex information processor that runs the program in solitude.

This cognitive tradition, adopted by the mainstream SLA community and dominated by Chomsky's theory of universal grammar, relies heavily on a linguistic notion of meaning that is similar to Frege's sense (Frege 1960; Rommetveit 1974; Chierchia and McConnell-Ginet 1992). Gottlob Frege (1960) argues that in addition to reference *(Bedeutung)*, sense *(Sinn)* is needed to provide a semantic analysis of language, to reveal the meaning of a given sentence. The reference of a sentence is its true value understood in a classic Aristotelian term:

> Every sentence has meaning, not as being the natural means by which a physical faculty is realized, but, as we have said, by convention. Yet every sentence is not a proposition; only such are propositions as have in them either truth or falsity. Thus a prayer is a sentence, but is neither true nor false.
>
> Let us therefore dismiss all other types of sentence but the proposition, for this last concerns our present inquiry, whereas the investigation of the others belongs rather to the study of rhetoric or of poetry.
> (in Edghill 1928, 16b–17a

From the perspective of reference, to know the meaning of a sentence is to be able to distinguish the circumstances in which it is true and in which it is not true. Frege (1960), however, argues that the Sinn (sense) meaning of a sentence is also needed to arrive at its meaning. Sense can be considered as thought, an abstract object, or an idea that is independent of the circumstances. Frege arrived at the need for including sense in a semantic analysis of language that is based on logical arguments, which are illustrated in the following example, discussed in Chierchia and McConnell-Ginet (1992, 57–59):

1. The morning star is the evening star.

From the astronomical perspective the morning star and the evening star are the same planet, Venus. Therefore, they both have the same referent. If reference were all there is to meaning, it would be possible to replace the evening star by its co-referential expression, to equate it with the morning star. This would result in the following sentence:

2. The morning star is the morning star.

We know, however, that sentences 1 and 2 do not carry the same message, although their reference is identical. Using the notion of sense, we can account for the fact that sentence 2 is uninformative because it has the same reference and the same sense. Sentence 1, however, is informative because, although it has the same reference, it does not have the same sense. Note that Frege's notion of sense is derived and accounted for *linguistically* and *logically;* it does not reflect social, historical, cultural, and institutional aspects of meaning-making; it is devoid of social contexts.

To summarize, the cognitive tradition, the most widely accepted scientific tradition in SLA, stresses the importance of mental processes. By the application of the logico-deductive method, which utilizes logical and mathematical reasoning, mental processes were made accessible to human investigation. The cognitive scientific tradition stresses the importance of human internal processes rather than external processes, thus reversing the well-established pattern of behaviorism, which, as you recall, focused on the external reality and disregarded the internal processes. In the cognitive tradition, the external environment is viewed as less important because human beings are born with the innate predisposition to evolve cognitively; we are born with the computer that is responsible for cognitive development. The external world serves as a trigger mechanism (see chapter 3 for more details), as a switch for the computer program to be activated. The individual is solely responsible for his or her cognitive development.

Both behaviorism and cognitivism embrace the Cartesian dualism of the human mind and body; however, whereas the former focuses on the body (the environment of the individual) as the source of cognitive development, the latter focuses on the mind (the individual's internal processes). Also, behaviorists and cognitivists rely on quantitative methods of scientific investigation, but only cognitivists use more subjectively oriented methods such as grammaticality judgment tasks to investigate the operation of mental processes.

The computational (information-processing) version of the cognitive tradition assumes the existence of rule-governed human mental processes, the so-called software program. It tends to look for the universality and homogeneity of human mental behaviors. The information-processing version of the cognitive tradition projects an image of a human being as a giant computer, self-sufficient and alone in the material world. It creates "an image of Man as an essentially asocial, but highly complex information-processing device" (Rommetveit 1992, 19). Such a perspective on human cognitive development, with its total disregard for "communicative social interaction and goal-oriented collective activity" (Rommetveit 1987, 79), has been criticized strongly and rejected by proponents of the third tradition.

The Dialogical Tradition

The dialogical tradition, which I endorse in this book, is based on the works of scholars such as Ludwig Wittgenstein, Jürgen Habermas, Jerome Bruner, Pierre Bourdieu, Ragnar Rommetveit, Rom Harré, Grant Gillett, Leo van Lier, and above all Lev Vygotsky and Mikhail Bakhtin. The works of these scholars have led to the development of a new approach that heals the Cartesian dualism and restores the proper balance between external and internal human realities (that is, between the body and the mind). This approach takes into consideration the dynamic role of social contexts, individuality, intentionality, and the sociocultural, historical, and institutional backgrounds of the individual involved in cognitive growth. This is the framework in which external and internal realities are united by the mediating power of the most elaborated system of signs—language. As Vygotsky points out in his theory of mind, the property of human mental functioning can be discovered by the investigation of the individual's environment and by the observation of mental and linguistic activities to which the individual has been exposed throughout his or her life.

This framework, unlike the cognitive tradition, assumes the existence of multiple realties that are interpreted differently by different individuals. These multiple realities exist because human beings are exposed in the course of their lives to different sociocultural and institutional settings, where they acquire different voices (or speech genres, to use Bakhtin's term). Because of this, intersubjectivity (Rommetveit 1974), coconstruction of the shared realities (Jacoby and Ochs 1995), and dialogized heteroglossia (Bakhtin 1981, 1986) are considered important characteristics of the dialogized approach.

Within this tradition, qualitative research methods are given higher status than statistically driven quantitative methods. Longitudinal case studies, diaries, journals, and personal narratives are considered to provide important insights into the individual's cognitive development. The dialogical approach focuses on *particularities* rather than on our ability to generalize findings to population at large. The investigation of the individual's behavior rather than the normalized and homogenized group's behavior is considered to represent the locus of scientific inquiry. Within this approach, the individual's "skewed" behavior is not marginalized and eliminated but is given special attention. The subjects' diverse voices, intentions, motives, and personal histories are not lost but are acknowledged and brought to the forefront of scientific inquiry.

This tradition stresses the importance of social, cultural, political, historical, and institutional contexts for the development of human cognition; it
highlights the importance for human cognitive development of social interaction in a variety of sociocultural and institutional settings.

As indicated above, the many versions of this tradition have their origin in
Vygotsky's sociocultural theory and Bakhtin's dialogized heteroglossia (see
Chapter 7 for more details). They are especially indebted to Vygotsky's sociocultural theory—the powerful theory of the social origin of the human mind.
Its power lies in the fact that it is not only about "the mind nor just about the
externally specifiable stimulus-response relations. It is about the *dialectic*
between the inter- and the intrapsychological and the transformations of one
into another" (Newman et al. 1989, 60, emphasis added).

Vygotsky's sociocultural theory lays a solid foundation for the third tradition, which gives a new power and voice to the realities and understanding
that the previous two traditions either suppressed or ignored. The dialogical
tradition also provides a unified framework for SLA theory, research, teaching, and testing, and for that reason it should be given serious consideration.

In this chapter I reviewed some major characteristics of the three scientific
traditions in order to set the stage for the discussion of major models and
theories of SLA that, as shown in the next several chapters, closely adhere to
the cognitive tradition. I also laid the groundwork for the development of a
new framework for SLA theory and practice that adheres to the dialogical
tradition—a framework that is based on Vygotsky's and Bakhtin's theories. I
advocate the building of a new model in which *dialectic* relations between
external and internal processes constitute the focal point of SLA theory and
research. This new model does not turn everything upside down, but by
acknowledging the social origin of the human mind, it focuses on the dialectic interaction that converts social processes into unique and creative internal
processes that, in turn, transform social realities.

2

Behaviorism and Second Language Learning

Contrastive Analysis

The origin of SLA as a scientific field is embedded in the behavioristic tradition, which dominated the field from the 1940s to the 1960s. It is also closely associated with contrastive analysis (CA), which had a great impact not only on SLA theory but also on second language classroom teaching.

Contrary to its counterpart in Europe, where CA was viewed as an integral part of a general linguistic theory (Fisiak 1981) and the goal was to understand and explain the nature of natural languages, CA in the United States had strong pedagogical roots. In addition, it adhered to the prevailing scientific tradition of its time—behaviorism.

Behaviorism was regarded as a general theory of learning, and language learning (whether first or second) was considered to adhere to the same principles. It was believed then that learning is advanced by making a stimulus-response connection, by creating new habits by means of reinforcement and practice of the established links between stimuli and responses. Behaviorism undermined the role of mental processes and viewed learning as the ability to inductively discover patterns of rule-governed behavior from the examples provided to the learner by his or her environment.

In accordance with the fundamental principle of behaviorism, first language learning was viewed as the imitation of utterances to which the child had been exposed in his or her environment. Children were believed to acquire their native language by repeating and imitating their caretakers' utterances. This idea of *habit formation* is illustrated in Leonard Bloomfield's (1933) explanation of the child's first language acquisition:

> Exactly how children learn to speak is not known; the process seems to be something like this:
>
> 1. Under various stimuli the child utters and repeats vocal sounds. This seems to be an inherited trait. Suppose he makes a noise which we may represent as *da*, although, of course, the actual movements and the resultant sounds differ from any that are used in conventional English speech. The sound-vibrations strike the child's ear-drums while he keeps repeating the movements. This results in a habit: whenever a similar sound strikes his ear, he is likely to make these same mouth-movements, repeating the sound *da*. This babbling trains him to reproduce vocal sounds which strike his ear.
>
> 2. Some person, say, the mother, utters in the child's presence a sound which resembles one of the child's babbling syllables. For instance, she says *doll*. When these sounds strike the child's ear, his habit (1) comes into play and he utters his nearest babbling syllable, *da*. We say that he is beginning to "imitate." Grown-ups seem to have observed this everywhere, for every language seems to contain certain nursery-words which resemble a child's babbling—words like *mama, dada*: doubtless these got their vogue because children easily learn to repeat them.
>
> 3. The mother, of course, uses her words when the appropriate stimulus is present. She says *doll* when she is actually showing or giving the infant his doll. The sight and handling of the doll and the hearing and saying of the word *doll* (that is, *da*) occur repeatedly together, until the child forms a new habit: the sight and feel of the doll suffice to make his say *da*. He has now the use of a word. To the adults it may not sound like any of their words, but this is due merely to its imperfection. It is not likely that children ever invent a word.
>
> 4. The habit of saying *da* at sight of the doll gives rise to further habits. Suppose, for instance, that day after day the child is given his doll (and says *da, da, da*) immediately after his bath. He has now a habit of saying *da, da* after his bath; that is, if one day the mother forgets to give him the doll, he may nevertheless cry *da, da* after his bath. "He is asking for his doll," says the mother, and she is right, since doubtless an adult's

"asking for" or "wanting" things is only a more complicated type of the same situation. The child has now embarked upon *abstract* or *displaced* speech: he names a thing even when that thing is not present.

5. The child's speech is perfected by its results. If he says *da, da* well enough, his elders understand him; that is, they give him his doll. When this happens, the sight and feel of the doll act as an additional stimulus, and the child repeats and practices his successful version of the word. On the other hand, if he says his *da, da* imperfectly—that is, at great variance from the adults' conventional form *doll*—then his elders are not stimulated to give him the doll. Instead of getting the added stimulus of seeing and handling the doll, the child is now subject to other distracting stimuli, or perhaps, in the unaccustomed situation of having no doll after his bath, he goes into a tantrum which disorders his recent impressions. In short, his more perfect attempts at speech are likely to be fortified by repetition, and his failures to be wiped out in confusion. This process never stops. At a much later stage, if he says *Daddy bringed it,* he merely gets a disappointing answer such as *No! You must say "Daddy brought it"*; but if he says *Daddy brought it,* he is likely to hear the form over again: *Yes, Daddy brought it,* and to get a favorable practical response.   (Bloomfield 1933, 29–31)

Note that Bloomfield was considered the most prominent representative of American structuralism. Thus, the two theories provided theoretical foundations for CA: a general theory of learning—behaviorism—and a theory of language—structural linguistics.

Structural linguistics assumed that oral language (speech) was more important than written language. Oral data were to be transcribed and analyzed according to a well-established system for determining structurally related elements that encode meaning. These elements, or structural units, which represent a given linguistic level, were connected; one literally built on the other. Thus, the phonetic level of a language led to the phonological level which, in turn, led to the morphological level, which led to the syntactic level. These interrelated linguistic levels were viewed as systems within systems.

Within this structural model of language organization, learning a language was viewed as the mastery of the structural units such as phones, phonemes, morphemes, phrases, clauses, and sentences and the rules for combining these elements. The building blocks of a language were pyramidally organized. That is, each minimal unit representing a different linguistic level subsumed the previous one, moving from the lower-level system to the higher-level system. A representation of this can be seen in figure 2.1.

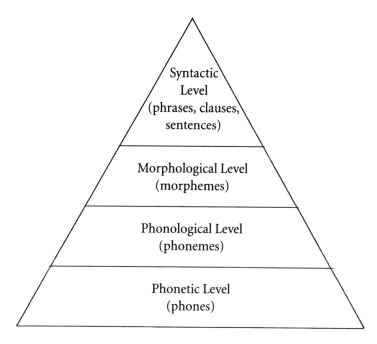

Fig. 2.1. A Structural View of Language Organization

Note that according to this model of the structural organization of natural languages, it was possible to conduct a thorough investigation of the structural characteristics of each linguistic level independent of other levels. For example, the syntactic level could be analyzed by itself. The structural organization of a language was determined on the basis of its surface structure, observable and verifiable by external examination. This surface structure does not have anything to do with deep-level structure, the mental representation of linguistic structures proposed by Chomsky (1959, 1965) in his linguistic theory of universal grammar, which eventually undermined both behaviorism and structural linguistics.

Because structural linguistics began the process of describing and analyzing a language at the lower levels (the phonetic level and the phonological level) and then moved to the higher-level systems, second language teaching followed the same method. That is, second language teaching began at the phonetic level. Once the building blocks of this level were mastered, then the student advanced to the next structural level.

In accordance with the fundamental principle of the behavioristic paradigm, second language learning was also viewed as the process of habit formation. The difficulty in learning a new habit was associated with interference from the old habit—the learner's first language. Charles Fries, in his foreword to Robert Lado's *Linguistics Across Cultures*, writes: "Learning a second language, therefore, constitutes a very different task from learning the first language. The basic problems arise not out of any essential difficulty in the features of the new language themselves but primarily out of the special 'set' created by the first language habits. Robert Lado was the first to grasp the significance of these basic facts for the building of efficient valid measures of achievement and progress in mastering a foreign language" (Lado 1957). Thus, the learner has a tendency to transfer his or her old habits to a new task—the task of learning a second language. Lado writes: "Individuals tend to transfer the forms and meanings, and the distribution of forms and meanings, of their native language and culture to the foreign language and culture—both productively when attempting to speak the language and to act in the culture, and receptively when attempting to grasp and understand the language and the culture as practiced by natives" (1957, 2). Although in a majority of cases the transfer of old habits will interfere with learning a second language, CA acknowledges that in some instances language transfer may be facilitative. When both languages, first and second, possess the same structures, language transfer will be positive, and the process of learning a second language will be facilitated and accelerated. On the other hand, the transfer of old habits will be negative when both languages do not possess the same grammatical structures. In such cases, the transfer of old habits will interfere with learning a second language. Since the goal of CA was to assist teachers in developing the most effective pedagogical materials, CA recommended that teaching materials be based on a careful examination of both languages. Fries (1945, 9) writes: "The most efficient materials are those that are based upon a scientific description of the language to be learned, carefully compared with a parallel description of the native language of the learner."

The contrastive analysis hypothesis (CAH) existed in two versions: strong version, also known as the a priori version, and a weak version, also known as the a posteriori version. The essence of the strong version of the CAH is captured in the following quotation from Lado's preface to *Linguistics Across Cultures*: "We can predict and describe the patterns that will cause difficulty in learning, and those that will not cause difficulty, by comparing systematically the language and culture to be learned with the native language and culture of the student. In our view, the preparation of up-to-date pedagogical and experimental materials must be based on this kind of comparison" (Lado 1957, vii). Thus, according to the strong version, it is possible to predict a priori (that is, in advance) all of the areas of difficulty in learning a second language. The grammatical structures that do not exist in the a quired second language but exist in the learner's first language will cause difficulty in learning. Thus, teaching materials should be based on a thorough scientific description of the learner's first language, which, in turn, should be carefully compared to the language to be acquired. This comparison should follow the well-established methodology of structural linguistics. For example, the morphological system of the target language should be compared with the morphological system of the learner's native language. Any target language structure that differs from the learner's native language should be given special attention in the preparation of pedagogical materials.

In sum, the proponents of the strong version claimed that, based on a careful examination of two languages, it would be possible to *predict* all difficulties in learning the second, and by doing so, it would be possible to help the teacher to create pedagogical materials that would alleviate in advance the learner's problems with learning the second language.

The strong version of the CAH was strongly criticized on both theoretical and empirical grounds. Theoretical critiques of the strong version were primarily aimed at the lack of universal grammatical systems, which would allow the teacher to objectively compare languages. Empirical findings contradicted the basic assumption of the strong version: Not all of the predicted areas of difficulty actually could be observed in the learner's performance. Also, some areas that should not have caused any difficulty in second language learning (that is, areas of positive transfer) in reality presented problems for the learner. Thus, the failure of the strong version to successfully predict difficulties in learning a second language contributed to its gradual rejection.

The weak version of the CAH was less "confident" in its power to predict and alleviate problems with learning a second language. Unlike the strong version, it did not begin with the process of comparing languages a priori, but began a posteriori—after the actual problem occurred. That is, based on the actual and recurring difficulties exhibited in the learner's performance, it attempted to account for their occurrence based on a careful analysis of the differences between the learner's native language and the target language.

The weak version of the CAH was treated less harshly by the critics than was the strong version. Ronald Wardhaugh writes: "The weak version requires of the linguist only that he use the best linguistic knowledge available to him in order to account for observed differences in second language learning. It does not require what the strong version requires, the prediction of those difficulties and, conversely, of those learning points which do not create any difficulties at all. The weak version leads to an approach which makes fewer demands on contrastive theory than does the strong version. It starts with the evidence provided by linguistic interference and uses such evidence to explain the similarities and differences between systems" (Wardhaugh 1970, 10).

The key points in the statement are "observed difficulties" and "linguistic interferences." Wardhaugh believes that the occurrence of observed difficulties in the learner's performance should initiate a contrastive investigation of the learner's two language systems. That is, if the learner's observed difficulties pertain to the phonology of the second language, the phonological systems of both languages ought to be compared and contrasted. Wardhaugh seems to have accepted the main premise of the weak version: its ability to predict the areas of difficulty in learning a posteriori. He considered the weak version of the CAH useful and appropriate for second language teaching.

Regardless of version, "area of difficulties" in CA theory was synonymous with "learner's errors." Errors were regarded as "sins" (Brooks 1964) and were to be avoided at all cost. The goal of CA was to develop teaching material that would prevent the learner from acquiring wrong habits—making errors.

In CA, errors were viewed as interference, or negative transfer of the learner's first language habits to the target language habits. Since language learning was viewed as a set of automatic habit formations, the learner errors provided evidence for the learner's bad habit formations. Also, since mental processes were totally disregarded in the behavioristic tradition, the occurrence of errors was to be examined and explained within the context of the learner's environment. That is, the failure of the learner to acquire new habits was perceived either as the learner's inability to imitate the language patterns presented to him or her by the teacher (the environment) or as the teacher's inability to provide appropriate assistance to the learner in the form of a right comparison between two language systems.

Error Analysis

Attitudes toward the learner's errors and their role in second language learning underwent major revisions in the approach that immediately followed CA: error analysis (EA). Error analysis exhibited some methodological similarities to the weak version of the CAH. In contrast to the weak version however, in EA the explanations for the learner's errors were sought not the learner's native language but in the target language. The methodological differences between the weak version of the CAH and EA are illustrated box 2.1.

Despite some apparent methodological similarities between the weak version of the CAH and EA, primarily because of their reliance on the observed

The weak version of the CAH
The observed learner's *errors* in the target language were compared with the learner's native language:

TL → NL

Error Analysis
The observed learner's *errors* in the target language structures were compared with the target language:

TL → TL

Box 2.1. A Methodological Difference Between the Weak Version of the CAH and EA

learner's errors, there is a major theoretical difference between them. This difference pertains to their treatments of the learner's errors. In EA, the learner's errors were not regarded as "sins" that needed to be avoided at all cost; errors gained a new status and significance.

In his seminal paper "The Significance of Learners' Errors," Stephen Corder defended the learner's errors, which he considered indispensable for second language learning. He also made a distinction between mistakes and errors:

> We are all aware that in normal adult speech in our native language we are continually committing errors of one sort or another. These . . . are due to memory lapses, physical states such as tiredness and psychological conditions such as strong emotion. These are adventitious artefacts of linguistic performance and do not reflect a defect in our knowledge of our own language. We are normally immediately aware of them when they occur and can correct them with more or less complete assurance. It would be quite unreasonable to expect the learner of a second language not to exhibit such slips of the tongue (or pen), since he is subject to similar external and internal conditions when performing in his first or second language. We must therefore make a distinction between those errors that are the product of such chance circumstances and those which reveal his underlying knowledge of the language to date, or, as we may call it, his *transitional competence*. The errors of performance will characteristically be unsystematic and the errors of competence, systematic. . . . It will be useful therefore

hereafter to refer to errors of performance as *mistakes,* reserving the term *error* to the systematic errors of the learner from which we are able to reconstruct his knowledge of the language to date, i.e., his *transitional competence.*   (Corder 1967, 166–67)

Thus, according to Corder, the focus of a scientific investigation should be on the learner's errors, not mistakes. He states, however, that from the learner's perspective, errors may not be perceived as such because they represent an integral part of the learner's "knowledge of the language to date." They are only errors from the native speaker's perspective. They are errors only if they are compared to the well-established norms of the target language system, which is yet not fully acquired or recognized by the second language learner.

Errors are not recognizable to the learner as errors because they are part of his or her current state of knowledge of the target language, or transitional competence, which represents an autonomous system of grammar with its own rules and regulations. Corder's transitional competence represents one of the first attempts to define the domain of SLA: the investigation of the processes of transitional competence. Although not well accepted, Corder's concept seems to have much in common with a similar construct, which Selinker (1972) called interlanguage, the term that has been widely used in the field of SLA.

According to Corder, the learner's errors are significant for three reasons. First, they provide important information to the teacher as to "how far towards the goal the learner has progressed and, consequently, what remains for him to learn" (1967, 167). Second, they provide to the researcher evidence of "how language is learned or acquired, what strategies or procedures the learner is employing in his discovery of the language" (ibid.). The learner's errors reveal some valuable insights as to the nature of an innate universal mechanism, which he calls the *built-in-syllabus,* that aids the learner in his or her second language learning. Third, they are important to the learner because they are used for "testing his hypotheses about the nature of the language he is learning" (ibid.).

Corder considers second language learning to be similar to first language acquisition, assuming that the learner is motivated: "Let us say therefore that *given motivation,* it is inevitable that a human being will learn a second language if he is exposed to the language data" (Corder 1967, 164, emphasis in original). For Corder, the learner's errors are similar to the child's native language errors. They represent the learner's attempts to test his or her hypotheses about the language being learned. The learner's errors should not be viewed as evidence of bad habit formations; they are not the result of language transfer (linguistic interference). He claims that "errors are not to be regarded as signs of inhibition, but simply as evidence of his strategies of learning" (168). Corder strongly defends the learner's right to test these hypotheses and advocates a shift in our attention "away from a preoccupation with *teaching* towards a study of *learning*" (163, emphasis in original), that is, away from the investigation of the learner's external environment to investigation of the learner's internal mental processes. He posits that until we learn more about how the learner's built-in-syllabus functions, we should refrain from imposing our preconceived notions regarding language learning on language teaching. Learners' errors should not be suppressed but should be carefully examined since they are the source of invaluable information about the nature of the learner's built-in-syllabus.

Corder's seminal paper provided a major theoretical setback for CA. His criticism of CA was reinforced by the findings obtained from a number of empirical studies that came to be collectively known as the morpheme order studies.

An Overview of the Morpheme Order Studies

The findings of the morpheme order studies contributed to the final rejection of CA's claim that language transfer is the main cause of errors in second language learning. In addition, the studies were conducted in order to empirically validate the claim that second language learning is similar to first language learning and is guided by universal, innate mechanisms. This hypothesis came to be known as the L1=L2 hypothesis. Corder, one of its proponents, writes: "I propose therefore as a working hypothesis that some at least of the *strategies* adopted by the learner of a second language are substantially the same as those by which a first language is acquired" (Corder 1967, 164–65). If such an innate mechanism exists, the grammatical features of the second language will be acquired in a predictable and invariant order, regardless of the learner's native language background.

In 1974, Heidi Dulay and Marina Burt replicated Roger Brown's longitudinal study (1973) of three children acquiring their first language. Dulay and Burt's (1974) study was not longitudinal, however, but cross-sectional. They replicated Brown's study based on the assumption that similar patterns of language development would be observed in children acquiring the L2. Dulay and Burt were guided by the hypothesis that the same innate mechanism operates in the L1 and the L2 (the L1=L2 hypothesis).

Their findings were based on the analysis of the data obtained from sixty

Spanish and fifty-five Chinese children, who were asked to provide responses to the questions posed by the researchers regarding selected pictures. These questions were aimed at eliciting the English grammatical morphemes in obligatory contexts such as the third person singular (*s*), past tense (*ed*), possessive (*'s*), and plural (*s*). In Dulay and Burt's study, L2 acquisition was operationalized as the accuracy order. That is, the thrust of their argument was that the more accurately a given morpheme was used, the earlier it was acquired.

The analysis of the elicited data with the Bilingual Syntax Measure (BSM) instrument revealed that despite their different linguistic backgrounds, Spanish and Chinese children showed a similar pattern in the acquisition of the English morpheme system; they underwent a similar pattern of development. Most of the errors produced by L2 children of different linguistic backgrounds were not due to L1 interference; instead, they represented developmental types of errors. The order of acquisition of the English morphemes by Spanish and Chinese children was similar. Since this was true irrespective of children's native language backgrounds, it was concluded that there must be an innate mechanism that aids the learner in L2 acquisition. Dulay and Burt called the process of second language learning guided by this innate mechanism *creative construction*, which they defined as "the process in which children gradually reconstruct rules for speech they hear, guided by universal innate mechanisms which cause them to formulate certain types of hypotheses about the language system being acquired, until the mismatch between what they are exposed to and what they produce is resolved" (Dulay and Burt 1974, 37). Creative construction rejected the behavioristic notion of learning as a set of automatic habit formations in which external rather than internal processes provided the bases for examination and explanation of second language learning.

In the same year, Dulay and Burt's study was replicated by Nathalie Bailey, Carolyn Madden, and Stephen Krashen with adult second language learners as subjects. These researchers used the BSM instrument to elicit the data from two groups: one consisting of thirty-three native Spanish speakers, and the other consisting of forty adult subjects of different language backgrounds such as Italian, Chinese, Greek, and Persian. The results of their study were similar to Dulay and Burt's (1974) findings. There were, however, some minor differences in the order of the acquisition of the English morphemes in obligatory contexts. For instance, in Dulay and Burt's study, children acquired English nominative and acquisitive cases prior to the progressive aspect (*ing*), which the adult L2 learners acquired first.

Bailey, Madden, and Krashen's (1974) findings confirmed Dulay and Burt findings regarding the limited role of the learner's native language in second language learning. Only 3 to 5 percent of the learner's errors could be attributed to native language transfer. The majority of the errors produced by children and adults were developmental in nature. The findings of these two studies, combined with other mostly longitudinal investigations of the acquisition of grammatical features such as relative clauses (Schumann 1980; Gass 1980), provided some empirical evidence as to the existence of the so-called natural route of acquisition, through which all L2 learners must go in order to learn a second language. The existence of the natural route of acquisition shifted the focus of attention from the learner's external environment to the learner's internal processes. It prompted interest in mental processes guided by the operation of a universal innate mechanism.

Despite some severe criticisms of the morpheme order studies aimed primarily at their methodologies, such as the validity of the BSM instrument and the equation of the construct of acquisition with the accuracy order, the findings of the morpheme order studies were accepted as the best evidence for the limitations of CA theory. These studies combined with Chomsky's (1959) attack on Skinner's behaviorism and Corder's seminal paper, brought about the fall of the behavioristic approach to second language learning. The behavioristic scientific tradition was replaced by the cognitive tradition. The field of SLA abandoned its preoccupation with the environment of the L2 learner and embraced the opposite extreme—the learner's mental world. The era of the cognitive tradition had begun.

3

The Cognitive Tradition and Second Language Acquisition

Chomsky's Theory of Universal Grammar

After rejecting behaviorism and structuralism, the field of SLA em braced the cognitive tradition. This trend in SLA theory is also linguistically based, owing to its heavy reliance on Noam Chomsky's linguistic theory o first language acquisition. Chomsky (1965, 1980, 1981a, 1981b) made a con vincing argument for the existence of an innate domain-specific languag faculty, which he called the language acquisition device (LAD). The LAI includes universal grammar (UG), which is indispensable for the child' ability to acquire his or her native language. Chomsky does not view languag as speech to be used in real-life communication but as a set of formal proper ties inherent in any natural language grammar.

Chomsky acknowledges that there is more to language than grammatica competence. The native speaker also possesses *pragmatic competence:* "W might say that pragmatic competence places language in the institutiona setting of its use, relating intentions and purposes to the linguistic means a hand" (Chomsky 1980, 225). His theory of first language acquisition based o the operation of UG is, however, exclusively limited to the child's acquisitio of grammatical competence. His theory does not attempt to explain th child's ability to use this grammatical knowledge in real-life situations; tha is, it does not deal with pragmatic competence, primarily because pragmatic competence contains variability and also is more concerned with "knowledge of conditions and manner of appropriate use, in conformity with various purposes" than with "the knowledge of form and meaning" (224), which is the main focus of his scientific inquiry.

For Chomsky, grammatical competence is confined to the domain of syntax, with some references to semantics and phonology. This knowledge of formal properties of grammar is implicit (that is, unconscious, intuitive). For example, the native speaker may be able to correctly determine that the sentence *Is raining?* is ungrammatical without being able to provide an explicit explanation as to why. Chomsky's theory of linguistic competence refers to the native speaker's implicit rather than explicit (conscious) knowledge of the formal properties of L1 grammar.

Note that Chomsky uses the term *pragmatic competence* rather than *communicative competence,* a term that was introduced by Dell Hymes in 1972. Hymes's communicative competence undermines Chomsky's grammatical competence (see Chapter 5 for more details) and has been widely accepted by linguists working within more socially oriented paradigms. Chomsky points out that there are many uses of language that go beyond the popular view of communication. He writes:

> Consider informal conversation conducted for the sole purpose of maintaining casual friendly relations, with no particular concern as to its content. Are these examples of "communication"? If so, what do we mean by "communication" in the absence of an audience, or with an audience assumed to be completely unresponsive, or with no intention to convey information or modify belief or attitude?
>
> It seems that either we must deprive the notion "communication" of all significance, or else we must reject the view that the purpose of language is communication.   (Chomsky 1980, 230)

He considers the separation of linguistic competence (that is, grammatical competence) from pragmatic competence indispensable for our ability to discover the formal properties of the genetically preprogrammed UG, which assists the child in the acquisition of what he calls "a core grammar" (Chomsky 1981b, 38). The following statement explains his justification for such a separation: "The descriptively adequate theory of UG gives an account of those real properties of the language faculty that would, under these idealized conditions, provide a core grammar, and that under the actual conditions of normal life, in interaction with other systems, provide the more complex systems that determine our knowledge of language. To discover the properties of

UG and core grammar we must attempt to abstract away from complicating factors of varied sorts, a course that has its hazards but is inescapable in serious inquiry, in linguistics no less than in other domains" (1981b, 39).

Chomsky and his followers base their claims regarding the existence of UG on observation and deduction that came to be known as the *logical problem of language acquisition* (Chomsky 1965, 1981a, 1981b; Cook 1985, 1988; Ellis 1994), which points to the gap that exists between what the child is able to attain in terms of his or her grammatical competence and the available input. The logical problem of acquisition, combined with the *poverty of the stimulus argument,* which claims that the input to which the child is exposed is "degenerate" and undetermined, serves as the basis for Chomsky's contention regarding the existence of an innate autonomous and domain-specific mental mechanism that aids the child in first language acquisition. Chomsky (1965, 58) states: "It seems plain that language acquisition is based on the child's discovery of what from a formal point of view is a deep and abstract theory—a generative grammar of his language—many of the concepts and principles of which are only remotely related to experience by long and intricate chains of unconscious quasi-inferential steps. A consideration of the character of the grammar that is acquired, the degenerate quality and narrowly limited extent of the available data, the striking uniformity of the resulting grammars, and their independence of intelligence, motivation, and emotional state, over wide ranges of variation, leave little hope that much of the structure of the language can be learned by an organism initially uninformed as to its general character." Thus, according to Chomsky, the available linguistic input or experience is often degenerate, incomplete, or ungrammatical. Based on the available input, it would be impossible for the child to determine which sentences are grammatical and which are ungrammatical. Also, the available input undermines the final grammar the child is able to acquire in a very short time.

In spite of the fact that the child is exposed to a limited number of sentences, the child is able to understand and produce an unlimited number of novel sentences. Also, according to Chomsky, the child is rarely provided with negative evidence. That is, explicit explanations as to why a given sentence is ungrammatical are rarely, if ever, provided. Thus, since the child, on the basis of a limited amount of positive evidence, is able to recognize understand, and create complex and novel grammatical sentences, there must be a mechanism that guides the child in the process of first language acquisition. This mechanism—UG—needs to be domain-specific and autonomous because at the age of four a child is able to fully use his or her native language. It needs to be solely responsible for analyzing linguistic data, and it needs to be independent of other cognitive mechanisms. This autonomy is evident in the child's ability to acquire his or her first language despite cognitive immaturity.

The autonomy of language faculty advocated by Chomsky raises the issue of a distinction between acquisition and development. Cook defines *development* as "the real-time learning of language by children" and *acquisition* as "language learning unaffected by maturation" (1985, 4–5). Development points to the interaction among various cognitive mechanisms such as cognition, UG, and social context. The claim that UG is autonomous excludes the possibility of such an interaction. Development is not the focus of Chomsky's theory of universal grammar, however. Acquisition, an idealized state, a formal abstraction, an innate knowledge of formal grammatical properties of language unaffected by time and experiences, is the focus of Chomsky's scientific inquiry.

Despite Chomsky's efforts to separate acquisition from development in order to justify the autonomous character of language faculty, his definition of acquisition raises a question regarding the "internal development" of UG (Cook 1985). Is UG available in its entirety from the very beginning or does it unfold gradually? White (1981) claims that UG is available to a child in its entirety from the very beginning. Others, however, such as Felix (1984), claim that UG unfolds in stages in a predetermined sequence. It simply grows, like hair or teeth. Some researchers, however, point to the fact that development cannot be separated from acquisition since the child does not produce all sentences with the same degree of complexity at the same time. More complex structures, such as relative clauses, appear later on in the child's language.

Chomsky claims that studies that investigate performance fall under the category of development rather than acquisition (Cook 1985). They cannot be characterized as examining the properties of the language faculty, which he defines as a " 'mental organ,' analogous to the heart or the vision system or the system of motor coordination and planning. There appears to be no clear demarcation line between physical organs, perceptual and motor systems, and cognitive faculties in the respects in question" (Chomsky 1980, 39). Like mental organs, it evolves according to its genetic code. Its growth is triggered by the environment, the input the child is provided with by his or her environment. Chomsky writes: "When external conditions are necessary for, or facilitate the unfolding of, an internally controlled process, we can speak of their 'triggering effect' " (1980, 32). The child does not learn the L1 the way the

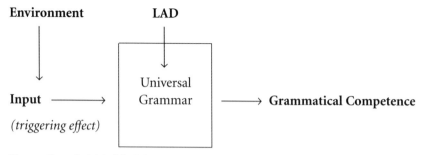

Fig. 3.1. Chomsky's Model of First Language Acquisition (after Chomsky 1981b; Ellis 1994)

child may learn to play the piano because his or her grammatical knowledge is dependent on the growth of a mental organ—UG—that is biologically predetermined.

This predetermined growth only needs to be triggered by the environment. Once triggered, grammatical knowledge proceeds; that is, it unfolds along a genetically determined course. Chomsky (1980, 33) writes: "a central part of what we call 'learning' is actually better understood as the growth of cognitive structures along an internally directed course under the triggering and partially shaping effect of the environment." The process of L1 acquisition is represented in figure 3.1.

Because of the existence of a genetically programmed language faculty, Chomsky's model of first language acquisition does not place much emphasis on the learner's environment or the social aspect of language in use. The external environment does not represent a necessary and sustainable condition for the growth of language faculty; human biology does. In Chomsky's theory of universal grammar, the focus is placed on human mental processes, on the structure and the operation of UG that are responsible for processing linguistic data and aiding the child in discovering formal properties of his or her native language. In order to investigate first language acquisition, one needs to rely more on logical than on empirical evidence. Thus, Chomsky's theory of first language acquisition may be categorized as a logico-deductive version (that is, the older version) of the cognitive paradigm.

What are the innate properties of the human mind that assist the child in L1 acquisition and can be logically deduced? Universal grammar consists of a set of abstract principles that apply to all natural languages and have language-specific parameters (Chomsky 1981a, 1981b; Cook 1985, 1988, 1994, 1997). Note that UG does not consist of a set of grammatical rules specific to a given language but consists of a set of principles and parameters that represent the properties of all natural languages. Although parameters may vary, UG sets the limits within which grammars of all natural languages can vary.

An example of a parameter is the *pro-drop parameter* (Cook 1985, 1988, 1994), which pertains to the way different languages realize their subject position in sentences. The pro-drop parameter has two values: the pro-drop and the non-pro-drop. Based on this value, languages fall into one of two categories. English, for example, is a non-pro-drop language; that is, a subject is required for all sentences. This explains the existence of the so-called dummy subjects—the expletives *it* and *there*. In a sentence such as *It is raining, It* does not carry any semantic value. It is present in the above sentence to fulfill the requirement of the pro-drop parameter that operates in English: all subject positions need to be filled. In contrast, a pro-drop language, such as Spanish, accepts an "empty" subject position.

The pro-drop parameter has an effect on other properties of L1 grammar. If a given language is a non-pro-drop language, then the subject-verb inversion is not possible in declarative sentences. On the other hand, if a language is a pro-drop language, then the subject-verb inversion is permissible.

The relation between principles and parameters is described by Cook:

> Overall there is a principle that drivers have to keep consistently to one side of the road, which is taken for granted by all drivers in all countries. Exceptions to this principle, such as people driving down motorways on the wrong side, rate stories in the media or car chases in action movies. The principle does not, however, say *which* side of the road people should drive on. A parameter of driving allows the side to be the left in England and Japan, and the right in the USA and France. The parameter has two values or "settings"—left and right. Once a country has opted for one side or the other, it sticks to its choice: a change of setting is a massively complex operation, whether it happens for a whole country, as in Sweden, or for the individual travelling from England to France. So a universal principle and a variable parameter together sum up the essence of driving. The principle states the universal requirement on driving; the parameter specifies the variation between different countries. (1997, 250–51)

Thus, UG makes certain elements obligatory in all natural languages, and other elements are free to vary within a well-established system of degrees of freedom. The selection of a particular value of the parameter is possible because of positive evidence provided to the child by the environment. For example, the child, based on the incoming English input (sentences), adjusts the pro-drop parameter value to a non-pro-drop value. Setting up the values of language-specific parameters may be visualized as tuning into a particular radio station. A radio may be visualized as the LAD. The radio needs to be plugged in and turned on, which is accomplished with the assistance of the environment. But in order to be able to listen to a jazz station—the grammar of a particular language—one needs to adjust the dial.

Note that UG does not assist the child in the acquisition of the entire grammar. It is responsible only for guiding the process of acquiring core grammar, the unmarked features of the child's native-language grammar. "Experience is necessary to fix the values of parameters of core grammar. In the absence of evidence to the contrary, unmarked options are selected" (Chomsky 1981a, 8). The marked rules, the periphery of grammar, need to be learned. An example of an unmarked rule that is discovered with the aid of UG is the English past-tense morpheme *ed* as in paint*ed*, work*ed*. Irregular verb forms such as *bought* or *taught*, however, are not acquired with the aid of UG. The child's reliance on the assistance of UG may explain frequent occurrences of such ungrammatical verb forms as *buyed* or *catched*. Children need to be explicitly taught that these particular verb forms are incorrect in English. Once the parameters of UG are fixed, "a particular grammar is determined, what I will call a 'core grammar' " (Chomsky 1981a, 7).

In sum, Chomsky's theory of first language acquisition has been developed in order to provide some answers to the logical problem of language acquisition: the gap that exists between the linguistic input to which the child is exposed and his or her ultimate level of language attainment. Based on the poverty-of-the-stimulus argument, Chomsky has deduced that there must be an innate language faculty that is independent of other mental faculties and that assists the child in first language acquisition. He confines L1 acquisition to the domain of grammatical competence. He separates linguistic competence from pragmatic competence. The language faculty (UG), which helps the child to acquire grammatical competence, consists of a set of abstract rules, universal principles, and language-specific parameters. Certain parameters vary within a well-defined set of values. The child's responsibility is to fix the value of certain parameters based on positive evidence provided by the environment. Universal grammar is responsible for the native speaker's implicit knowledge of the formal grammatical properties of his or her native language and the native speaker's intuition about the grammaticality or ungrammaticality of sentences. In the Chomsky theory, the environment is relegated to the role of a trigger mechanism that initiates the operation of UG. Once "turned on," UG unfolds in a genetically predetermined way.

Chomsky's theory of universal grammar has undergone many changes and appeared in many forms. First, it was given the name of transformational-generative grammar (Chomsky 1965; Radford 1988) and then was considered within the government and binding theory (Chomsky 1981a; Haegeman 1991). Currently, it is being revised and reexamined under the name of the minimalist program (Chomsky 1995), in which L1 acquisition is reduced to the acquisition of "the argument structure of a head, indicating how many arguments the head licenses and what semantic role each receives. For example, the verb *give* must be specified as assigning an agent role, a theme role, and a goal/recipient role" (Chomsky 1995, 30).

In all these different versions of the linguistic theory that aims at explaining the operation of UG, the role of the environment in L1 acquisition remains the same. The external environment is viewed as a trigger device. Thus, regardless of the version, Chomsky's theory of linguistic competence is focused on mental processes and on the operation of an innate, autonomous, language-specific mechanism responsible for the native speaker's implicit knowledge of formal properties of grammar.

Chomsky's UG and Second Language Acquisition

Chomsky's theory of language acquisition has not gone unnoticed by some researchers working in the field of SLA. Kevin Gregg, one of the staunchest proponents of Chomsky's linguistic theory, calls for its application to SLA. Gregg claims that the field of SLA suffers in two areas: the area of its unspecified domain and that of its theory. With regard to the first problem, he states that the domain of SLA should be restricted to linguistic competence and not include linguistic performance. He writes: "Having fixed our domain as the acquisition of linguistic competence, we now need a linguistic theory to account for that competence." This linguistic theory needs to be "a theory of grammar" (Gregg 1989, 24), which is autonomous and modular. By *autonomous* Gregg means that it is separated from other more "holistic" approaches to language such as "discourse-based or discourse-functional approaches" (26), which view language as communication. The theory of grammar, in Gregg's opinion, should be a formal theory modeled on Chomsky's generative grammar. Gregg considers the formality of Chomsky's generative grammar to constitute "one of its major strengths" (30). In addition, such a formal theory would "add both clarity and explanatory power to the research being carried out in SLA. Beyond that, by relating SLA research to first language acquisition theory and linguistic theory, such a perspective can give our field something else it could do with: a sense of direction" (34–35).

Gregg strongly criticizes the variable competence model (Tarone 1984; Ellis

1985), which deals with the variability in the learner's performance. He points to many flaws of this model, which claims to account for the learner's heterogeneous competence, or varied language competence in different social contexts. The main shortcoming of the model, in Gregg's opinion, is associated with its confusion of competence with performance. That is, the learner's behavior is falsely argued to represent competence (knowledge) rather than performance. Gregg sees a similar flaw in Tarone's (1984) capability continuum. This refers to a continuum of styles that the L2 learner exhibits in different social contexts.

Gregg claims that although the data concerning variability may be interesting to study, once we establish "the domain of a theory of second language acquisition so that it is confined to the acquisition of linguistic competence, then we will not be compelled to account for those data on variability as far as that theory is concerned; and by ignoring them we can avoid the conceptual contradictions and confusions exemplified in such terms as 'heterogeneous competence' or 'capability continuum' " (1989, 22).

In summary, Gregg recommends that SLA define its domain within the boundaries of linguistic competence and develop a theory of grammar that explains that domain. Such a theory of grammar needs to be linguistic and formal in nature. According to Gregg, the application of Chomsky's generative grammar would add "rigor to SLA theory" (1989, 30) because of its formalism. Formalism, in Gregg's opinion, is required of any cognitive activity. Drawing on Pylyshyn (1973), Gregg claims that any cognitive system is characterized by a set of formal logical rules. To be able to understand any cognitive system is to be able to describe it and explain it in terms of formal and logical rules. Because the linguistic competence that is acquired by the L2 learner represents such a cognitive system, SLA needs a set of formal and logical rules that describe and explain L2 linguistic competence. Gregg complains that "in the absence of a formal theory, we get not only informal description, but also a proliferation of terminology, either produced ad hoc ('creative construction,' Krashen's 'output filter' [1985], Tarone's 'capability continuum,' the various 'competences,' etc.; my favorite invention is 'semantic clout') or imported unthinking from other disciplines; added to this are a lot of flow charts and diagrams" (1989, 31).

Gregg calls for more research into the L2 learner's access to UG principles and parameters. Several researchers, following his lead, have conducted studies to determine such access. Most of these studies investigated such principles as subjacency, which put constraints on the movement of a constituent within sentences, and parameters such as the pro-drop parameter. Also, most of these studies elicited their data utilizing the so-called grammaticality judgment task, in which L2 learners were asked to use their intuition to determine the grammaticality of the selected sentences. Grammaticality judgment tasks have been criticized because of their inability to show the difference between explicit and implicit knowledge (Birdsong 1989). That is, it is difficult to determine whether L2 learners are basing their decisions on their explicit knowledge of L2 grammar or their implicit knowledge of L2 grammar. Also, such tasks are inappropriate for learners at the lower levels of L2 proficiency and L2 learners who are illiterate.

Because the results of studies that examined the L2 learner's access to UG are controversial and inconclusive, some researchers openly deny that L2 learners have access to UG. For example, Robert Bley-Vroman (1989) considers the logical problem of adult second language acquisition (see above for a discussion of Chomsky's logical problem of language acquisition) to be only somewhat similar to the child's first language acquisition. He acknowledges the existence of some kind of internal mechanism that assists the learner in second language acquisition. Contrary to the proponents of UG, however, Bley-Vroman does not believe that L2 learners have access to UG.

The Fundamental Difference Hypothesis

Robert Bley-Vroman (1989) describes nine fundamentally different characteristics of adult second language learners to justify his position that they have no access to UG. These nine characteristics are meant to illustrate Bley-Vroman's point that adult learners do not acquire a second language with the assistance of UG.

The major difference between childhood first language acquisition and adult second language acquisition is the lack of "general guaranteed success" (Bley-Vroman 1989, 43) on the part of L2 learners. All children achieve perfect mastery of the L1; however, the same cannot be stated regarding L2 learners. In spite of years of classroom instruction, exposure to L2 input, and motivation, many adult L2 learners are not able to acquire the target language. If UG were operative during the process of L2 learning, such a lack of guaranteed success would not be possible. This lack supports Bley-Vroman's claim that L2 acquisition is guided by "general human cognitive learning capacities rather than by the same domain-specific module which guarantees child success in first language acquisition" (44).

There is also substantial variation in "degree of attainment, in course of learning, and in strategies of learning" (Bley-Vroman 1989, 45). Such a degree of variation in the ultimate attainment of the L2 further supports Bley-Vroman's contentions that UG is not available to adult L2 learners and that no domain-specific cognitive mechanism must be utilized by adult foreign language learners.

Unlike children, adult second language learners set up different goals as to their desired level of L2 mastery. For example, some adult learners may be satisfied with a rudimentary level of L2 proficiency that allows them to survive in the target culture; others may wish to acquire the L2 only to be able to read in the target language. Children do not experience this type of flexibility because their goals are under control of language faculty that unfolds along a genetically programmed sequence.

Adult L2 learners also differ from children acquiring the L1 in terms of "fossilization" (Bley-Vroman 1989, 46). Adult learners may reach a certain plateau that cannot be surpassed no matter how hard the individual may try to overcome it. Also, adult L2 learners at the very advanced level of proficiency do not exhibit the same level of intuition as to the grammaticality of sentences that native speakers do. Children, unlike adult L2 learners, do not require formal grammar lessons to acquire the native language. Neither do they require corrective negative evidence to learn their native language. They simply need some exposure to linguistic input. Children's success in the L1 is also unaffected by such factors as personality, motivation, attitude, and aptitude, which play important roles in adult second language acquisition.

All these different characteristics led Bley-Vroman to the conclusion that "the domain-specific language acquisition system of children ceases to operate in adults, and in addition, that adult foreign language acquisition resembles general adult learning in fields for which no domain-specific learning system is believed to exist" (1989, 49). He claims that the domain-specific role of language faculty in adults is replaced by a general (non-domain-specific) cognitive system—a general abstract problem-solving system.

Bley-Vroman proposes the fundamental difference hypothesis, which not only describes differences between child and adult language acquisition but also asserts that these differences are internal, linguistic, and qualitative in nature:

> *Internal:* It is caused by differences in the internal cognitive state of adults [and] children, not by some external factor or factors (insufficient input, for example).
> *Linguistic:* It is caused by a change in the language faculty specifically not by some general change in learning ability.
> *Qualitative, not quantitative:* The difference is not merely quantitative: the domain-specific acquisition system is not just attenuated, it is unavailable. Period.   (1989, 50)

These differences between child and adult language acquisition are illustrated as follows:

Child language development	Adult foreign language learning
A. Universal Grammar	A. Native language knowledge
B. Domain-specific learning procedures	B. General problem-solving systems

(1989, 51)

Thus, according to Bley-Vroman, adult language learners do not have access to Chomsky's UG; therefore, they must construct "a kind of surrogate for Universal Grammar from knowledge of the native language" (1989, 52). And because the ability to construct a surrogate for UG is very individual, there are many individual variations in L2 attainment. Also, this variability may be associated with the nature of a general cognitive system, which because of its non-domain-specific function accounts for a varying degree of success in L2 attainment. In sum, according to Bley-Vroman's fundamental difference hypothesis, adult L2 learners lack access to UG, and the operation of UG is replaced with the general cognitive problem-solving mechanism.

Bley-Vroman's position is supported by Clahsen and Muysken (1986). Their findings reveal that native children and adult L2 learners do not acquire German word order in the same way. Children start with the SOV word order, which is characteristic of German subordinate clauses, then gradually learn to move the verb to the second position (SVO) in independent clauses. In contrast, adult L2 learners start with the SVO word order in independent and subordinate clauses and then gradually learn to move the verb to the final position (SOV) in subordinate clauses. These differences in the acquisition of the German word order point to the operation of two different cognitive mechanisms in children and adults.

There are other researchers, however, who disagree with the position advocated by Bley-Vroman. Flynn (1987), for example, claims that adult L2 learners have full access to UG. White (1989), however, believes that L2 learners only have access to the parameters that have been activated in their first language. That is, access to UG is only available through the L2 learner's native language. Felix (1985) agrees that adult L2 learners have access to UG, but he claims that L2 learners have access to both UG and a general problem-solving module. These two cognitive mechanisms compete with each other for processing "rights" to the incoming linguistic input. In this competition, a general problem-solving module always wins. All these various positions regarding adult second language learners' access to UG can be graphically represented as shown in figure 3.2.

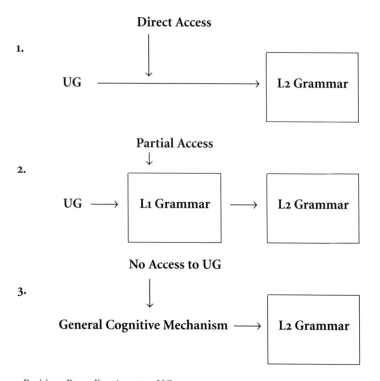

Fig. 3.2. Positions Regarding Access to UG

Despite this ongoing controversy regarding the L2 learner's access to UG. Chomsky's theory has had a profound impact on SLA theory and research. For example, most of the existing information processing models, such as VanPatten's information processing model and Gass and Selinker's second language acquisition model, make explicit references to UG.

Long's Call for a Cognitive Approach to SLA

Although some mainstream researchers disagree as to the applicability and appropriateness of Chomsky's linguistic theory for SLA, they do not advocate the replacement of Chomsky's theory with another theory that may be more "environmentally" friendly or more socially oriented. Rather, they call for its replacement with another cognitively oriented theory. They claim that the focus of SLA should be on describing and explaining mental processes responsible for second language acquisition. Long's (1997) response to Firth and Wagner's criticism of the mainstream preoccupation with cognitive approaches to SLA may serve as an illustration of the current cognitive trend in SLA and the power of the mainstream researchers to silence "alternative voices." Long writes: "Most SLA research, F&W complain (echoing Rampton), is preoccupied with the relationship between a speaker and his or her interlanguage grammar, not that between speakers and the world around them, this despite research in sociolinguistics having 'irrefutably established and documented [a] reflexive relationship between *language use* and *social context*...' And who would deny it? The question, again, however, is what any of this has to do with the appropriate focus for research on SLA" (1997, 318, emphasis in original). Long then proclaims that because most SLA researchers work within a cognitive approach, such an approach should be accepted as the norm for the entire field. He writes: "Whether F&W like it or not (they do not), most SLA researchers view the object of inquiry as in large part an internal, mental process: *the acquisition of new (linguistic) knowledge*" (319, emphasis in original).

In the same response to Firth and Wagner, Long also makes clear that he wishes to distance himself from a controversial debate about Gregg's (1989) attempt to confine the domain of SLA within Chomsky's UG theory. He states that "by far the majority of 'cognitively oriented' SLA researchers are not UG-ers" (322). It seems to me that Long needs to separate himself from Chomsky's UG because of his belief in the facilitative power of implicit negative feedback in second language acquisition, which he included in his newer version of the interaction hypothesis (see Chapter 4 for details). This facilitative role of negative feedback contradicts the notion that the L2 learner has access to UG. Recall that although children do not receive corrective (negative) feedback from their caretakers, they are still able to acquire their native language.

According to Long (1997), the main object of SLA inquiry should be the acquisition of linguistic knowledge, which he associates with the acquisition of phonology, lexicon, and morphosyntactic rules. The SLA research community should concentrate its efforts on understanding the nature of the learner's mental processes, which may not necessarily be governed by UG. A social setting in such a cognitive approach is acknowledged, but only superficially. It almost exists for the sake of existence: "SLA is a process that (often) takes place in a social setting, of course, but then so do most internal processes—learning, thinking, remembering, sexual arousal, and digestion, for example—and that neither obviates the need for theories of those processes, nor shifts the goal of inquiry to a theory of the settings"(Long 1997, 319).

This cognitive bias toward SLA theory and its prevailing experimental research methodology are reinforced even further in Long's next statement:

"Given, then, that most SLA researchers are, in my view, correctly, endeavoring to understand a mental process and a changing mental representation of the L2, or interlanguage grammar, *cognitive* variables are for them inevitably and justifiably the central focus, and what F&W call 'cognitive oriented theories and methodologies' are inevitably and appropriately those researchers' central theories and methodologies" (ibid.). It is not surprising that existing communicative competence models used in SLA (see Chapter 5 for more detail) tend to treat social contexts "abstractly," in terms of stable and defined features in advance. Such an approach to social context is consistent with the quantitative "bias" toward SLA: Something that cannot be measured and quantified is either treated superficially or is simply excluded from a study design. Most of the study designs used within the cognitive approach to SLA fall under the category of experimental research method designs with well-defined variables and inferential statistical procedures.

Long gives a "blessing" to the mainstream SLA research and theories, and he undermines the value of any theory, particularly any that is social in nature, that tries to account for the same complex processes of second language acquisition. He writes: "Social and affective factors, the L2 *acquisition* literature suggests, are important, but relatively minor in their impact, in both naturalistic and classroom settings, and most current theories of and in SLA reflect that fact" (ibid.). This statement is particularly harmful for SLA researchers working within a more socially oriented paradigm. It sends a signal that the theories that do not conform to cognitive norms and by extension to experimental and quantitative research norms should not be treated as providing useful contributions to our understanding of SLA processes. And thus they should not represent the main object of the mainstream SLA research.

Long concludes his criticism of noncognitively oriented theories by stating that the field of SLA will continue focusing on a cognitive, psycholinguistic approach given the fact that "to date insights into SL acquisition from sociolinguistically oriented research have been relatively minor" (1997, 322) Long's position is typical of the current cognitive bias toward SLA theory and research; it reflects the mainstream researchers' mistrust of more socially oriented approaches to SLA whose contributions are viewed as "relatively minor" and whose findings, which are primarily qualitative, are viewed as being "unscientific."

In sum, Long's rebuttal of Firth and Wagner's criticism of mainstream SLA research supports my main contention that current SLA theory and research is primarily focused on the following:

1. the understanding of mental processes;
2. the acquisition of linguistic knowledge; and
3. the investigation of cognitive variables within a well-established experimental type of research design.

I have selected Long's response to Firth and Wagner as an illustration of my general point concerning the prevailing attitude on the part of the mainstream community regarding the superiority of the cognitive approach to the social approach. Also, I do not necessarily believe that one is superior to the other or that one excludes the other. I believe that they can be easily reconciled and united under a new framework, which is based on Vygotsky's sociocultural theory (I describe this framework in Chapter 9). I find the position held by Long and his followers dangerous, however, because it hinders progress in our field. The exclusion of insights that differ from the position held by the majority does disservice to our efforts to understand the complex processes of SLA. Any progress in science is based on constructive criticism, on experimenting with new ideas no matter how insignificant or "minor," as Long put it, they may seem to those in the majority position. After all, we were once forced to believe that the Sun turns around the Earth because of the fear of some to look through a telescope.

The current debate about the superiority of one paradigm to the other reminds me of the state of confusion that currently exists in the diet industry, in which proponents of one type of diet claim to have found the Holy Grail and disregard the rest. The truth is that we all may be right; "our truth" may be appropriate for one group of learners but not necessarily for another. The problem with the cognitive approach is that most of the researchers working within this paradigm exclude the possibility that the so-called alternative voices have something "major" to offer and, in the process, they try to silence these voices. I hope that the time has come to begin a true dialogue, to work on building a new model—a dialogically based model of SLA.

In this chapter I provided a brief overview of the older version of the cognitive tradition—the logico-deductive version, which is primarily associated with Chomsky's UG. In the next chapter I discuss the latest trend in SLA theory, which is associated with the newer version of the cognitive tradition: information processing.

4

Information Processing Models

In this chapter I discuss SLA models that adhere to the information-processing paradigm—the newer version of the cognitive tradition. The selected models include Bill VanPatten's (1996) input processing model and Susan Gass and Larry Selinker's (2001) model of second language acquisition. The discussion of these models is preceded by a description of two theories: Stephen Krashen's input hypothesis (1985) and Michael Long's (1983b, 1996) interaction hypothesis, which influenced the selected information processing models and the field of SLA in general.

Krashen's Input Hypothesis

The impact of Krashen's input hypothesis on the field of second language acquisition and teaching has been profound. His hypothesis has been to a large extent responsible for the introduction of two of the most controversial issues in SLA theory and practice. These two issues are connected with the roles of input and grammar instruction in second language acquisition. Krashen's input hypothesis is part of his larger theoretical framework, which attempts to account for second language acquisition processes. It consists of five hypotheses:

1. Acquisition-Learning
2. Natural Order
3. Monitor
4. Input
5. Affective Filter

The first hypothesis claims that second language acquisition can be developed in two ways, by means of two independent processes: *acquisition,* which refers to subconscious processes that result in acquired knowledge, and *learning,* which refers to conscious processes that result in explicit knowledge about the grammatical properties of a second language. Krashen adheres to the noninterference position with respect to learning and acquisition; that is, knowledge about the formal properties of a second language, such as one's ability to explain the form of the English present perfect tense, does not lead to acquisition. In contrast to acquisition, learning requires the formal teaching of grammatical rules and structures. Since this formal teaching does not lead to acquisition, the teaching of grammar is relegated in Krashen's framework to the periphery and is associated with the operation of the monitor hypothesis.

Krashen's second hypothesis, the natural order hypothesis, states that SLA proceeds according to a well-defined order. That is, the second language is acquired in a predetermined way; it unfolds along a natural path of development that cannot be altered. This hypothesis sets the stage for an information processing view of second language acquisition: If there is a natural order of acquisition, there must be a mechanism that processes the incoming information according to an innate, universal, and rule-governed system.

The monitor hypothesis accounts for the existence and the operation of learned knowledge. Krashen writes: "Our ability to produce utterances in another language comes from our acquired competence, from our subconscious knowledge. Learning, conscious knowledge, serves only as an editor, or Monitor. We appeal to learning to make corrections, to change the output of the acquired system before we speak or write (or sometimes after we speak or write, as in self-correction" (1985, 1–2). Access to the monitor is available only under a limited set of conditions. The learner must have enough time to apply the learned knowledge, "must be consciously concerned about correctness" (2), and must know a grammatical rule.

The fourth hypothesis, the input hypothesis, claims that "humans acquire language in only one way—by understanding messages, or by receiving 'comprehensible input'" (ibid.). Comprehensible input is operationalized as $i + 1$, where i represents the learner's current level of language competence and 1 the next level of competence in the natural order of development. Here the natural order and input hypotheses merge because, according to Krashen, we move along the natural order of development by understanding the input that contains structures at the next level ($i + 1$).

Note that Krashen's input hypothesis refers to acquisition, not learning. Krashen claims that if there is enough comprehensible input "the necessary grammar is automatically provided" (ibid.). There is no need to teach grammar deliberately because it can be acquired subconsciously with the assistance of the internal language processor—Chomsky's LAD.

Krashen believes that the operation of Chomsky's UG extends beyond the L1; he disagrees with the researchers who undermine its value for second language acquisition. He writes: "The idea that we acquire in only one way may not be fashionable in this age of individual variation. . . . The extensive evidence for the Input Hypothesis . . . supports Chomsky's position, and extends it to second-language acquisition. We may see individual variation 'on the surface'—different sources of comprehensible input, different strategies for obtaining input, different messages, and of course different languages— and this variation may be of practical concern. But deep down, the 'mental organ' for language (Chomsky 1975) produces one basic product, a human language, in one fundamental way" (Krashen 1985, 3). Thus, Krashen's position regarding the operation of Chomsky's UG in second language acquisition makes him one of the supporters of the full-access-to-UG position.

The last hypothesis—the affective filter hypothesis—claims that although comprehensible input is the necessary condition for, indeed the cause of, moving along the natural order of development, there is another factor that affects SLA: the affective filter. This affective filter is "a mental block that prevents acquirers from fully utilizing the comprehensible input they receive for language acquisition" (ibid.). When the affective filter is "up," the input, although understood, will not reach the LAD. This mental block is associated with the following factors: anxiety, lack of confidence, and lack of motivation. When the affective filter is "down," the input will be delivered to the LAD, and second language acquisition will take place subconsciously. The operation of the affective filter in Krashen's model of second language acquisition is represented in figure 4.1.

Owing to Krashen's heavy reliance on the LAD and subconscious processes, his model of SLA is part of the cognitive paradigm. His model also represents one of the earliest versions of the information processing model; it contains three classic elements of any information processing model: input,

Affective Filter

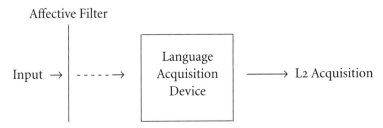

Fig. 4.1. The Role of the Affective Filter in Krashen's Model of SLA (based on Krashen 1985; Gass 2001)

cognitive mechanism (here the LAD), and output. A diagram of Krashen's input hypothesis is illustrated in figure 4.2.

In Krashen's model, acquisition (that is, acquired competence) is not distinguished from the learner's performance. In other words, it is difficult to determine how this acquired competence differs from the learner's performance. Also, it is not clear to what the learner's acquired competence refers. Recall that in Chomsky's theory, UG is responsible for assisting the child in the acquisition of grammatical competence. In Krashen's model, acquired competence seems to refer to all aspects of second language; it seems to go beyond Chomsky's grammatical competence.

Krashen's input hypothesis has been criticized extensively, and since these criticisms have been reported widely in many SLA textbooks (for example, Gass and Selinker 2001; Ellis 1994), in this section I focus on some of the flaws of his theory of SLA that are relevant to my discussion of information processing models that use Krashen's model as their points of reference.

For example, based on Krashen's claim that "humans acquire language in only one way—by understanding the message, or by receiving 'comprehensible input'" (Krashen 1985, 2), it is difficult to determine who is responsible for second language acquisition. After all, understanding is the individual's internal act, whereas receiving comprehensible input depends greatly on what happens in the learner's external environment. Thus, according to this operational definition of SLA, either the environment could be blamed for the learner's inability to acquire the language or the learner could blame himself or herself for the inability to understand (that is, acquire) the language.

Although his definition explicitly states that there is "only one way" to acquire the language, the remainder of his statement identifies two processes: understanding the message and receiving comprehensible input. Since the Input Hypothesis predicts that actual two-way interaction with native

INPUT ⎯⎯⎯⎯⎯⎯⎯⎯⎯→ **LAD** ⎯⎯⎯⎯⎯⎯⎯⎯⎯→ **OUTPUT**

Fig. 4.2. Krashen's Input Hypothesis as an Information-Processing Model

speakers is not necessary for acquisition" (Krashen 1985, 33), there is a logical flaw in his statement. His position that there is only one way is contradicted by his insistence on the existence of both understanding (internal) and re- ceiving comprehensible input (external). It is unclear how these two pro- cesses were to be reconciled.

Input gains a more prestigious status in Krashen's input hypothesis than it does in Chomsky's UG. Since his comprehensible input is in a cause-and- effect relation with acquisition, it cannot be viewed as a trigger device (as is the case in UG). Therefore, it is difficult to see how the active role of Krashen's comprehensible input can be reconciled with the passive role of Chomsky's input. Are we to assume that the LAD needs one amount of input in the L1 and a different amount in the L2 in order to begin its operation?

Simply stated, Krashen confuses two paradigms (cognitive and social). Although he claims that cognitive processes are responsible for SLA, he unintentionally brings to the fore the need to examine the interaction be- tween the learner's external and internal realities. He unintentionally points to the fact that there exists a more complex relation between these realities than he is willing to admit.

There are also some inconsistencies in Krashen's affective filter hypothesis. Krashen claims that if the affective filter is up, "the acquirer may understand what he hears and reads, but the input will not reach the LAD" (1985, 3). If this is the case, there are two ways to interpret this statement. Either the pro- cess of understanding is accomplished outside the learner's mind or under- standing represents a stage that precedes the LAD. Also, his statement seems to imply that SLA equals one's ability to *access* the LAD.

Krashen's definition of the affective filter is imprecise and rather confus- ing. Please recall that the affective filter is "a mental block that prevents acquirers from fully utilizing the comprehensible input they receive for lan- guage acquisition" (1985, 3). Defined that way, the mental block can only represent the result, *not* the cause, of the learner's inability to access the LAD. Lack of motivation, self-confidence, and anxiety cause the learner's mental block. It is the result of the learner's emotional states. These emotional states, not the mental block, prevent the learner from accessing the mental organ, LAD.

Krashen's affective filter hypothesis indirectly points to the need to exam- ine the relation between the emotional state and the mental state of the learner. Note that even the learner's emotional states are defined in terms of the learner's internal reality. The operation of the affective filter is viewed solely as the learner's responsibility. That is, the learner alone is responsible for being anxious, unmotivated, or unconfident. The possibility that these states could be caused by the external environment is not taken into consideration in Krashen's model.

Despite its theoretical shortcomings, Krashen's input hypothesis has been very popular. Its popularity may have something to do with the natural approach (Krashen and Terrell 1983; Richards and Rodgers 2001), a method of teaching English as a second language that is based on Krashen's theory. In sum, Krashen's input hypothesis is responsible for

1. initiating the debate regarding the role of input—one-way versus two-way interaction—in second language acquisition;
2. triggering the research on the role of grammar instruction in SLA;
3. identifying the processes that are responsible for the conversion of input into output; and
4. perhaps unintentionally, examining the relation between comprehensible input and mental processes (the learner's external and internal processes).

Thus, despite its apparent flaws, one needs to acknowledge that his theory has contributed to scientific progress in our field. It has planted the seeds for a fruitful discussion regarding the complex process of second language acquisition. It has prompted some research in the area of the roles of input, output, and formal grammar instruction in SLA. Our field has substantially improved in its ability to understand and explain the processes of SLA because of Krashen's controversial stand regarding the roles of input and grammar instruction, and for these reasons, Krashen's input hypothesis should be given recognition.

Swain's Comprehensible Output Theory

Merrill Swain (1985, 1993, 1995) proposed that not only comprehensible input but also *comprehensible output* is required for second language acquisition. She disagrees with Krashen's (1989) claim that output represents the result of acquired competence, and as such it does not play an important role in SLA. She writes: "It has been argued that output is nothing more than a sign of the second language acquisition that has already taken place, and that output serves no useful role in SLA except possibly as one source of (self-) input to the learner" (1995, 125). In her opinion, the production of comprehensible output forces the learner to notice a gap between "what they *want* to say and what they *can* say" (126, emphasis in original). In other words, comprehensible output may help the learner to consciously recognize that there is a gap in his or her knowledge of the linguistic properties of the target language, and this recognition may prompt a desire to work on improving the quality of his or her acquired competence. Comprehensible output thus plays a crucial role in changing the quality of (that is, restructuring; McLaughlin 1990) the learner's interlanguage. This "pushed out" input is necessary for the learner to engage in a syntactic processing of the incoming input rather than in a semantic processing, which is characteristic of comprehension. Comprehensible output, with its focus on syntactic processing, contributes to a higher level of grammatical accuracy.

Swain (1995, 128) identifies three functions of comprehensible output, which, she hypothesizes, relate to "accuracy rather than fluency":

1. the "the noticing/triggering" function, or what might be referred to as its consciousness-raising role;
2. the hypothesis-testing function;
3. the metalinguistic function, or what might be referred to as its "reflective" role.

The first function, "noticing the gap," was first introduced to the field of SLA by Schmidt and Frota (1986) in their diary study of the acquisition of Portuguese as a second language. In producing the target language, learners may notice the mismatch between what they know and what they do not know in the target language. This noticed gap may raise the learner's consciousness regarding the target language forms, which otherwise may not have been noticed. It may make him or her aware of something he or she needs to find out about L2 grammar.

The second function of comprehensible output is in line with the research that claims that, in order to be able to acquire the target language, the learner has to test hypotheses about the language (Corder 1967). And in order to do that, the learner needs to produce the language to determine what is possible and what is not possible in the target language.

The third function is metalinguistic in nature. It provides the learner with an opportunity to reflect on the target language's forms and structures which, in turn, may lead to the improvement of the quality of the learner's interlanguage because the internalized forms will have a chance to be revised according to the target language's norms.

Note that in her latest work, Swain (2000) investigates the role of output from a Vygotskian perspective. She even calls for the replacement of the term *output* with a different term that more accurately reflects the dialogic nature of output. I return to Swain's comments on Vygotsky in Chapter 8.

Long's Interaction Hypothesis

Michael Long (1983a, 1983b) expanded on Krashen's comprehensible input by introducing conversational adjustments (recall his three-step hypothesis, described in Chapter 1). His ideas regarding the role of conversational adjustments in SLA evolved from the work of Hatch (1978). He agrees with Hatch that conversational interaction and, in particular, conversational modifications can provide contexts not only for the practice of grammatical rules but also for the acquisition of these rules. That is, knowledge of grammatical rules develops from conversational interaction, not from grammatical rules that are acquired independent of conversational interaction.

Long's original hypothesis regarding the role of conversational adjustments in SLA has been revised in his updated version of the interaction hypothesis (IH). Long defines the IH as follows: "It is proposed that environmental contributions to acquisition are mediated by selective attention and the learner's developing L2 processing capacity, and that these resources are brought together most usefully, although not exclusively, during *negotiation for meaning*. Negative feedback obtained during negotiation work or elsewhere may be facilitative of L2 development, at least for vocabulary, morphology, and language-specific syntax, and essential for learning certain specifiable L1-L2 contrasts" (Long 1996, 414, emphasis in original).

Regardless of whether one agrees or disagrees with the appropriateness of the selected variables—environmental contributions, selective attention, and negotiation for meaning—there is a logical problem in Long's definition of the IH. The nature of any mediational system requires that the selected mediational device be independent of the parties involved and be equally distributed between the parties involved. According to Long's definition, environmental contributions are mediated by selective attention and the learner's developing L2 processing capacity. Both these mediational devices are part of the learner's mind. They are extracted from the learner's mind to play the role of mediator between the learner's internal and external worlds. Environmental contributions do not have any representation in Long's mediational device. This is illustrated in figure 4.3.

The flaw in Long's reasoning can be remedied by reshuffling the elements of his IH. If Long's negotiation for meaning were to be assigned the role of mediator between environmental contributions and the learner's internal

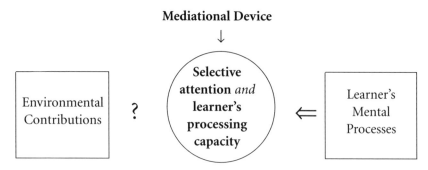

Fig. 4.3. Long's Mediational Device

processes, we would have a device that adheres to the basic requirement of any mediational system. Such a change in Long's mediational device is graphically illustrated in figure 4.4.

If negotiation for meaning were to be assigned the role of an "independent" mediator between the learner's external and internal environments then the rest of Long's IH would make more sense. That is, negotiation for meaning provides the opportunity for negative feedback. The obtained negative feedback draws the learner's attention to the target language's linguistic structures, and this attention, in turn, may lead the learner to noticing the gap in his or her linguistic competence and to converting the incoming input into intake.

Also, Long describes these environmental contributions in an idealized, abstract, and universal manner. In such an environment, one is expected to find negotiation for meaning to be a natural human condition. The appearance of negotiation for meaning sets up an expectation of the automatic occurrence of negative feedback. His definition assumes a linear progression from the environment to negotiation for meaning to negative feedback to the acquisition of linguistic forms. Long's IH sounds like a natural law of physics that asserts that the appearance of one phenomenon presupposes the appearance of another. Our daily experience contradicts such an assumption, however. Depending on the social situation (a real and not an imaginary one), we may find some participants who are unwilling to negotiate. Any real negotiation for meaning presupposes some kind of tension, the asymmetry of power among interlocutors. Some participants may have more power and status than the others; some may have more of a vested interest in negotiating than the others, which, in turn, may affect the quantity and quality of the negative feedback. It seems that in the process of not addressing the social

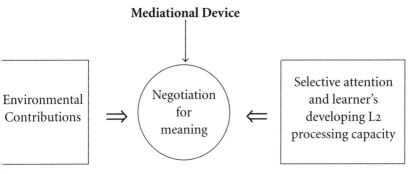

Mediational Device

Environmental Contributions ⟹ Negotiation for meaning ⟸ Selective attention and learner's developing L2 processing capacity

Fig. 4.4. *Negotiation for Meaning* as the Mediator Between the Learner's External and Internal Environments

spects of environmental contributions, Long has created an abstraction that may satisfy the requirements of the cognitive scientific tradition but does not reflect the reality of human communication.

In addition to the idea of negotiation for meaning, Long's IH also includes negative feedback, which he considers essential for second language acquisition. Note that Long advocates the application of implicit rather than explicit negative feedback. Long disagrees with Krashen (1985) as to the role of grammar teaching in SLA. He does not, however, subscribe to traditional grammar teaching, which he calls *focus on forms* (Long and Robinson 1998). Focus on forms is typical of the synthetic approach (Wilkins 1976), in which grammatical items are presented "as models to learners in linear, additive fashion according to such criteria as (usually intuitively assessed) frequency, valence, or difficulty" (Long and Robinson 1998, 15).

Long and Robinson propose a different approach, which they call *focus on form.* "*Focus on form* refers to how attentional resources are allocated. Although there are degrees of attention, and although attention to forms and attention to meaning are not always mutually exclusive, during an otherwise meaning-focused classroom lesson, focus on form often consists of an occasional shift of attention to linguistic code features—by the teacher and/or one or more students—triggered by perceived problems with comprehension or production" (1998, 23).

Negotiation for meaning that results in implicit negative feedback serves the function of the attention-focusing devices that increase "the saliency of otherwise problematic items and cause learners to focus on form." Negotiation for meaning draws the learner's attention to "language as object during a generally meaning-oriented activity" (Long 1996, 429).

Focus on form draws the learner's attention to both form and meaning. It

"involves learners' orientation being drawn to language as object, but i
context. In other words, it is a claim that learners need to attend to a task i
acquisition is to occur, but that their orientation can best be to both form
and meaning, not to either form or meaning alone" (ibid.). This raises
question regarding Long's interpretation of meaning within his negotiatio
for meaning. It is not clear whether it refers to semantic meaning or prag
matic meaning. Because Long insists on restricting the object of SLA to th
domain of linguistic competence, however (see Chapter 3 for details), i
appears that *meaning* in *negotiation for meaning* is interpreted within th
boundaries of semantics rather than pragmatics. If this is the case, Wid
dowson's observation regarding focus on form is correct. He writes: "Th
point, then, is that the structural approach did focus on meaning but o
meaning in form, informed meaning, one might say. That is to say, the focu
was on semantic meaning, that which is encoded as general concepts an
principles in the language itself" (1998, 707).

In the context of semantics, Long's insistence on helping the learner to pa
attention to both form and meaning is self-evident and redundant. Semant
meaning requires the ability to make a connection between form and mean
ing on the sentential level. Only if Long's interpretation of meaning were t
go beyond semantic meaning—that is, only if his *meaning* in *negotiation f*
meaning were to enter the field of pragmatics, where contextual feature
provide extralinguistic clues to the proper interpretation of the conveye
message—could the orientation toward both form and meaning be justifie
on theoretical grounds.

In accordance with Richard Schmidt's (1990, 1993, 1994) research findin;
regarding the role of noticing in SLA, Long (1996) claims that implicit neg
tive feedback obtained during negotiation for meaning brings the learne
attention to the target language forms. In the older version of the IH (Lor
1983b), negotiation for meaning was viewed primarily as a means of obtaii
ing comprehensible input (that is, positive evidence). In the newer version
the IH, negotiation for meaning provides negative feedback (that is, negati
evidence), which Long defines as input that provides "direct or indire
information about what is ungrammatical. This may be explicit (e.g., gram
matical explanation or overt error correction) or implicit (e.g., failure
understand, incidental error correction in a response, such as a confirmatic
check, which reformulates the learner's previous utterance without inte
rupting the flow of conversation—in which case, the negative feedback simu
taneously provides additional positive evidence—and perhaps also the a
sence of items in the input)" (Long 1996, 413). One type of evidence
implicit negative feedback is the *recast*, which he defines as "utterances th

ephrase a child's utterance by changing one or more sentence components subject, verb, or object) while still referring to its central meanings" (434). Recasts allow the learner to compare his or her ungrammatical utterances with the grammatical utterances offered by others. The learner can notice the gap between input and his or her interlanguage.

Some Research Studies of the Role of Recasts in SLA

In "The Role of Implicit Negative Feedback in SLA: Models and Recasts n Japanese and Spanish," Long, Inagaki, and Ortega (1998) report on two xperiments that were conducted in order to assess the effectiveness of mod-ls and recasts in Japanese and Spanish. In the first study, twenty-four adult earners of Japanese enrolled in a second-semester course were randomly ssigned to five groups, which were later collapsed into two groups (models nd recasts) and a control group. The study utilized a pretest, posttest, and ontrol group design. Two structures were selected for the experiment: Japa-ese adjective ordering and a locative construction.

In the treatment groups, the structures were delivered "via a communica-on game, played either in a model or in a recast version, by researcher and articipant separated by a screen." The participants also communicated by eadphones, which the authors consider beneficial because they created "an iformation gap between participant and researcher" (Long, Inagaki, and Ortega 1998, 361).

For adjective ordering, in the model treatment group the participants eard the model structure and were given a chance to repeat it, and after that ie researcher and the participants held up the appropriate piece of paper. In ie recast treatment group, the participants viewed a picture on a screen and ere asked to describe it. The researcher provided a recast following the articipants' responses.

For the locative construction treatment, the researcher and the partici-ants were asked to place four dolls on "a drawing of a room containing two ows of seats, two seats per row, matching each other's configuration while eparated by a screen" (362).

The results for the two Japanese syntactic structures reflected in the par-cipants' gain scores (the difference between their performance on a pretest ıd a posttest) were not statistically different. That is, there was no difference ı the acquisition of these constructions among the model, recast, and con-ol groups.

The authors conducted another study, one that also utilized a pretest, osttest, and control group design, with thirty subjects enrolled in a third-

semester Spanish course. The subjects were assigned to five groups: four treatment groups that were later combined for statistical purposes into two group:
(recast and model) and a control group. The selected Spanish structure:
included direct object topicalization and adverb placement. Two commu
nicative tasks were developed for the treatment groups in which the prompt:
were delivered using headphones. In both of these tasks, the participants anc
the researcher were separated by a screen. The participants were asked t(
"communicate about characters, objects, and habitual actions symbolised b\
cardboard cutouts whose disposition they manipulated on felt boards" (365)

The results for the second experiment revealed no significant differenc
among groups regarding the acquisition of direct object topicalization. Th(
findings for adverb placement revealed that learners in the treatment group
(recast and model) outperformed learners in the control group, and learner
in the recast group scored significantly higher than the learners who hear(
modeled structures.

The combined results of both studies, as the authors themselves admit, ar
disappointing. They claim, however, that the findings "nevertheless provid
some evidence in support of the claim that implicit negative feedback plays
facilitative role in L2 acquisition" (367).

I find this final "appraisal" of the facilitative role of implicit negativ(
feedback unjustified and rather typical of the research conducted on thi
topic. Most of the studies of recasts, as shown below, produce inconclusiv(
results; however, like Long and colleagues, they tend to interpret their in
conclusive and often contradictory findings as providing some positive ev:
dence as to the facilitative role of implicit negative feedback.

Considering the controlled nature of these experiments (pretest, posttes
control group), the limited number of grammatical structures that partici
pants were supposed to acquire, and the artificiality of the so-called con
munication games, which one hardly expects to find in a real-life situatio
(such as seeing participants isolated by a screen and communicating v:
headphones) unless one is interacting with an inmate in prison, the fina
results point toward a negative or at best neutral role for implicit negativ(
feedback rather than a facilitative role in second language acquisition.

In the study titled "Conversational Interaction and Second Language Deve(
opment: Recast, Responses, and Red Herrings?" Alison Mackey and Jenef(
Philp (1998) investigated two research questions: "Do learners who partic
pate in task-based interaction with intensive recasts show an increase i
developmentally more advanced structures? and What is the role of the learr
er's response to the recasts?" (Mackey and Philp 1998, 343).

Like Long and colleagues (1998), they used a design that employed a pre-test, a posttest (delayed posttest), and a control group. Second language development was operationalized as changes in question formation and was determined quantitatively by the appearance (production) of at least two higher-level question forms in more than one of the posttests (there were three posttests).

The participants were divided into two groups: "ready" and "unready." Those who began their participation at stage three of Pienemann and Johnston's (1987) six-stage scale for question formation were deemed not ready to acquire question-type structures at stage five or six because the scale is progressive. That is, the individual can accelerate his or her progress within each stage but cannot skip a stage. Stage four has to be acquired prior to stage five, and so on.

In order to obtain answers to their research questions, investigators implemented the following research design (Mackey and Philp 1998, 347):

Group Assignment

Group	Treatment	Group Size
Control	no treatment	6
Interactor Ready	negotiated interaction	6
Interactor Unready	negotiated interaction	6
Recast Ready	interaction with intensive recasts of nontarget-like forms	9
Recast Unready	interaction with intensive recasts of nontarget-like forms	8

Experimental Procedures

Week 1	Week 1	Week 1	Week 1	Week 1	Week 2	Week 5
Day 1	Day 2	Day 3	Day 4	Day 5	Day 5	Day 5
Pretest	Treatment	Treatment	Treatment	Posttest 1	Posttest 2	Posttest 3
Picture	1	2	3	*Picture*	*Picture*	*Picture*
Differences	*Story*	*Story*	*Story*	*Differences*	*Differences*	*Differences*
	Completion	*Completion*	*Completion*			
	Picture	*Picture*	*Picture*			
	Sequencing	*Sequencing*	*Sequencing*			
	Picture	*Picture*	*Picture*			
	Drawing	*Drawing*	*Drawing*			
examples				3 examples	3 examples	3 examples
	(1 example of each)	(1 example of each)	(1 example of each)			

Their findings indicate that no statistically significant difference between the interactor-unready group and the recast-unready group was noted. The significant statistical difference was found to be between the interactor-ready group and the recast-ready group. Owing to the small number of participants in each group, however, and the imprecise nature of the first research question, which affects the reader's ability to determine the appropriateness of the selected statistical procedures (for example, chi square versus one-way ANOVA), these significant results should be treated cautiously. I suggest that they be treated more descriptively than inferentially.

Also, the behavior of the participants in the interactor-unready group undermines the validity of investigators' operational definition of L2 development. Please recall that an increase in the participant's development was operationalized as the production of at least two questions at the next higher level on the six-stage scale on one of the three posttests. An increase in question formations by the unready participants, who managed to acquire question forms not only at the next stage (stage four) but also at stage five (that is, two stages above their current level), calls into question the validity of Pienemann and Johnston's scale. Recall that according to this scale, the "unready" participants were not supposed to acquire question forms beyond stage four.

The findings for the second research question indicate that a great majority of the participants did not modify their output in response to the recasts. They continued to talk. The recasts did not affect their production of more developmentally advanced structures. Despite these findings, Mackey and Philp (1998) still express their support for Long's recasts. They state: "It seems that recasts can provide learners with some of the processes and conditions necessary for L2 learning" (352). But they admit that "it is difficult to identify the process by which recasts may have been incorporated into the database and also to what extent the database was usable" (353). These two statements seem to contradict each other: On one hand, recasts can provide learners with some of the processes necessary for L2 learning, and on the other, it is difficult to determine the process by which recasts may be incorporated into L2 learners' interlanguage. It seems to me that their findings regarding the role of recasts in second language acquisition suggest that this form of implicit negative feedback plays a role in obtaining positive evidence (that is, comprehensible input) rather than in acquiring linguistic forms.

Mackey (1999) also investigates Long's IH in a study titled "Input, Interaction, and Second Language Development: An Empirical Study of Question Formation in ESL." In this study, however, because the researcher found it difficult to distinguish between negotiations and recasts, the focus is on "interaction containing negotiation rather than recasts, although in some cases recasts and negotiation co-occur" (561). There are two main research questions in this study: (a) Does conversational interaction facilitate language development? and (b) Are the developmental outcomes related to the nature of conversational interaction and the level of learner involvement? (565).

The design of the study is very similar to that in Mackey and Philp (1998). It consists of a pretest, a posttest (delayed posttest), and a control group, with the same types of treatment activities as Mackey and Philp's activities (picture differences, story completion, and picture sequencing).

As in Mackey and Philp (1998), L2 development was operationalized as movement through the sequence of developmental stages of Pienemann and Johnston's (1987) scale, and Mackey (1999) imposed "the more stringent criterion of requiring the presence of at least two examples of structures in two different posttests, to strengthen the likelihood that sustained development had occurred" (567).

Mackey makes an attempt to define *interaction*. She writes: "Interaction was operationalized following Long (1996), who claimed, as discussed above, that it is beneficial because it can provide implicit reactive negative feedback that may contain data for language learning. Such feedback can be obtained through interactional adjustments that occur in negotiated interaction" (1999, 565–66). I find her definition of interaction rather ambiguous. It deals more with the results of interaction, such as "it is beneficial," than with its operational definition; *it* still needs to be clearly defined. And the definition of this unknown *it* needs to go beyond "following Long (1996)."

The participants in her study, thirty-four adult ESL learners in Sydney, Australia, were assigned to four treatment groups (interactors, interactor unreadies, observers, scripteds) and a control group. The interactors and the interactor unreadies participated in a task that was carried out in native-speaker–learner pairs in which interactionally modified input was presented to the participants. The observers did not participate directly in a task but observed the interactor group. The scripted group participated in the same task as the interactor group; however, the input was premodified (scripted) and no interactionally modified exchanges were allowed.

The results for developmental stage increases (research question a) indicate that the "Interactor and the Interactor Unready groups made large gains: 5 out of 7 Interactors (71%) and 6 out of 7 Interactor Unreadies (86%) increased in stage. The Observer group made some gains: 4 out of 7 (57%) showed an increase in stage" (Mackey 1999, 571). The scripted group and the control group, however, did not make much progress.

Acknowledging that "second language development is a complex con struct" (573), the researcher conducted an additional statistical investigation of specific question forms to determine the overall interlanguage change in each group. That is, the production of question types characteristic of stages four and five such as "Where does your cat sit?" or "Can you tell me where the cat is?" was analyzed for each group. The results of an ANOVA procedure revealed that "although all groups appear to slightly increase production of question forms during the first posttest, it is only the two interactor group and the Scripted group that appear to maintain this increase during the subsequent tests" (574).

As in Mackey and Philp (1998), the behavior of the interactor unready group is "unexpected." That is, the "unready" participants' increase in L development contradicts the theoretical assumptions of the Pienemann and Johnston scale. It raises the question of the validity of this scale and th appropriateness of using it as the theoretical foundation for the definition of L2 development in the studies that investigate Long's IH.

Also, on the basis of Mackey's (1999) graphic description of the production of questions at stages four and five by the interactor groups, it is unclear wh the interactor unreadies performed better on the last posttest (posttest three than on posttest two and why the interactors performed better on posttest two than on posttest three. These results seem to contradict the so-called de velopmental gains of these two groups. Their behavior is inconsistent with the author's insistence that there were developmental gains for both groups If some progress (development) were to be acknowledged, the interactor should have consistently outperformed the interactor unreadies in questio formations on all three posttests. But the interactors performed worse o the last posttest than did the interactor unreadies; this seems to indicat that there is something going on internally. There must have been som confounding variables that affected their performance. Within this contex Mackey's last statement—"None of the groups demonstrated unambiguou development except the Interactors" (576)—requires closer scrutiny.

As far as the role of the learner's involvement (research question b) i concerned, the author claims that participation in the tasks that were inter actionally modified had a positive effect on the production of developmen tally advanced questions. Even the participants in the observer group bene fited from their passive observations of the modified interaction.

In conclusion, the author claims that the study provides "direct empiric support for the claims of the interaction hypothesis (Long 1996): Inter actional modifications led to SL development and more active involvemer in negotiated interaction led to greater development" (Mackey 1999, 583). It difficult to accept that she found "direct empirical support" for Long's IH, however, because of the following shortcomings of the study: a small number of participants in each group; some reservations as to the appropriateness of the statistical procedures used, such as chi-square; the lack of an operational definition of conversational interaction; the contradictory findings as to the validity of the Pienemann and Johnston scale; and the lack of distinction between language competence and language performance (that is, between acquisition and production).

In addition, I would like to suggest that the production of questions at levels four and five, which was viewed as an increase in L2 development, could have been the result of the effect of task types rather than L2 development. It could have come from memorization of certain question types characteristic of spot-the-differences-in-pictures tasks rather than acquisition of more advanced question forms. Therefore, there is a need to make a clear distinction between acquisition and performance so that it becomes possible to determine which has been measured in her study.

Alison Mackey, Susan Gass, and Kim McDonough (2000) continue to investigate the role of interaction in SLA as proposed by Long (1996) in his interaction hypothesis. Specifically, they examine the issue of perception of implicit negative feedback (recasts) by the learner and the effect of this perception on the learner's subsequent performance.

The participants in this study included ten learners of English as a second language and seven learners of Italian as a foreign language. All were beginners or low-intermediate students. Each participated in what the authors call "communication tasks." As in the studies described above, these tasks involved spotting the differences in pictures. The participants had to identify together the differences between the pictures they viewed. During the interaction the English and Italian interviewers were instructed to provide interactional feedback whenever the participants produced nontarget-like utterances. The interactions were videotaped. The feedback was provided in two forms, negotiation and recast, and it was provided in response to the participants' morphosyntactic, lexical, and phonological errors.

After the completion of the task, the learners had a chance to reflect on their performance. They were asked to recall their thoughts in reaction to the interactional feedback provided to them. Their responses, elicited in order to examine the participants' perceptions about interactional feedback, were recorded. Feedback was categorized into various interactional feedback episodes. Different types of categories were identified on the basis of "the error type that had triggered the feedback" (Mackey, Gass, and McDonough 2000, 480).

The data revealed that in the ESL components the morphosyntactic type of feedback was most frequently provided to the participants, followed by phonological feedback and lexical feedback. The Italian data revealed that the lexical type of feedback was most frequently provided to the participants, followed by morphosyntactic feedback and phonological feedback.

The results of learners' perceptions regarding morphosyntactic feedback suggest that most of the participants in the ESL group perceived it as semantic feedback (that is, they did not regard morphosyntactic feedback as an attempt on the part of the ESL interviewer to draw their attention to the linguistic forms), and the Italian participants perceived it as lexical feedback (that is, as an attempt on the part of the Italian interviewer to provide them with the necessary vocabulary). Thus, the overall results suggest that *neither* group perceived morphosyntactic feedback accurately. The ESL participants seemed to perceive phonological feedback accurately, but the learners of Italian had difficulty recognizing this type of feedback. They tended to perceive it as the lexical type of feedback. The authors suggested that this could be explained by their backgrounds. Most of the Italian participants had some background in Italian, and their interviewer was a nonnative speaker of Italian.

Mackey, Gass, and McDonough (2000) claim that "proponents of the Interaction Hypothesis (Gass, 1997; Long, 1996; Pica, 1994) have suggested that interaction can result in feedback that focuses learners' attention on aspects of their language that deviate from the target language. If learners' reports about their perceptions can be equated with attention, then the findings in this study are consistent with the claims of the Interaction Hypothesis, at least with regard to the lexicon and phonology. In terms of morphosyntax, however, these findings are less consistent with researchers' claims about the benefits of interaction, at least at first glance" (490). The problem with their claim, however, is that in order to accept their proposition, one needs to equate perception with attention. Since the learner's perception and the learner's attention represent the results of two different activities, the former obtained during interaction, the latter while watching the selected feedback episodes, the equation of perception with attention seems to be theoretically implausible. Also, it is not clear whether the authors refer to attention given during the moment of interaction or to attention given while viewing the videotaped episodes. We are confronted here with two different types of attention that have been obtained at different times and places.

Even if one is willing to accept the authors' proposition that perception equals attention, their claim that the findings "are consistent with the claims of the Interaction Hypothesis, at least with regard to the lexicon" (ibid.)

directly undermines their support for the IH because lexicon points in the direction of comprehension, *not* in the direction of attention to linguistic forms (the fundamental claim of the IH). Had the learners recognized morphosyntactic feedback, the authors would have been able to claim their support for the value of the IH in second language acquisition. Their findings undermine the importance of recasts in SLA because their additional analysis of the distribution of feedback type and error type revealed that recasts were most frequently used in response to the participants' morphosyntactic errors, whereas negotiation was most frequently used in response to phonological errors. Had the learners recognized morphosyntactic feedback, the authors would have been able to claim their support for the value of the IH in second language acquisition. But since (1) morphosyntactic feedback in their study was provided most frequently in the form of recasts, and (2) this type of feedback was not appropriately perceived as morphosyntactic feedback but as semantic feedback (as comprehension), then (3) one has to deduce that recasts are not useful devices for providing negative implicit feedback. Recasts do not contribute to focusing the learner's attention on linguistic forms.

The results of the Mackey, Gass, and McDonough (2000) study seem to suggest that the recast represents another interactional device that assists the learner in *comprehension*. Lexis is essential for semantic meaning, which is important for comprehension. This is precisely how the participants perceived morphosyntactic feedback presented in the form of recasts. Since different processes are involved in a syntactic analysis of language in which morphosyntactic structures play an important role, and different processes are involved in a semantic analysis of language in which lexicon plays an important role, basically these findings, unintentionally, I am sure, support my contention that the IH is all about comprehension. These findings also indirectly seem to validate VanPatten's claim (see below) that the learner cannot attend to form and function at same time, a notion that Long's IH seems to reject.

Mackey and colleagues call for reappraisal of the type of design that most of the IH studies utilize. It is clear that most of the studies discussed in this section follow one type of design: pretest, posttest, and control group. I understand the need to impose some scientific rigor on SLA research. Because we are dealing with human beings, however, who will most likely communicate in real-life situations where screens, headphones, and spot-the-difference tasks are not the norm for communication, it is necessary to test the premise of the IH in real-life contexts, under new conditions, within different research paradigms, and in tasks that resemble real-life interaction.

As one of my graduate students pointed out, reading the studies that investigate the role of implicit negative feedback is like reading a map of a Napoleonic war. They are unnecessarily complicated and quite predictable at the same time. They build up expectations as to their scientific importance; they stir up the feeling that we are about to witness the unraveling of one of the greatest mysteries of SLA, only to be disappointed when the findings are presented. The defensiveness of the researchers' explanations of their contradictory findings leaves one with an impression that no matter how statistically insignificant their results turn out to be, they will always be interpreted as providing "some positive evidence for L2 learning."

In conclusion, I suggest that no matter how much the proponents of Long's IH try to "spin" the importance of recasts for the L2, the time has come to give it a rest and accept the reality. The reality is that even under experimental conditions (pretest, posttest, control groups) that elicit highly controlled behavior in one type of task—the information gap task—in which the operational definitions of L2 development, attention as perception, and interaction are full of inconsistencies, these studies still cannot provide clear results as to the positive role of recasts—the centerpiece of Long's IH—in the L2.

VanPatten's Input Processing Model

VanPatten's input processing model of second language acquisition is a classic example of a model that draws heavily on ideas from cognitive psychology. In fact, VanPatten explicitly acknowledges the roots of the ideas utilized in his model. He writes: "We will draw upon various constructs from cognitive psychology, most notably attention, and argue that second language learners are limited capacity processors. As such, they can only attend to so much linguistic data at a time in the input during on-line comprehension" (1996, 14). The metaphors of limited capacity processors, on-line comprehension, input, and linguistic data clearly point in the direction of viewing the learner as a machine, a computer; they are characteristic of the information-processing paradigm.

VanPatten's input processing model is based on three principles:

P1. Learners process input for meaning before they process it for form.
  P1(a). Learners process content words in the input before anything else.
  P1(b). Learners prefer processing lexical items to grammatical items (e.g., morphological markings) for semantic information.
  P1(c). Learners prefer processing "more meaningful" morphology before "less" or "nonmeaningful morphology."

P2. For learners to process form that is not meaningful, they must be able to process informational or communicative content at no (or little) cost to attention.   (VanPatten 1996, 14–15)

P3. Learners possess a default strategy that assigns the role of agent to the first noun (phrase) they encounter in a sentence. We call this "first noun strategy."

   P3(a). The first noun strategy can be overridden by lexical semantics and event probabilities.

   P3(b). Learners will adopt other processing strategies for grammatical role assignment only after their developing system has incorporated other cues (e.g., case marking, acoustic stress).   (1996, 32)

The first principle (P1) draws on attention as a construct of cognitive psychology. Relying on L1 research findings that claim that learning takes place via attention (one has to pay attention to the incoming stimulus in order to learn), Schmidt (1990, 1993, 1994), a leading expert on the role of attention and consciousness in SLA, states that subconscious and subliminal learning, advocated by Krashen and his followers, do not exist. Schmidt writes: "The existing data are compatible with a very strong hypothesis: you can't learn a foreign language (or anything else, for that matter) through subliminal perception" (1990, 142). Tomlin and Villa also claim that during attentional processing one process is of extreme importance for potential second language acquisition—detection—which they define as "the process that selects, or engages, a particular and specific bit of information" (1994, 192). Building on the work of Tomlin, Villa, and Schmidt, VanPatten operationalizes processing as "attending to and detecting linguistic data in the input" (VanPatten 1996, 17).

In P1 VanPatten claims that meaning and form compete for attentional processing resources, with meaning generally prevailing. He writes: "When all else is equal, form and meaning compete for detection—with meaning generally winning out" (1996, 18). This "competition" is based on the assumption that "attention is effortful, and cognitive psychologists generally agree that attention involves a limited capacity to deal with stimuli: Only so much incoming data can be attended to at a given time" (16). In other words, not everything in the input can be attended to and thus potentially detected.

Item P1(a) states that while processing the input for meaning, learners process content words before anything else. The evidence for that comes from studies of child L1 acquisition, as well as from research in second language acquisition (Mangubhai 1991), that shows that beginning L2 learners acquire content words first before they are able to put these words together.

In part P1(b) VanPatten acknowledges that some grammatical features, for example, the English past-tense morpheme *(ed)* encode semantic meaning. In many cases, however, semantic meaning may be conveyed by lexical items rather than by syntactic features. For example, the meaning of the English simple past tense may be conveyed by lexical items such as *ago, yesterday,* or *last year*. This portion of the model assumes that learners prefer lexical items to grammatical items for gleaning semantic information. This is evident in beginning ESL students' uttering **I work yesterday* before *I worked yesterday*. Thus, both P1(a) and P1(b) claim that because the learner's primary attention during processing of the incoming linguistic information is on meaning rather than form, lexical items are given priority over grammatical items.

Item P1(c) addresses the issue of "the relative communicative value of grammatical form" (VanPatten 1996, 24), which is attended to and deduced during input processing. "Communicative value refers to the relative contribution a form makes to the referential meaning of an utterance and is based on the presence or absence of two features: inherent semantic value and redundancy within the sentence-utterance" (ibid.). This notion may be illustrated by the English morpheme *ing*, which tends to be used frequently in daily communication. This morpheme is also salient as far its phonology is concerned; that is, *ing* is more audible than, for example, the English morpheme *ed*. Therefore, the grammatical items that carry a greater relative communicative value will be noticed prior to other grammatical items with less communicative value. They will simply have a better chance to be detected first.

In P2 VanPatten builds on the notion that the learner's limited processing capacities do not allow for detection of forms that are not communicatively meaningful, such as the English third-person singular *s*, before other more communicatively important stimuli are processed. The detection of grammatical features that are not "meaningful" takes up a lot of the energy and resources of a human processor; therefore, they require special attention.

Item P3 is based on the competition model (Bates and MacWhinney 1989). In the competition model, language acquisition is not dependent on a language-specific mechanism such as Chomsky's LAD but on a nonfaculty-specific cognitive information processing mechanism that uses the patterns of the incoming cues during on-line comprehension and production to establish form-function mappings. This process is frequently illustrated by making references to the function of "agency."

Different languages use different devices (cues) to signal the "agent" of a sentence. For example, in the English language there is a tendency to assign the role of agent to the first noun phrase in a sentence. This strategy may be overridden, however, by lexical semantics and real-life experiences or event

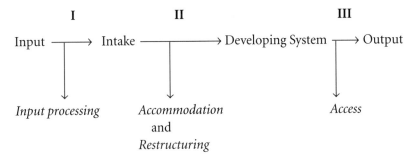

Fig. 4.5. Three Sets of Processes in Second Language Acquisition and Use (based on VanPatten 1996, 154)

probabilities, as exemplified in the following sentence: *A sandwich ate a boy.* The verb *eat* requires an animate agent. In such a case, the first-noun strategy will be overridden and the role of the agent will be assigned to *boy* and not to *sandwich.*

To summarize, according to the first two principles (P1 and P2), the learner, as a limited-capacity processor, favors processing input for meaningful communication prior to processing it for less communicative grammatical features. Only grammatical features that possess high communicative value can easily be detected. In this system, something that is not detected is not given a chance to be acquired. Although detection does not guarantee acquisition, it is considered the prerequisite for acquisition. Grammatical forms will be detected when the learner is able to acquire the meaning of the input effortlessly. When such a process is automatized, the processing resources will be released to attend to and detect other features in the input. VanPatten's (1996) input processing model accounts for the process of making a link (mapping) between form and meaning. Once such a link is detected, the processed input can be delivered to the next stage—intake—to be further processed later on by the developing system.

VanPatten's input processing model consists of three sets of processes that convert input into output: input processing (I), accommodation and restructuring (II), and access (III). These processes are illustrated in figure 4.5. These three principles, with their corollaries, were utilized in VanPatten's expanded model of second language acquisition and use, in which both Chomsky's UG and the learner's native language play an active role. Figure 4.6 illustrates VanPatten's model (1996, 144).

According to this model, first the incoming information is processed for content words. Grammatical categories such as "noun" and "verb" are assigned to the incoming linguistic information (P1a). If there are no available

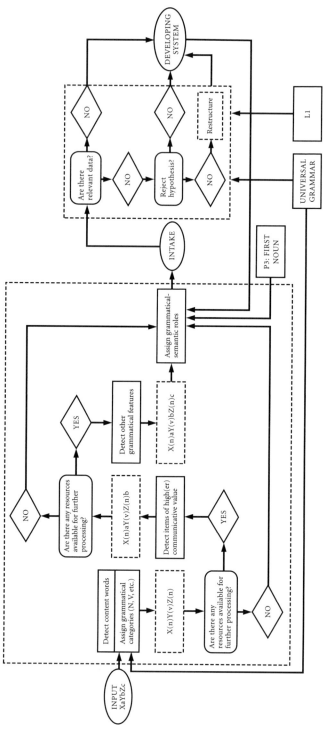

Fig. 4.6. VanPatten's Expanded Model of Second Language Acquisition and Use. (*Source: Bill VanPatten*, Input Processing and Grammar Instruction: Theory and Research. *Norwood, N.J.: Ablex Publishing Corporation, 1996, 144. An imprint of Greenwood Publishing Group, Inc, Westport, CT. Reproduced with permission.*)

resources, then the input is not processed further but is stored in the developing system as lexicon. If there are available resources, however, then there is a possibility that items of higher communicative value are detected (P1b). If there are still available resources in the limited-capacity processor, then the information is processed further, and the detection of grammatical features in the incoming information may occur (P2). This process is followed by the assignment of semantic roles (P3).

Only after all these processes (P1, P2, and P3) have been completed is the detected input converted into intake. Intake is now available to be "fed" into the developing system by passing through two subprocesses: accommodation (adding or rejection) and restructuring. Chomsky's UG plays a decisive role in the operation of accommodation processes. VanPatten claims that "input processing relies on certain knowledge sources such as Universal Grammar (which contains the abstract grammatical categories)" (1996, 42). If intake is accepted, then restructuring processes are most likely going to take place. Access processes are responsible for converting the developing system into output. That is, the entire process of converting input culminates in the output stage, at which the acquired knowledge is used in real-life situations.

As noted above, VanPatten's model is a classic example of an information processing model. It includes typical metaphors that are associated with the information processing model: The learner is viewed as a machine, a limited-capacity processor, and human communication is reduced to the notion of input that needs to be processed according to well-established computational rules. Meaning is reduced primarily to a sentence-level type of information. The model is also linguistically oriented, with the focus placed on the learner's ability to process linguistic structures, and it seems to equate competence with performance.

The relation between output and intake is not explored in VanPatten's model. Are we to assume that there is no relation between access (III) and input processing (I) simply because his model is linear (that is, it leads progressively from one stage to another and the stages rarely interact)? It is also not clear whether VanPatten subscribes to an interface or a noninterface position. Does his model advocate the separation of learning and acquisition, as proposed by Krashen (1985)?

There is also a problem with VanPatten's application of UG to his model. Recall that he places universal grammar in the developing system in connection with accommodation processes. Such a placement would indicate that UG operates on *intake* rather than input. This raises the issue of the relation between VanPatten's UG and Chomsky's. How does VanPatten plan to reconcile this apparent discrepancy between Chomsky's UG, which operates on input, and his UG, which operates on intake?

VanPatten (1996, 133) presents a graph in which he describes the relations among input, UG, and the child's L1. In this graph, UG operates on input, not on intake. In VanPatten's (1996) expanded model of second language acquisition and use, however, the operation of UG seems to be delayed until intake is ready to be transported into his developing system. If this is the case, then we are confronted with two different types of UG: one for children learning the L1 and one for adult learning the L2.

I also take issue with his application of the learner's L1 to the developing system. Recall that the operation of the learner's L1 is associated with restructuring processes that follow accommodation processes within VanPatten's developing system. My questions are: Why is the L1 assigned to restructuring processes and not to these accommodation processes? Why does the L1 follow UG? Recall from Chapter 3 that there are some researchers who claim that UG only operates through the L1. If this is the case, then most of the syntactic analyses of the L1 will likely be based on the parameters established by UG; thus, the processes of the learner's L1 seem to be duplicated. The positing of a relation between Chomsky's UG and the learner's L1 needs some theoretical and empirical justification.

Some explanation of the relation between long-term and short-term memory is needed. VanPatten (1996) claims that information that has not been processed beyond content words is stored as lexicon. But where? Where is this place that stores all of the unprocessed information obtained from the various stages of his model? Also, it is not clear where the information processed by the developing system is stored. Is it stored in long-term memory or short-term memory? The developing system includes two drastically different processes: accommodation (adding information) and restructuring (which changes the quality of the existing developing system) Obviously, the outcomes of these two processes need to be stored differently All of these issues need to be examined more thoroughly on both theoretica and empirical grounds so that the internal validity of the model can be enhanced.

The Application of VanPatten's Model
to L2 Grammar Teaching

VanPatten and Cadierno (1993) use the input processing model to poin to the shortcomings of traditional grammar teaching, which tends to con centrate on access rather than on input processing. This traditional approach is illustrated in figure 4.7. They propose an approach to second languag grammar teaching that focuses on processes that convert input into intake This is illustrated in figure 4.8.

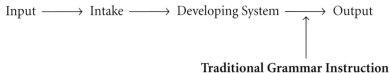

Input ⟶ Intake ⟶ Developing System ⟶ Output

Traditional Grammar Instruction

Fig. 4.7. Traditional Instruction in Foreign Language Teaching (after VanPatten and Cadierno 1993, 227)

VanPatten and Cadierno criticize traditional approaches to teaching grammar that, in their opinion, follow a flawed pattern: introduction of a linguistic problem, practice exercises, and production. These approaches focus on the processes that convert the developing system into output while ignoring the processes that precede the output stage (the processes that convert input into intake).

In his book *Input Processing and Grammar Instruction,* VanPatten (1996) reports on several studies that have been conducted to investigate the effectiveness of his input processing model in grammar teaching. These studies use basically the same research design and similar statistical procedures, and they frequently use the same set of materials developed for the earlier studies. Also, the findings of all these studies assert the "superiority" of input processing instruction to traditional approaches to teaching grammar.

The studies reported in VanPatten (1996) include, among others, VanPatten and Cadierno's (1993) research study, which represents the first empirical investigation of processing instruction and which focused on Spanish object pronouns and word order; Cadierno's (1995) study, which focused on the Spanish past tense; VanPatten and Sanz's (1995) study, which examined the effect of input processing on a variety of communicative tasks; and VanPatten and Oikkenon's (1996) study, which investigated the role of explicit information in processing instruction.

All of these studies elicited data using activities developed for the sole purpose of enhancing and facilitating the transfer of input into intake. These activities are called *structured input* activities. VanPatten provides some guidelines for developing structured input activities that help the learner to detect a connection between form and meaning in the provided input:

. Teach only one thing at a time.
. Keep meaning in focus.
. Learners must do something with the input.
. Use both oral and written input.
. Move from sentences to connected discourse.
. Keep the psycholinguistic processing strategies in mind.

(VanPatten 1996, 67–69)

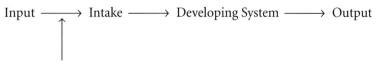

Input Processing Instruction

Fig. 4.8. Input Processing Instruction in Foreign Language Teaching (after VanPatten and Cadierno 1993, 227)

Thus, according to these guidelines, the developer of structured input activities needs to make sure that the learner is given a chance to attend to meaning-oriented input. The activities should be confined to sentence-level input rather than connected discourse, which should be reserved for further teaching. VanPatten claims that "connected discourse may hinder learners' initial processing of the targeted form because of their limited capacity to process incoming data. Connected discourse may not give learners sufficient 'processing time' as the sentences in the discourse occur one after the other to form a larger narrative or text. The result may be that much of the input is 'noise' and the learners may have difficulty in attending to and detecting the relevant grammatical item" (1996, 69). He presents sample lesson plans that illustrate the major components of a lesson based on his input processing model. Such a lesson must include explanation of processing strategies during which learners are informed about the need to pay attention to the grammatical features of the target language that differ from those of their native language. This part of the lesson is followed by structured input activities that include *referentially oriented activities* and *affectively oriented activities*. A referentially oriented activity is one that has right or wrong answers. An affectively oriented activity does not have right or wrong answers, but it asks the learner to indicate "agreement-disagreement, true for me–not true for me, check boxes in surveys, in short, they provide indications of their opinions, beliefs, feelings, and personal circumstances" (64).

The idea behind structured input activities is to draw attention to a connection between form and meaning, one structure at a time. These activities, in contrast to traditional instruction, do not require any production on the part of the learner; they simply make an attempt to make form-meaning connections more accessible (salient) to the learner so that input may be converted into intake.

As I indicated above, most of the studies that applied VanPatten's input processing model to classroom instruction claim that processing instruction is more effective for overall second language acquisition than are traditional approaches. Also, most of them have the same research design; that is, based on one study's design, one can easily predict the design of another. For example, VanPatten and Cadierno's (1993) study, reported in VanPatten (1996, 94), had the following design:

Two Independent Variables:

1. Instruction with Three Levels: Control, Traditional, and Processing
2. Time with Two Levels: Pretest and Posttest

VanPatten and Sanz's (1995) study, reported in VanPatten (1996, 106), had the following design:

Three Independent Variables:

1. Mode with Two Levels: Oral and Written
2. Task with Three Levels: Sentence Level, Question-Answer, and Video Narration
3. Time with Two Levels: Pretest and Posttest

Because of the similarities in these studies' designs, the statistical analyses are also similar. Most of these studies used ANOVA (one-way or two-way, depending on the number of independent variables). And their findings always show that processing instruction is more effective than traditional approaches. For example, processing instruction was more effective in teaching Spanish word order (VanPatten and Cadierno 1993). It was more effective in teaching the Spanish simple past test (Cadierno 1995). It was also more effective in connection with different task types such as the video narration task, the question-answer task, and the sentence-level task (VanPatten and Sanz 1995).

All the positive findings reported in VanPatten (1996) pertain not only to comprehension but also to production. That is, although the students in the processing groups in all of these studies were not asked to produce output during their treatment sessions, the effect of processing instruction was such that not only their ability to make a connection between form and meaning but also their ability to use the selected grammatical structures in output was improved.

In spite of all these "positive findings," however, I would like to point to the very controlled nature of all of these experiments, which are not communicative in nature. For example, consider the tasks used in VanPatten and Sanz's (1995) study. The design of this particular study was such that the tasks differed as to the degree of their "communicativeness." The sentence-level task was less communicative than the question-answer task, which was less so than the video narration task. The students performed better on the video narration task than on the question-answer task, and this raises questions as to the nature of the communicativeness of these tasks. That is, it seems reasonable to expect that the learner who could perform the video narration task successfully would be able to provide sentence-level answers in the question-answer task. Perhaps the contrived nature of these tasks may explain why, although the subjects in the processing group improved, "they performed better in the written mode than the oral mode on the sentence-level completion task and the video narration tasks, but no difference was found for mode on the question-answer task" (VanPatten 1996, 107).

An explanation of these contradictory results may also lie in the coding system used in VanPatten and Sanz's study. That is, the subjective and convoluted scoring system may have had something to do with these "unpredictable" results. VanPatten describes the scoring system as follows: "The use of three different production tasks, with varying numbers of items and types of responses, created a problem in comparability. To solve this, VanPatten and Sanz first transformed all scores into ratios. To do this, they formed a denominator using the number of critical items multiplied by two. They then calculated the numerator by adding the amount of correct responses multiplied by two, the amount of incorrect attempts multiplied by one and the amount of cases in which the item was not supplied at all multiplied by o" (VanPatten 1996, 106).

Also, VanPatten's claim that the learner is unable to attend to both form and meaning simultaneously needs to be reconciled with Doughty's (1991) study results, according to which the subjects of her experiment were able to attend to both, and Long and Robinson's (1998) contention that attention to form and attention to meaning are not always mutually exclusive. Because VanPatten's, Doughty's, and Long's studies are categorized as part of the focus-on-form framework, in which grammar teaching is considered to aid the learner in second language acquisition, it is important that the issue of the learner's ability to pay attention to either form or meaning *or* to both simultaneously be given serious consideration. The lack of a resolution to this theoretical issue affects the teacher's ability to develop efficient classroom activities aimed at assisting learners in grammar acquisition in the focus-on-form framework.

Gass and Selinker's Model

In the last chapter of their book *Second Language Acquisition: An Introductory Course,* Gass and Selinker (2001) present a model of SLA that attempts to integrate all the different subareas of SLA. This integrated model was first introduced by Gass in 1988, and then it was reintroduced in Gass (1997) and in the first edition of *Second Language Acquisition*. Thus, the integrated model of second language acquisition has been in use for almost a decade. Note that although the model was published in Gass and Selinker (2001), Gass is its author. Therefore, in my appraisal of the model, I refer to Gass as its sole author, although all my quotations will be from Gass and Selinker (2001). Figure 4.9 represents Gass's integrated model of second language acquisition.

Gass's model identifies five major stages that are involved "in conversion of input to output: apperceived input, comprehended input, intake, integration, and output" (Gass and Selinker 2001, 400). Each contains stage-specific features. Thus, for example, comprehended input includes universals and prior linguistic knowledge that assist the learner in completing this stage of the analysis of input data, and the intake phase includes hypothesis formation, hypothesis testing, and hypothesis modification and confirmation. Also, each major stage subsumes within its boundaries the preceding stage. Thus, comprehended input cannot exist without apperceived input, intake without comprehended input, and so on.

The first major stage is called the *apperceived stage*. Gass claims that "apperception is the process of understanding by which newly observed qualities of an object are related to past experiences." She continues: "In other words, past experiences relate to the selection of what might be called *noticed* material" (Gass and Selinker 2001, 400). In these two statements, *apperception* is defined as the process of understanding and as the selection of noticed material. The theoretical implications of these two different operational definitions are significant. If the first stage is associated with understanding, then there is no need to grade the process of the conversion of apperceived input into intake by adding another stage—comprehended input. Understanding assumes that the message has been comprehended; therefore, the introduction of the comprehended input stage duplicates the process. If, on the other hand, apperception is viewed as noticing without understanding, adding the stage between apperceived input and intake is justified on theoretical grounds.

In connection with apperceived input, Gass poses the following questions: "Why are some aspects of language noticed by a learner, whereas others are not? What are the mediating factors at this initial stage?" (ibid.). She identifies these factors as frequency, affect (social distance, status, motivation, and attitude), prior knowledge, and attention. I agree with Gass that the last factor, attention, plays an important role in the individual's ability to notice features in the input. I find it difficult, however, to accept her rationale for

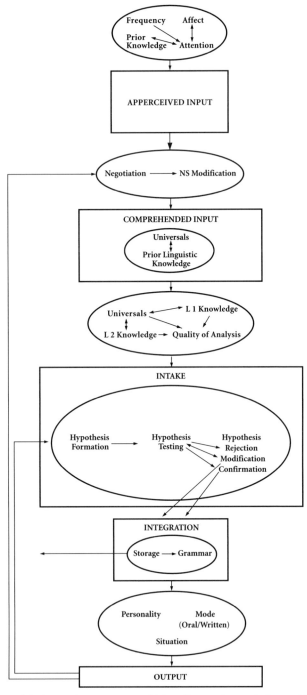

Fig. 4.9. A Model of Second Language Acquisition. *(Source: Susan M. Gass and Larry Selinker, Second Language Acquisition: An Introductory Course, 2d ed. Mahwah, N.J.: Lawrence Erlbaum Associates, 2001, 401. Reprinted with permission.)*

including affective factors such as social distance, status, and motivation at this initial stage of the model. These factors may play a significant role in the learner's ability to get access to input but not necessarily in the learner's ability to notice something in the input. If apperception is to be viewed as an internal cognitive act, noticing something in the input should be viewed as occurring independent of the individual's social or emotional state.

Prior knowledge, the third factor influencing apperception, is defined broadly and "can include knowledge of the native language, knowledge of other languages, existing knowledge of the second language, world knowledge, language universals, and so forth. All of these play a role in a learner's success or lack of success in interpreting language data, in that they ultimately determine whether a learner understands and what level of understanding takes place" (402). The last sentence is rather ambiguous because there is no direct object. "Whether a learner understands" begs a question: understands what?

In connection with the second stage, *comprehended input*, the author distinguishes between Krashen's comprehensible input and comprehended input to order to be able to separate the agents of making the input comprehensible from the agent who is doing the work of "comprehending." Gass states that "comprehensible input is controlled by the person providing input, generally (but not necessarily) a native speaker of the second language, whereas comprehended input is learner-controlled; that is, it is the learner who is or who is not doing the 'work' to understand" (404). Please note that the author again equates comprehended input with understanding, the process that is also expected to take place, as stated above, in the previous stage—apperceived input.

Gass considers the distinction between comprehended input and comprehensible input crucial because of their relation to intake. She writes: "This distinction is crucial in the eventual relationship to intake, because it is the learner who ultimately controls that intake" (404). This distinction, however, requires some explanation as to a possible interaction between comprehensible input and comprehended input. That is, the separation of comprehensible input, which is controlled by the one who provides input, from comprehended input, which is controlled by the learner, raises several questions: Are they indeed totally separated from each other? Or are they interrelated? And what is the effect of this relation on intake?

Another difference between Gass's comprehended input and Krashen's 1985) comprehensible input is associated with the notion of comprehension. Gass claims that in Krashen's definition, comprehensible input is "a dichotomous variable; that is, it is either comprehensible or it is not" (Gass and

Selinker 2001, 404). Gass points out that there are many different levels of comprehension and that it represents "a continuum of possibilities ranging from semantics to detailed structural analyses" (ibid.). Her definition is ambiguous, however, because comprehension seems to be defined in terms of possibilities, not in terms of internal processes. If one were to eliminate the word *possibilities* from her statement, comprehension would equal a continuum of unknown processes.

Gass also claims that "the most typical meaning of *comprehension* is at the level of semantics. However, there is a broader sense of the word, one that includes comprehension of structure as well as meaning" (ibid.). This statement illustrates my point that Gass's *comprehension* is defined more in terms of the word's dictionary meaning than in terms of mental processes.

In order to acknowledge that there are many different levels of analysis and thus of comprehension, Gass claims that "the most common way of getting at a syntactic analysis is by first having an understanding of the meaning. However, one can also imagine having an understanding of the syntax yet not being able to arrive at a meaning. This would be so in the case of idioms, for example, or a proverb" (ibid.). This statement needs some clarification: Does the author imply arriving at the appropriate meaning (that is, appropriate according to cultural and social norms of a given target language culture)? There seems to be some confusion as to semantic meaning and pragmatic meaning. That is, someone may understand syntactic structures essential for encoding semantic meaning but, because of lack of knowledge of sociocultural norms, for example, be unable to arrive at the appropriate pragmatic meaning. This confusion as to semantic and pragmatic meaning is also reflected in Gass's interchanging of the terms *utterance* and *sentence*. In semantics, the minimal unit of analysis is a sentence. The same pertains to syntax. An utterance, on the other hand, is a unit of analysis of pragmatics. Pragmatic meaning goes beyond sentence-level semantic meaning and is dependent on a variety of contextual and textual features. Using the terms *utterance* and *sentence* interchangeably is inappropriate and confusing since, in the earlier chapters of their book, the authors make a clear distinction among different units of analysis: phonology, morphology, lexicon, syntax, semantic, and pragmatics.

Also, according to Gass, "not all input that is comprehended becomes intake. For example, input may be comprehended only for the immediate purpose of a conversational interaction, or it may be used for purposes of learning" (Gass and Selinker 2001, 405). Following Faerch and Kasper (1980) she further states that in her model, intake "refers to the process of attempted integration of linguistic information. Thus, input that is only used in conversation and for the sake of that conversation is not regarded as intake" (ibid.). I am not sure what the author means by "conversation . . . not regarded as intake." According to her model, input cannot become intake unless it passes through two stages, apperceived input and comprehended input, regardless of whether it was originally presented in the form of conversation or some other form. This statement also contradicts her previous statement that "there are also factors specific to conversational interactions that are relevant to how the input can be shaped so that it can be comprehended. Here are included the concepts of negotiation and foreigner talk" (403).

In any conversation, even one held only for the sake of conversation, some negotiations of meaning or modification can take place. Frequently in conversation one can observe real involvement and note that attention is being paid to what someone is saying. Using the author's previous claim that attention is the prerequisite for the conversion of comprehended input to intake, I do not understand why the author dismisses the value of this type of interactional exchange. If "a conversation for the sake of that conversation" is deprived of any value for second language acquisition, are we to assume that L2 acquisition cannot take place in natural contexts? or that a second language can only be acquired under very controlled circumstances or in artificial types of interactions such as spot-the-difference tasks?

Gass defines the third stage of her model, intake, as "the *process* of attempted integration of linguistic information" (405). If that is the case, I do not see the need to include another stage, integration, unless there are two different types: integration at the stage of intake and integration at the stage of integration. Gass writes: "After there is language intake, there are at least two possible outcomes, both of which are a form of integration: the development per se of one's second language grammar, and storage. The distinction made here is between integration and nonintegration of new linguistic information" (407). She claims that "there are essentially four possibilities for dealing with input" (ibid.). The first two, hypothesis confirmation or rejection and apparent nonuse, take place in intake, the third and fourth in the integration component of the model. Integration includes storage and nonuse. In connection with integration, Gass states that "input is put into storage, perhaps because some level of understanding has taken place, yet it is not clear how integration into a learner's grammar can or should take place" (408). She illustrates this point by giving an example of a Spanish-speaking ESL student who has heard the word *so* in a sentence such as *So, what did you do last night?* Because the student is not sure about the meaning of the word *so*, he or she "stores" this information and waits for the next opportunity to ask the teacher about the meaning of this word. The stored information "waits" until its proper interpretation takes place so that it can be integrated into the learner's grammar.

The problem with her explanation of the process of storage in the integration component of her model is that according to the model, if the learner is not able to comprehend what the word *so* in the sentence quoted above means, then we are *not* dealing with the stage of integration (recall that the model is progressive)—we are dealing with the stage of apperceived input that has not yet been comprehended. In addition, her definition of integration raises a question of storage of information in general. Why does storage have to be an integral part of integration and not intake, for example? The nature of processes associated with intake, such as hypothesis testing, modification, and rejection, requires some storage of the compared and tested information. That is, in order to be able to reject, compare, or modify information, one needs to be able to hold or store the new information, even if temporarily. Also, if the learner needs to store the input because of an inability to integrate it into his or her grammar, should not this input be regarded as part of the previous stage (intake) and not integration?

The process of understanding is also identified with the stage of integration (recall "because some level of understanding has taken place . . ."). These different levels of understanding are neither defined nor distinguished from one another. The process of understanding at the level of comprehended input is not differentiated from understanding at the levels of intake and integration. This treatment of the process of understanding illustrates my larger point that Gass's model includes too many stages, processes, and factors that are not clearly operationalized, and this seriously undermines the internal validity of her integrated model of second language acquisition.

The same factors that mediate comprehended input, intake, and integration also operate at the level of apperception. That is, the same factors that influence the least complex stage, apperceived input (the stage of noticing influence the outcomes of more complex stages, such as intake, in which hypothesis formation takes place. Even if one were to accept Gass's proposition that indeed the same factors operate at all levels of linguistic analysis considering the fact that the outcomes of each stage are different, the various factors' contributions to the outcomes must be different. Therefore, listing set of factors that supposedly influence each major stage of her model does not help us in understanding the nature of these factors and their impact; it does not explain how the same factors may produce different results at the different stages.

In Gass's model, the last stage, output, interacts with intake. One may wonder, however, Why not extend its interaction to apperceived input since

1.   Krashen's Model

Input ———→ LAD ———→ Output

2.   VanPatten's Model

Input ———→ Intake ———→ Developing System ———→ Output

3.   Gass's Model

Input → Apperceived → Comprehended → Intake → Integration → Output
         Input   Input

Fig. 4.10. A Comparison of Information Processing Models

self-generated input may be used to notice the gap in the learner's grammatical knowledge? At the end of her discussion of the effects of different factors on output, the author claims that "different grammatical information may be used in different genres" (Gass and Selinker 2001, 410). Since the model is based on the assumption that the learner has access to stored information that is "universal" in nature, are we to assume from her statement that *one* universal grammatical system is able to produce different speech genres? If so, then her model does not explain how the learner is able to use one uniform grammatical system in genres that may require different grammatical systems. Here linguistic competence is confused with linguistic performance, as it is in all information processing models. The processes that are associated with linguistic competence are not distinguished from those that are associated with linguistic performance. That is, although the model focuses on linguistic competence, it also claims to account for the use of this knowledge in real-life situations—in which speech genres vary—without identifying processes that pertain to linguistic performance.

Gass's model complements and expands on Krashen's and VanPatten's models. In her model, apperceived input is transformed into comprehended input, which then is transformed into intake, which is integrated into the learner's grammar before it can be utilized in output. Output can be recycled to become intake. Interaction is viewed primarily as a cognitive issue, not as a social issue, as the interaction among internal components of the model. Interaction is presented in a linear and progressive fashion. It leads from apperceived input to comprehended input to intake to integration to output. Figure 4.10 represents a comparison of Gass's model with Krashen's and VanPatten's models.

Simply stated, Gass's model retains Krashen's input and output and Van-

Patten's intake but grades the processes that lead to intake by adding apperceived input and comprehended input. Integration, despite its different label, is similar to VanPatten's developing system.

All of these models include the metaphors typical of models that adhere to the information processing paradigm. These metaphors include input, intake, output, storage, data processing mechanisms, limited-capacity processors, language data, attention-getting devices, and databases. In all these models, the focus is on the learner's cognitive processes. The process of analyzing the incoming information is viewed as being mechanistic, predictable, stable, and universal. The outside reality, or social context, is acknowledged indirectly, abstractly, and superficially, mainly in the stage associated with input or apperceived input. Input presented to the learner takes on the form of data entry, which is processed in a mechanistic and predictable fashion, according to a programmed sequence in which no individual variation is allowed to take place. Any real human interaction is viewed as "a conversation for the sake of that conversation" that does not contribute to the acquisition of linguistic forms. Interaction is not viewed as a social issue but as a cognitive issue, for which the individual is solely responsible. It is viewed primarily in terms of the interaction among different components of the model in the individual's mind.

I continue discussing the role of interaction in Chapter 5, in which several communicative competence models are described in order to further illustrate my point that most influential models of SLA are cognitively oriented and in these models interaction is viewed as a cognitive issue and not as a social issue.

5

Communicative Competence Versus Interactional Competence

In this chapter I describe two of the most popular and influential models of communicative competence. Their descriptions will be preceded by a historical overview of the notion of communicative competence. At the end of this chapter I also describe interactional competence (Young 1999), which represents an alternative framework. The purpose of this chapter is to further illustrate the current cognitive "bias" in SLA theory and research.

As illustrated below, despite having a name that may give the impression that these models adhere to a communicative view of language, communication (that is, interaction) is viewed as a cognitive issue. In these models *interaction* refers mainly to the interaction among various language competencies, placed directly in the mind of the learner. Also, the learner is solely responsible for his or her interaction with the external world. Communicative competence models are only communicatively or interactionally based on the surface. They are monologically based because the learner is interacting with himself or herself. The learner is a loner in an artificially created social context that tends to be described in terms of stable features identified a priori. Since these social features are viewed as being stable and are assumed to be understood by all participants in the interaction in the same fashion, there is no need for coconstruction, or building an understanding of the shared reality based on dialogically negotiated interaction. These models adhere primarily to the transmission model of passing the information (that is, the conduit metaphor). The information is encoded by the speaker, who sends a message to the hearer, who, in turn, decodes the message.

Also, communicative competence models send a false message to second language learners that once various language competencies included in these models are acquired, language performance in a real-life situation is achieved automatically. These models present an idealized, homogenized view of the researcher's vision of what human communication should represent. It is almost as if this artificial and abstract depiction of human communication was developed in a laboratory where objects and different substances can be observed, measured, and added and subtracted from one another in a uniform and predictable fashion or as if communication were "objectified" and "normalized" to satisfy the requirements of an experiment. Such a view of human communication is devoid of the unpredictability of real-life interaction and totally ignores "the messy, ambiguous, and context-sensitive processes of meaning making" (Bruner 1996, 5).

A Historical Overview of the Concept of Communicative Competence

Noam Chomsky is considered to be the originator of the notion of linguistic competence, which he associates with an ideal speaker's tacit knowledge of his or her native language's grammatical structures only. Chomsky writes: "Linguistic theory is concerned primarily with an ideal speaker-listener, in a completely homogeneous speech-community, who knows its language perfectly and is unaffected by such grammatically irrelevant conditions as memory limitations, distractions, shifts of attention and interest, and errors (random or characteristic) in applying his knowledge of the language in actual performance" (Chomsky 1965, 3). The ultimate goal of linguistic theory is to explain first language acquisition. By *first language acquisition* Chomsky and his proponents refer to the acquisition of grammatical competence only. Note also that Chomsky (1988) in *Language and Problems of Knowledge* openly admits that he does not know how a second language is acquired. His theory of universal grammar attempts to account for the acquisition of the child's native language grammar.

Recall that according to Chomsky, all human beings are born with an innate propensity to learn language. We all are born with the language acquisition device (LAD), which is responsible for analyzing linguistic input. The LAD contains universal grammar (UG), which consists of a set of universal principles, abstract rules, and language-specific parameters. Univers grammar assists the child with the acquisition of his or her native language grammar and helps the child to create an unlimited number of novel sentences based on a limited number of abstract rules and principles.

Chomsky divides linguistic theory into two parts: linguistic competence and linguistic performance. The former concerns the tacit knowledge of grammar, the latter the realization of this knowledge in actual performance. Chomsky distinctly relegates linguistic performance to the peripherals of linguistic inquiry. Linguistic performance as the actual use of language in concrete situations is viewed as "fairly degenerate in quality" (Chomsky 1965, 31) because performance is full of errors.

Chomsky's constructs of linguistic competence and performance can be traced back to the nineteenth-century French structural linguist de Saussure (1959), who divided language into *la langue* (that is, a system of signs) and *la parole* (that is, the realization of this system in a particular situation). Chomsky's linguistic competence corresponds to *la langue*, and Chomsky's linguistic performance corresponds to *la parole*. Chomsky's linguistic competence, however, because it is concerned primarily with the underlying competence, is viewed as superior to de Saussure's *la langue.*

As discussed in Chapter 3, Chomsky's theory of UG has had a great impact on the field of linguistics. Precisely because of its importance, some researchers (for example, Gregg 1989; Cook 1985, 1988; Flynn 1987) advocate its application to the field of second language acquisition.

A competing view—communicative competence—has its roots in an ongoing debate about the value and appropriateness of Chomsky's theory for SLA and is closely associated with Hymes's notion of communicative competence.

Hymes's Communicative Competence

Dell Hymes (1972) objected to Chomsky's definition of linguistic competence. He introduced the term *communicative competence* in order to expand Chomsky's definition of competence beyond the knowledge of tacit grammatical rules. Hymes stated that "there are rules of use without which the rules of grammar would be useless" (1972, 278). Contrary to Chomsky, Hymes claims that when a child acquires his or her native language, the child acquires "knowledge of sentences, not only as grammatical, but also as appropriate. He or she acquires competence as to when to speak, when not, and as to what to talk about with whom, when, where, in what manner" (277). He calls this ability to use the grammatical rules that are appropriate to a given social context *sociolinguistic competence,* which introduces the notion of a

Table 5.1 Comparison of the Functional and the Structural Views of Language

Structural or Formalist	Functional
1. Structure of language (*code*) seen as grammar	1. Structure of speech (act, event) seen as ways of speaking
2. Analysis of language code precedes analysis of use	2. Analysis of use precedes analysis of language code
3. Referential function is the norm	3. Gamut of social functions is the *norm*
4. Single homogeneous code and community	4. Heterogeneous speech and community

Source: After Hymes 1974; Johnson 2001, 43

heterogeneous speech community and the notion of a heterogeneou speaker. Hymes's sociolinguistic competence stands in sharp contrast to Chomsky's notions of a completely homogeneous speech community and a ideal, homogeneous speaker and listener.

Hymes's view of language as functional also differs from Chomsky's view of language as structural (that is, formal). Hymes (1974) provides a list of the major characteristics of these two views of language, which are summarized in table 5.1.

Hymes (1974) adheres to the functional paradigm, in which language i viewed not as a code but as ways of speaking, the structure of language i not grammar but a speech act or speech event, and language code and language use are in a dialectical relationship. Within this functional paradigm, single homogeneous ("idealized") speech community is replaced by a speech community regarded as running the gamut of speech styles. Also, language is viewed as a societal phenomenon rather than a mental phenomenon which tends to be primarily associated with the formalist (structural) view o language.

He also questions Chomsky's definition of performance, specifically it inability to distinguish

(1) (underlying) competence v. (actual) performance and
(2) (underlying) grammatical competence v. (underlying) models/rules o performance.   (Hymes 1972, 280

According to Hymes, Chomsky does not make clear whether performanc should be viewed as "the actual use of language in concrete situations (Chomsky 1965, 4) or as the underlying rules (that is, states or abilities) o

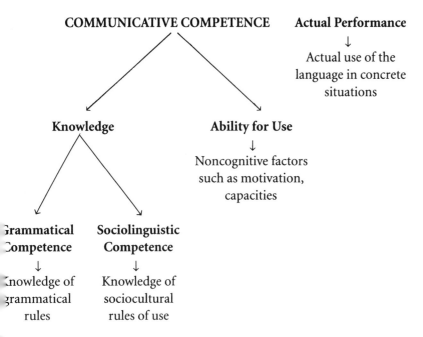

COMMUNICATIVE COMPETENCE

Actual Performance
↓
Actual use of the
language in concrete
situations

Knowledge

Ability for Use
↓
Noncognitive factors
such as motivation,
capacities

Grammatical Competence
↓
Knowledge of
grammatical
rules

Sociolinguistic Competence
↓
Knowledge of
sociocultural
rules of use

Fig. 5.1. Hymes's Communicative Competence Model. *(Source: Marysia Johnson,* The Art of
Nonconversation: A Reexamination of the Validity of the Oral Proficiency Interview. *New
Haven: Yale University Press, 2001, 157.)*

performance not yet realized in the actual performance. Hymes (1972) calls
these underlying rules of performance *ability for use,* which he places within
his new model of communicative competence. He defines *ability for use* as
"Noncognitive factors, such as motivation" and other factors such as those
identified by Goffman (1967): "Courage, gameness, gallantry, composure,
presence of mind, dignity, stage confidence, capacities" (Hymes 1972, 283).

Thus, Hymes's communicative competence is "dependent upon both
(tacit) knowledge and (ability) for use" (282). This tacit knowledge includes
both grammatical competence and sociolinguistic competence. Hymes's
communicative competence is illustrated in figure 5.1.

Canale and Swain's Communicative Competence Models

Some researchers working in the field of SLA found Hymes's communicative competence relevant for the second language learning context.
Michael Canale and Merrill Swain expanded Hymes's model into a model of
communicative competence for SLA.

Canale and Swain's (1980) original second language communicative competence model consisted of three components: grammatical competence, sociolinguistic competence, and strategic competence. In 1983, Canale added discourse competence to their original model.

In the four-component model, *grammatical competence* is defined as "knowledge of lexical items and rules of morphology, syntax, and sentence grammar semantics, and phonology" (Canale and Swain 1980, 29). Their *sociolinguistic competence* is similar to Hymes's (knowledge of the rules of language use). *Strategic competence* is defined as "verbal and non-verbal communication strategies that may be called into action to compensate for breakdowns in communication due to performance variables or to insufficient competence" (30). *Discourse competence* is defined as knowledge of how to achieve cohesion and coherence in a text and is based on the work of Halliday and Hasan (1976).

The Canale and Swain model does not include Hymes's ability for use. The authors provide the following reasons why they decided to exclude this notion from their model: "(i) to our knowledge this notion has not been pursued rigorously in any research on communicative competence (or considered directly relevant in such research), and (ii) we doubt that there is any theory of human action that can adequately explicate 'ability for use' and support principles of syllabus design intended to reflect this notion" (1980, 7).

In contrast to Hymes, Canale and Swain placed ability for use within communicative performance, which they defined as "the realization of these competencies and their interaction in the actual production and comprehension of utterances (under general psychological constraints that are unique to performance)" (6). It seems that because of its complex nature they decided to place ability for use in "the actual production and comprehension." They also indirectly seem to support the view of ability for use as "the actual use of language in concrete situations" (Chomsky 1965, 4) rather than as Hymes's underlying states and abilities of linguistic performance not yet realized in the actual performance. The combined models (Canale and Swain 1980 and Canale 1983) are illustrated in figure 5.2.

As Johnson (2001) points out, despite Canale and Swain's efforts to exclude ability for use from their model, at least two of their competencies, strategic and discourse, make implicit references to it. It is difficult to imagine that nonverbal strategies, for example, represent only an individual's knowledge and not skills, such as the individual's ability in drawing or in using gestures. The same reservation can apply to the notion of coherence. It is difficult to imagine that the ability to create coherence in a text is only a matter of

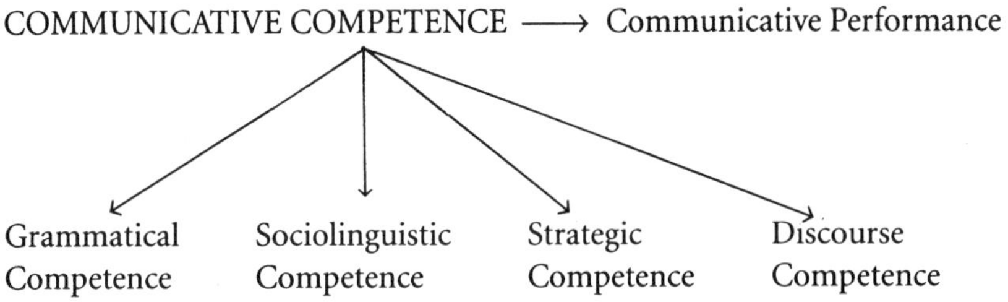

COMMUNICATIVE COMPETENCE ⟶ Communicative Performance

Grammatical   Sociolinguistic   Strategic   Discourse
Competence   Competence   Competence Competence

Fig. 5.2. Canale and Swain's Communicative Competence Model. *(Source: Marysia Johnson, The Art of Nonconversation: A Reexamination of the Validity of the Oral Proficiency Interview. New Haven: Yale University Press, 2001, 159.)*

knowledge and not of skills such as logical thinking. Thus, despite their explicit refusal to open what McNamara (1996) rightly called a Pandora's box, Canale and Swain implicitly introduced ability for use into their communicative competence model.

In addition to the problem of ability for use, there are some other problems with the model. For example, the mechanism responsible for interaction among the competencies is not identified or explained. Therefore, it is not clear how this interaction is conducted in the individual's mind or how it is implemented in social contexts. Moreover, based on their definition of communicative competence, it is not clear whether these four competencies contribute *equally* to all the outcomes of interaction or whether each competence's contribution differs depending on the context of interaction.

Contrary to the structural model of language organization, discussed in Chapter 2, in which interaction among components such as phonetics, phonology, morphology, and syntax is clearly described, in Canale and Swain's 1980) communicative competence model, interaction among different competencies is vaguely described. These competencies are linearly, not pyramidally, structured (recall figure 2.1). It is not clear how much each of the identified competencies contributes to the total outcome of interaction and whether they all need to be present in order for a communicative goal to be achieved, although it is not difficult to image that in some social situations, reliance on one or two competencies such as the sociolinguistic and the strategic could outperform the remaining competencies in achieving communicative goals. Schmidt's (1983) case study of Wes is a classic example of such an occurrence.

Moreover, there is some ambiguity associated with Canale and Swain's definition of interaction. It is difficult to determine whether they refer to the interaction that takes place in the individual's mind, to the interaction with the outside environment, or both. Recall, for example, that the authors definition of strategic competence refers to the successful implementation o verbal and nonverbal strategies to compensate for a breakdown in communi-cation. Thus, their strategic competence seems to point in the direction o interaction with other interlocutors because the successful implementatior of strategic competence requires that the interlocutor signal his or her lack o comprehension of the speaker's message; it requires some assistance on the part of the interlocutor. On the other hand, Canale and Swain's separation o communicative competence from actual performance and their focus on the former seem to point in the direction of the view that interaction among different competencies takes place in the mind of the learner—it is a cognitive issue, not a social issue.

To summarize, Canale and Swain expanded Hymes's communicative com petence model by adding two other competencies: discourse competence and strategic competence. Canale and Swain are also responsible for introducing perhaps unintentionally, the notion of interaction, which they viewed pri marily as a cognitive issue rather than a social issue. By doing so, they also raised a question regarding the nature of the mechanism responsible for such interaction. The popularity of Canale and Swain's model remained unchal lenged until Bachman (1990) introduced his communicative language abilit model (CLA).

Bachman's Communicative Language Ability Model

Lyle Bachman describes CLA as "consisting of both knowledge, o competence, and the capacity for implementing, or executing that compe tence in appropriate, contextualized communicative language use" (199c 84). His model consists of three competencies: language competence, strate gic competence, and psychophysiological mechanisms. Of these three, th most important is strategic competence, which drastically differs from Ca nale and Swain's strategic competence.

Bachman's strategic competence pertains to general underlying cognitiv skills in language use such as assessing, planning, and executing, which ar instrumental for achieving communicative goals. In Bachman's CLA, strate gic competence is separated from language competence and assigned non linguistic, cognitive functions. The main function of Bachman's strategi competence is to relate language competence to the speaker's knowledge c the world and to the features of the context in which language use takes place Thus, the shortcoming of Canale and Swain's model regarding the lack of mechanism responsible for the interaction of their competencies is resolve

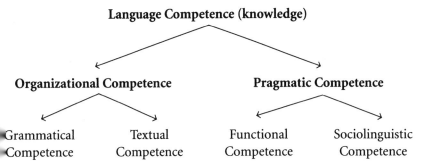

Fig. 5.3. Bachman's Language Competence Model (after Bachman 1990, 87; Bachman and Palmer 1996, 68; Johnson 2001, 164)

n Bachman's strategic competence, which represents the mechanism responsible for such interaction.

Bachman's language competence is divided into two major components: *organizational competence* and *pragmatic competence*. The first consists of two subcomponents: *grammatical competence,* defined as the knowledge of vocabulary, morphology, syntax, and phonology, and *textual competence,* defined as "the knowledge of the conventions for joining utterances together to form a text" (1990, 88). The second is divided into two subcomponents: *illocutionary competence* and *sociolinguistic competence*. Illocutionary competence is essential for a wide range of language functions such as ideational, manipulative, regulatory, interactional, heuristic, and imaginative functions. Note that Bachman and Palmer (1996) replaced the name *illocutionary competence* with *functional knowledge*. They state: "Functional knowledge, or what Bachman (1990) calls 'illocutionary competence', enables us to interpret relationships between utterances or sentences and texts and the intentions of language users" (69). They also replaced the word *competence* with *knowledge;* that is, grammatical competence was replaced with grammatical knowledge, textual competence with textual knowledge, and so on.

The last subcomponent of Bachman's pragmatic competence—sociolinguistic competence—is defined as "sensitivity to, or control of the conventions of language use that are determined by the features of the specific language use context" (1990, 94). Bachman further defines the abilities subsumed under sociolinguistic competence as "sensitivity to differences in dialect or variety, to differences in register and to naturalness, and the ability to interpret cultural references and figures of speech" (95). The major components of Bachman's language competence are illustrated in figure 5.3.

Although Bachman's CLA may be regarded as an improved and expanded version of the Canale and Swain model, there are still some problems with it. Like the Canale and Swain model, Bachman's model presents a cognitive view of interaction. Furthermore, by placing cohesion under organizational competence and coherence under pragmatic competence, Bachman separates the features of language competence that are in a reciprocal relationship in real-life communication. As Johnson (2001) points out, although this separation may be justified on logical grounds, it cannot be justified on practical grounds. In real-life communication, it is not uncommon to produce a coherent text without employing any cohesive devices. Grice's conversational implicature may serve as an illustration of this point:

> A: Smith doesn't seem to have a girlfriend these days.
> B: He has been paying a lot of visits to New York lately.
>
> (Grice 1975, 51)

If one were to adhere to Bachman's separation of cohesion and coherence in a testing situation, for example, one could obtain a high score on cohesion and a low score on coherence. The interpretation of the test taker's score for these features would be difficult to achieve in a real-life context.

As indicated above, Bachman and Palmer (1996) replaced the name *illocutionary competence* with *functional knowledge*. Despite this name change, however, their definition of functional knowledge is still unclear: the word *relationships* is ambiguous. It is not clear whether they view "relationships between utterances or sentences" in terms of cohesion and coherence, in terms of the speaker's intentions, or both.

In addition, their usage of the word *sentences* is inappropriate in the context of pragmatics. Recall that in their CLA model functional knowledge is included under pragmatic knowledge. It is a well-accepted fact that what distinguishes semantics from pragmatics is a different unit of analysis. A sentence is associated with semantics, and an utterance is associated with pragmatics. This distinction is important because it has profound theoretical implications for another fundamental concept—that of *context.*

In semantics, context is limited to a grammatical context (that is, the meaning of a sentence is confined to the context of the sentence). On the other hand, when one uses the term *utterance,* one moves away from the territory of sentence-level semantics, from the literal meaning of a sentence toward the broader interpretation of context in pragmatics, where the meaning of the same utterance may differ depending on the context in which it was uttered.

Because of major theoretical research findings in the field of discourse analysis (for example, Schiffrin 1990, 1994; Brown and Yule 1983; Stubbs 1983; Levinson 1983; Goffman 1967, 1974, 1976, 1981; Gumperz 1982; Goodwin and Duranti 1992; Goodwin and Goodman 1992), our understanding of the notion of context has been broadened substantially. Context is essential for our ability to interpret the intended meaning of the speaker's utterances (Goodwin and Duranti 1992). Students of discourse analysis are familiar with a definition of context that changes depending on the type of discourse approach one chooses. The choice among different discourse approaches is important because these approaches, owing to their different treatments of the notion of context, will produce different interpretations of the same text (Schiffrin 1994). Pragmatics, viewed primarily as Grice's pragmatics (Schiffrin 1994), is one of many approaches to discourse analysis. Speech act theory, interactional sociolinguistics, variation analysis, the ethnography of communications, and conversation analysis represent other approaches to discourse analysis (Schiffrin 1994). Given these developments in the field of discourse analysis, it seems that the choice of the term *pragmatic knowledge* by Bachman (1990) and Bachman and Palmer (1996) is rather obsolete and loosely defined.

Also, according to the latest developments in discourse analysis, the functions used by Bachman and Palmer, which appear to be based on the work of Jakobson (1972) and Halliday (1973, 1976), are not appropriate. This set of functions, identified as ideational, manipulative, regulatory, interactional, heuristic, and imaginative, gives an impression of being constant and stable across various social contexts. If these functions are to be constant and stable, the definition of social context needs to be stable as well. And this is precisely how the authors define context in their model. They define it a priori in terms of stable features such as register, dialect, and variety. Social context is viewed as being autonomous and separated from other components. The possibility that language can create social context and vice versa during actual interaction is not addressed in their model.

It seems as if Bachman (1990) was more concerned with "normalizing" context by enumerating its stable characteristics than with trying to understand what that social context means to different individuals engaged in real-life communication. This understanding of how the individual views social context is essential for our ability to understand the individual's behavior, or performance, in a particular social context. Perhaps Bachman's background in language testing has something to do with this static view of social context. The fundamental principle of language testing—reliability—demands that scores be consistent across different times or different tests, or among different testers. Therefore, the skills or abilities to be measured and the context in which they are to be measured need to be "stabilized" and normalized to eliminate the possibility of error.

As Johnson (2001) points out, there is also a problem with Bachman's definition of sociolinguistic competence: "sensitivity to, or control of the conventions of language use." He goes on to identify the abilities subsumed under sociolinguistic competence as "sensitivity to differences in dialect or variety, to differences in register and naturalness, and the ability to interpret cultural references and figures of speech" (1990, 95). From this definition, however, it is not clear "whether his notion of sensitivity and control should fall under the category of language competence. Sensitivity, after all, can be viewed as a personality trait, as a person's ability to feel empathy, and not a language knowledge" (Johnson 2001, 169). Therefore, one may argue that Bachman's definition of sociolinguistic competence mixes the underlying rules of performance (that is, Hymes's ability for use) with underlying language competence, and perhaps some of its elements should be placed under Bachman's strategic competence.

Note that Bachman's (1990) CLA model and Canale and Swain's (1980) communicative competence model have not been empirically validated, although Bachman and Palmer (1982) found some empirical evidence for their distinction between pragmatic, grammatical, and sociolinguistic competencies (Bachman 1990).

The lack of empirical evidence as to these models' validity, the models' abstractness and theoretical complexity, and their almost exclusive focus on language competence, coupled with their disregard for actual language performance in real-life contexts, have contributed to the current state of dissatisfaction with the existing models of communicative competence. This dissatisfaction with the models' view of interaction as a cognitive issue rather than a social issue led to the development of a new model—the interactional competence model (Hall 1993, 1995; He and Young 1998; Young 1999).

Interactional Competence

Interactional competence is "a theory of the knowledge that participants bring to and realize in interaction and includes an account of how such knowledge is acquired" (Young 1999, 118). The fundamental principle of interactional competence asserts that general language competence does not exist; only local, context-specific competence exists. Such treatment of the *local* nature of language competence differs fundamentally from communicative competence models, which assume the existence of *universal* competence. Interactional competence is located in specific instances of locally bound interaction, which Joan Hall (1993, 144) has called "oral practices." She defines these oral practices as speech events that are "socioculturally conventionalized configurations of face-to-face interaction by which and within which group members communicate." Hall (1995) replaced oral practices with interactive practices. "Interactive practices are recurring episodes of talk that share a particular structure and are of sociocultural significance to a community of speakers" (Young 1999, 118). During participation in interactive practices, the individual acquires many resources of various types, such as vocabulary and syntax, knowledge of how to manage turns and topics, and knowledge of rhetorical scripts and skills (Young 1999; Hall 1993, 1995). Once acquired, these resources can be generalized to the same type of interactive practices. For example, once the individual acquires the interactional competence to participate in a formal interview, the individual will be able to transfer this knowledge to interactive practices in which formal interviews take place.

Interaction in this model is viewed not as a cognitive issue but as a social issue. That is, interaction is not viewed abstractly, as a process of combining different competencies that takes place inside the individual's mind, but is viewed as face-to-face interaction among all participants in interactive practices. Thus, interaction takes on a different form—the form of human communication among people in real-life sociocultural settings.

Face-to-face interaction and the local nature of language competence are combined with another fundamental principle of the theory of interactional competence: coconstruction. *Coconstruction* is defined as "the joint creation of a form, interpretation, stance, action, activity, identity, institution, skill, ideology, emotion, or other culturally meaningful reality" (Jacoby and Ochs 1995, 171). According to interactional competence, knowledge of language is jointly co-created by all participants in interaction (He and Young 1998; Young 1999). Note that this notion does not assume that all coconstruction needs to be friendly (Jacoby and Ochs 1995). An argument is just as coconstructed as a friendly dialogue or a conversation.

The notion of coconstruction releases the individual from his or her sole responsibility for conducting a successful and appropriate interaction for a given social context. The responsibility for such interaction is shared by all participants. Also, in the theory of interactional competence, meaning does not exist independent of social reality. It is not fixed in advance. Meaning is negotiated through face-to-face interaction and is jointly coconstructed in a locally bound social context.

As indicated above, the theory of interactional competence also accounts

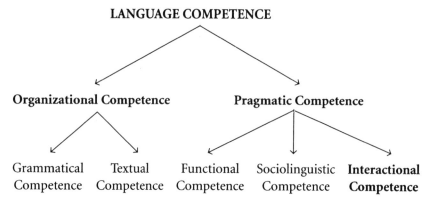

Fig. 5.4. Interactional Competence and Bachman's Language Competence Model

for how such knowledge is acquired. According to Hall (1995), interactional competence is acquired through three processes or stages, which can be summarized as discovery, observation-reflection, and construction. The first involves "the discovery (other-and-self-guided) of interactive patterns in the practices in which we engage with other" (Hall 1995, 218). The second involves "observation and reflection on others' participatory moves and the responses to these moves" (ibid.). The last stage involves "our own active constructions of responses to these patterns" (ibid.).

To summarize, interactional competence is a theory of the knowledge of language that one needs to possess in order to participate in interactive practices. It is a theory of second language acquisition because it identifies processes (stages) that lead to the acquisition of resources that are indispensable for the development and use of interactional competence. Interactional competence is locally developed and jointly constructed by all participants in interactive practices. Interactional competence proposes a view of inter-

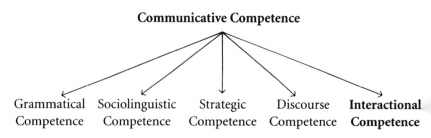

Fig. 5.5. Interactional Competence and Canale and Swain's Communicative Competence Model

action that is social, not cognitive. It also states that general (universal) language competence does not exist; only local competencies exist. The domain of the theory of interactional competence is face-to-face interaction.

Interactional competence, as its name indicates, focuses on *competence* rather than performance. Therefore, it can be regarded as an expansion of communicative competence models. One may argue that interactional competence can easily be added to Bachman's (1990) language competence model as an aspect of his pragmatic competence. If so, then Bachman's *pragmatic competence* would then be comprised of three competencies: functional, sociolinguistic, and interactional. This is illustrated in figure 5.4. Or interactional competence can be added to Canale and Swain's model, which would then be comprised of five competencies: grammatical, strategic, discourse, sociolinguistic, and interactional, as illustrated in figure 5.5.

As Johnson (2001) points out, although interactional competence offers new insights into the nature of second language acquisition, these insights have their roots in Vygotsky's sociocultural theory. In order to fully understand and appreciate the fundamental principles of interactional competence, such as the notion of locally developed competencies, the role of social, cultural, and institutional settings in the development of interactional competence, and the origin of Hall's (1995) three stages in the acquisition of interactional competence, one needs to refer to the work of Vygotsky. In my opinion, interactional competence can easily be subsumed within Vygotsky's sociocultural theory, which offers a more powerful and comprehensive view of language ability.

In Chapter 6 I provide an overview of Vygotsky's sociocultural theory in order to give the reader a chance to see some of the vital connections between his theory and interactional competence and to lay the foundation for my claim that his theory offers a unique theoretical framework for the entire field of second language acquisition (second language theory, research, teaching, and testing). Vygotsky's theory offers a new understanding of what second language knowledge is, how it is acquired, and how it should be taught and assessed.

PART **II**

A Dialogical Approach to SLA

6

Fundamental Principles of Vygotsky's Sociocultural Theory

In this chapter I describe the major tenets of Lev Vygotsky's sociocultural theory (SCT). I also present some biographical information about Vygotsky in support of his claim that we are all products of the social, cultural, and historical environments to which we have been exposed in the course of our lives. As one would expect of a genius, some of his ideas transcend time and space; some, however, are a clear reflection of his time: they are rooted in the political and social climate of his era.

Vygotsky: Biographical Notes

Vygotsky was born Lev Vygodsky on November 5, 1896, in Orsha, a small town near Minsk in Belorussia. A year later, his family moved to Gomel, where his father worked as a department chief at the bank. In Gomel, Lev Semenovich Vygotsky went to the private Jewish Gymnasium, graduating with a gold medal in 1913. In that year he entered Moscow University, where he studied law. He also attended the Shanyavskii People's University, an unofficial school taught by faculty members who had been expelled from Moscow University for their involvement in an antitsarist movement. Here Vygotsky pursued his interests in philosophy, literature, theater, and psychology. Having received his degree in law from Moscow University, he returned to Gomel. Vygotsky could not practice law because of major political changes that were taking place in Russia during that time. The abolishment of the tsarist government and creation of a new state—the Soviet Union—made his law degree worthless. Instead, Vygotsky taught literature and psychology in various state schools, including Gomel's Teacher College, where he conducted his first psychological experiments, which became the basis for his *Pedagogical Psychology*.

In Gomel, Vygotsky held various positions that made him one of the most prominent cultural figures. He gave talks on the topics of literature, art history, science, and theater. Throughout his life Vygotsky was interested in theater. He even wrote a paper on the psychology of the actor. These varied interests were crucial for the development of his unified theory of human higher mental functions.

Vygotsky spent seven years in Gomel after his return from Moscow. The outbreak of Russian Revolution in 1917 and the subsequent political and economic changes must have had as great an impact on his life as they had on the lives of millions of Russians who endured the unspeakable atrocities of Stalin's regime, including the death of thirty million people from persecution, starvation, and exile to Siberian concentration camps.

Little is known about Vygotsky's political affiliations during this time. Some suggest that Vygotsky was critical of the new Bolshevik Party, although this claim cannot be substantiated. If he was opposed to the new emerging totalitarian regime, his political views must have been kept secret. He simply would not have survived had he been critical of the new Soviet regime.

For Vygotsky, 1924 was a very important year from both a personal and a professional point of view. He married that year, and he also made a presentation at the Second All-Russian Psychoneurological Congress in Leningrad. His presentation at the congress was so impressive that the director of the Psychological Institute in Moscow invited him to join the institute's faculty, sparking the second period of Vygotsky's career. By accepting the position, Vygotsky shifted the focus of his interests from literature, arts, and theater to problems in psychology and pedagogy.

The years between 1924 and 1934 (the time of his death) were very productive. During these years, he wrote most of his now-famous books, including *Mind in Society*. At the institute in Moscow, Vygotsky was very much involved in developing a new kind of psychology, one based on Marxist philosophy. Luria, one of his colleagues and followers, claims that Vygotsky was a leading Marxist theoretician. This claim seems to be supported by Wertsch (1985a) and by the flourishing of Vygotsky's career during the formation of the Soviet Union. As indicated above, his success would not have been possible had h expressed even the slightest objection to the official Soviet doctrine. The fact that he was working on the new Marxist psychology to be used by the regime to control the masses most likely saved his life.

During his last ten years, in addition to working on his research and writings, Vygotsky traveled extensively, gave lectures in various academic institutions, set up research laboratories, and trained teachers and psychologists in many parts of the Soviet Union. Some of his research activities were moved to Kharkov, in the Ukraine, where one of his students and followers—Leont'ev—developed a school of psychology called activity theory.

Vygotsky died in 1934 of tuberculosis. After his death, his writings were banned for more than twenty years. The publication of his work resumed after Stalin's death. Vygotsky left behind many articles, several books, and many unpublished manuscripts. He also left behind a group of students and collaborators who went on to promote his ideas.

Vygotsky's theory of human higher mental functioning is currently enjoying great popularity in the West. Many researchers working in the fields of psychology, education, and second language acquisition find his ideas very appealing and useful. This growing interest in his work at the dawn of a new century seems to represent the best evidence of his genius.

Vygotsky's Sociocultural Theory

In this section I describe the fundamental principles of sociocultural theory. At the end of this chapter, I also address the relation between SCT and activity theory.

Vygotsky's sociocultural theory can be summarized in terms of three major tenets (Wertsch 1990, 1985a; Johnson 2001):

1. the developmental analysis of mental processes;
2. the social origin of human mental processes; and
3. the role of sign systems in the development of human higher mental functions.

Note that although these tenets may be analyzed and investigated separately, all are closely interrelated. That is, the understanding of one requires a full understanding of the others and the way they interact with one another.

The first tenet refers to the type of analysis (that is, scientific method) Vygotsky advocated for the investigation, understanding, and interpretation of human psychological functions. He called for a search for a new method because "the search for method becomes one of the most important problems of the entire enterprise of understanding the uniquely human forms of psychological activity" (1978, 65), and "any fundamentally new approach to a scientific problem inevitably leads to new methods of investigation and analysis" (58). Vygotsky, thus, saw a close relation between the method used in the analysis of a scientific problem and our interpretation and understanding of the problem itself.

He criticized various schools of psychology of his time, Piaget's in particular. He objected to both the introspective and the objective methods used by an experimental type of psychology in the investigation of human higher mental development. Dissatisfied with the existing methods of analysis, Vygotsky developed a fundamentally different method based on Engels's *dialectic* philosophy, which stresses the importance of change as the main factor in human social development. For Engels, this change is brought about by a constant conflict between opposite forces such as nature affecting humans and humans affecting nature. In the process of interaction and tension between opposite forces, new conditions for human social existence are developed. Vygotsky found Engels's ideas applicable to his new method. They constitute the foundation on which his new method is based. He writes: "The dialectical approach, while admitting the influence of nature on man, asserts that man, in turn, affects nature and creates through his changes in nature new natural conditions for his existence (Engels, *Dialectics in Nature*). This position is the keystone of our approach to the study and interpretation of man's higher psychological functions and serves as the basis for the new methods of experimentation and analysis that we advocate" (Vygotsky 1978, 60–61). He claims that "we need to concentrate not on the *product* of development but on the very *process* by which higher forms are established" (64).

Vygotsky's dialectical method requires an investigation of all major points in the history of human mental development. It requires the investigation of this process "in all its phases and changes—from birth to death" (65). For that reason, the method is called historical. This method studies higher mental processes on many levels. All are governed by their own explanatory principles. Because all these levels are interrelated, however, the development of higher mental functions cannot be fully explained by the principles or laws that govern only one level. Vygotsky's method captures the nature of human mental development at all levels *simultaneously.*

Vygotsky identified and described four such levels: phylogenesis, sociocultural history, ontogenesis, and microgenesis (Wertsch 1985a). The first, phylogenesis, refers to the *evolutionary* development of humans. Vygotsky agreed with Marx that the ability to use tools, in addition to the obvious biological differences in brain development, distinguishes humans from higher apes. Although Vygotsky acknowledged the significance of phylogenesis in the development of higher mental functions, he considered other levels to be more significant in this development. He subscribed to the position reflected in the following statement of his student and follower, Leont'ev: "Man learns from the errors—and still more from the successes—of other people while each generation of animal can learn solely from its own. . . . It is mankind as a whole, but not a separate human being, who interacts with the biological environment; therefore such laws of evolution as, for example, the law of natural selection become invalid inside the human society" (Leont'ev 1970, 124).

Although Vygotsky did not see the continuation of the development of human higher mental functions between the levels of phylogenesis and sociocultural history, he did see the continuation of the processes between sociocultural history and ontogenesis. For him, the processes undergone in these two levels coincide because the ability to use tools and sign systems by society as a whole (the sociocultural domain) affects ontogenesis—the individual level of human mental development.

Vygotsky viewed the third level, *ontogenesis,* in terms of two forces: natural (biological) and cultural. The former is responsible for lower-level mental functions such as perception and involuntary attention, and the latter for higher mental functions such as voluntary attention, planning, monitoring, rational thought, and learning. These two forces, although difficult to separate from an empirical point of view, nevertheless operate independently and are governed by different sets of rules. What distinguishes these two forces is the degree and type of regulation. The lower (elementary) functions are regulated by the environment, and the higher mental functions are self-regulated. He writes: "The central characteristic of elementary functions is that they are totally and directly determined by stimulation from the environment. For higher functions, the central feature is self-generated stimulation, that is, the creation and use of artificial stimuli which become the immediate causes of behavior" (1978, 39).

The fourth level of Vygotsky's new method is called *microgenesis.* According to Vygotsky, human higher mental functioning should be investigated not only longitudinally but also in a very short period of time, for example, during the individual's first reactions to a task in an experiment. Such observations, characteristic of the domain of microgenesis, allow the investigator to "grasp the process in flight" (1978, 68). They allow us to investigate human mental processes in which the first and most critical mental links are established. Vygotsky criticizes scientific research studies that tend to disregard the value of such observations and pay too much attention to the behavior that has already been "fossilized" by the individual.

In sum, the first tenet of Vygotsky's SCT, his genetic method of analysis of human mental functions, states that only by a thorough analysis of human mental processes at all four levels—phylogenesis, sociocultural history, ontogenesis, and microgenesis—simultaneously can we arrive at a complete and accurate interpretation and understanding of human mental functioning. Note that although Vygotsky identified four levels, most of his research was conducted at that of ontogenesis—the individual level of human mental development.

Sociocultural Origin of Human Higher Mental Functions

The second tenet of Vygotsky's SCT claims that higher mental functions, such as rational thought and learning, originate in social activity. This claim is captured in the *general genetic law of cultural development:* "Any function in the child's cultural development appears twice, or on two planes. First it appears on the social plane, and then on the psychological plane. First it appears between people as an interpsychological category, and then within the child as an intrapsychological category. This is equally true with regard to voluntary attention, logical memory, the formation of concepts, and the development of volition. We may consider this position as a law in the full sense of the word, but it goes without saying that internalization transforms the process itself and changes its structure and functions. Social relations or relations among people genetically underline all higher functions and their relationships" (Vygotsky 1981, 163). Thus, according to the general genetic law of cultural development, higher mental functions originate on the interpersonal (that is, the social, historical, or institutional) plane—on the plane external to the individual. While participating in many social activities on the interpersonal plane, the individual internalizes the patterns of these social activities. The process of internalization of patterns of social activities is very complex and dynamic. It can be described as a gradual movement from the initial stage, at which the individual is solely controlled by the environment (the object-regulated stage), to the other-regulated stage, at which the individual's mental functioning depends on the adult's assistance, and finally to the self-regulated stage, at which the individual takes control of his or her higher mental processes.

The transition from the interpersonal to the intrapersonal plane is dependent on the mediated function of sign systems, in which language plays a crucial role. I will return to the role of language in the development of human higher mental functions in the section pertaining to the third tenet of Vygotsky's SCT.

Vygotsky's assertion that higher mental functions originate on the social plane was revolutionary. It undermined Piaget's claim that higher mental functions unfold independent of social contexts and they are not influenced by external processes. By *external processes* Vygotsky meant learning that is available to a child in a variety of social, cultural, and institutional settings. Vygotsky considered the natural or biological line of development "raw material" for sociocultural forces, raw material that is transformed by learning available to a child on the sociocultural plane. The sociocultural plane thus provides the necessary foundation for the development of higher mental functions; it transforms lower functions into higher mental functions. For Vygotsky, higher mental functions do *not* originate on the biological plane; they originate on the social plane.

Higher mental functions develop by means of a process of internalization of many patterns observed on the social plane. This internalization, although originated on the interpersonal plane, does not represent a replica of the interpersonal plane because, as Vygotsky points out, "internalization transforms the process itself and changes its structure and functions" (ibid.). That is, internal processes reflect external processes, but they are not identical because external processes are transformed during their appropriation. Although not identical, these two processes—interpersonal and intrapersonal—are closely related. Thus, in order to understand higher mental functions, we need to investigate their origins—the sociocultural contexts to which the individual has been exposed in the course of his or her life.

To explain the relation between the interpersonal and the intrapersonal plane, Vygotsky developed the concept of the zone of proximal development (ZPD), which he defined as "the distance between the actual developmental level as determined by independent problem solving and the level of potential development as determined through problem solving under adult guidance or in collaboration with more capable peers" (1978, 86). Thus, he distinguished between two crucial levels of development: actual and potential. The former represents children's ability to perform mental activities without help from a more capable peer. This independence indicates that the functions associated with the independently performed activities have been stabilized; no intervention from another person is necessary. The latter level, the potential level of development, indicates that certain mental functions have not been stabilized; therefore, some intervention (assistance from a more capable peer or tutor) is required. The difference between these two levels can be mathematically presented as follows:

The potential level *minus* the actual level *equals* the zone of proximal development. It can be graphically represented as shown in figure 6.1.

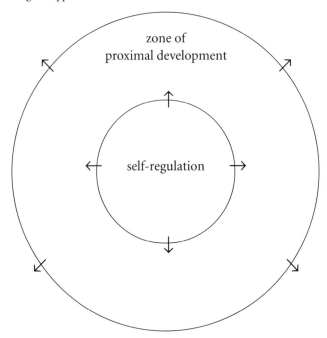

Fig. 6.1. Zone of Proximal Development (Source: Leo van Lier, *Interaction in the Languag* *Curriculum: Awareness, Autonomy, and Authenticity*. London: Longman, 1996: 190. An im print of Pearson Education, Inc., White Plains, N.Y. Reproduced with permission.)

Vygotsky was more interested in the individual's (that is, the child's) po tential level of development than in his or her current (actual) level of de velopment. Two individuals may be at the same level of actual developme as determined by their test scores, for example, but may exhibit differe levels of potential development as determined by their differing abilities solve the same problem with a different degree of assistance from an adu Vygotsky criticized common practices in education and testing that focu primarily on the child's actual level of development and pay little attention the child's potential level of development. He called the latter "the buds" "flowers" rather than the "fruits" of development (ibid.). These "buds" nee to be cultivated and nourished in the zone of proximal development.

Vygotsky claims that "an essential feature of learning is that it creates t zone of proximal development; that is, learning awakens a variety of intern developmental processes that are able to operate only when the child interacting with people in his environment and in cooperation with h peers. Once these processes are internalized, they become part of the chil independent developmental achievement." He continues: "Learning is a ne essary and universal aspect of the process of developing culturally organized, specifically human, psychological functions" (1978, 90).

To summarize, all higher mental functions originate in a social activity— on the interpersonal plane. The interpersonal plane is transformed into the intrapersonal plane by the gradual, dynamic process of internalization of the patterns of social activities to which the individual has been exposed in the course of his or her entire life. The process of internalization of these socially originated human behaviors is possible because of the mediated function of sign systems. Contrary to the proponents of the cognitive paradigm, Vygotsky maintains that sociocultural factors occupy the central position in the development of human higher functioning. Although he recognizes the importance of biological constraints on human mental development, he denies the human brain the central position in cognitive development. For Vygotsky, the development of higher mental functioning such as voluntary attention, logical memory, rational thought, and learning represents not the unfolding of innate cognitive abilities but the *transformation* of these capacities that is initiated by the child's sociocultural environment. Socioculturally constructed mediational signs such as algebraic symbols and above all, language, generate this transformation. According to SCT, the study of human mental development is the study of how mediated means, which are symbolic and sociocultural in nature, are internalized (that is, appropriated) by the individual. This appropriation of mediational means is the result of dialogic interaction between children and other members of their sociocultural worlds such as parents, teachers, coaches, and friends. This leads us to the third tenet of Vygotsky's SCT: the role of semiotics (sign systems), in particular, language, in human higher mental functions.

The Mediated Role of Language in the Development of Human Higher Mental Functions

Vygotsky's fundamental theoretical insight is that language, in addition to fulfilling its communicative function, serves as a means of organizing mental activities. According to Vygotsky, language regulates and facilitates not only the child's manipulation of objects but also his or her behavior. The main function of speech is to serve as a mediator between two planes: the interpersonal (between people) and the intrapersonal (within the individual). The function of speech as an organizer of private mental functioning is evident in the emergence of egocentric (private) speech.

At the age of seven, the child is able to distinguish between two functions of speech: speech for oneself and speech for the other. The emergence of the so-called egocentric speech signals the beginning of the transition from the interpersonal plane to the intrapersonal plane. When this transition is completed, egocentric speech becomes *inner speech*. "Egocentric speech is a stage of development preceding inner speech: Both fulfill intellectual functions; their structures are similar . . . one changes into the other" (Vygotsky 1986, 226).

Egocentric speech appears when the child is confronted with a task that exceeds his or her current level of development. In such situations, the child develops a method of behavior—egocentric speech—that, combined with the child's appeal for help from an adult, guides the child through a problem-solving activity that exceeds his or her actual level of development.

Egocentric speech resembles the patterns of speech behavior to which the child has been exposed on the interpersonal plane, but it lacks all grammatical features of social speech. The child may, for example, utter the word *red* while looking for a red piece to complete a puzzle. *Red* thus stands for the entire statement *I am looking for a red piece*. The emergence of egocentric speech is important because it reveals some insights about the structure of human higher mental functions. It provides an explanation as to how interaction on the interpersonal plane, combined with the child's biological endowment, constitutes the source of the development of higher mental functions.

In contrast to Piaget, Vygotsky does not accept the notion that egocentric speech simply disappears with the child's cognitive development. Vygotsky claims that egocentric speech turns "inward" and becomes verbal thought-inner speech—a silent and inaudible dialogue in the mind of the individual.

Egocentric speech can be viewed as a transitional vehicle from the interpersonal to the intrapersonal plane. Once this transition is completed, egocentric (private) speech takes on the form of inner speech, "speech for oneself" (Vygotsky 1986, 225), which is inaccessible to human observation. Egocentric speech thus provides us with invaluable insights as to the nature and structure of verbal thoughts, which Vygotsky termed "speech without words." Because one changes into another and their structures are similar, "egocentric speech provides the key to the study of inner speech" (226).

In order to discover the main characteristics of egocentric speech, one must observe speech patterns on the social plane, and to understand the structure of inner speech, one needs to turn to egocentric speech. Vygotsky thus establishes a close link between the inner speech of the adult and the egocentric speech of the child. He provides an answer to the question of why speech goes inward. It goes inward "because its function changes" (1986, 86). Different functions of speech are associated with different forms of speech: external, egocentric, and inner. Therefore, the line of progression proceeds from external speech to egocentric speech, and finally to inner speech.

Although all these different forms of speech are related, they are not the same. Vygotsky (1986) warns us against premature equation of inner speech with external speech, speech for communication among people. He writes of "inner speech, which is neither an antecedent of external speech nor its reproduction in memory, but is, in a sense, the opposite of external speech. The latter is the turning of thoughts into words, their materialization and objectification. With inner speech, the process is reversed, going from out-side to inside. Overt speech sublimates into thoughts" (226).

The distinction between inner processes and external speech processes described in the quotation above is important. Vygotsky discourages us from equating these two processes because if they were to be equated, his socio-cultural theory would have resembled the behavioristic theory of stimuli and responses. Absorbing speech into thoughts should be viewed not as the individual's passive assimilation of the outside stimuli but as his or her active process of transforming external speech into thoughts. The exposure to the external speech initiates and activates an ever-present process of convert-ing speech into thoughts in which the individual, an active agent, plays an important role. One also needs to be reminded that "verbal thought, how-ever, does not by any means include all forms of thought or all forms of speech. There is a vast area of thought that has no direct relation to speech" (Vygotsky 1986, 88).

Cognitive development requires that the child move from reliance on others to reliance on his or her inner speech, in which the control over his or her mental functioning takes place. The beginning of the child's quest for self-regulation and cognitive independence is signaled by the emergence of egocentric speech—a vocalized form of inner speech—in which the first attempt at self-regulation emerges. Private speech provides the child with metacognitive tools such as planning, guiding, and monitoring of activity that exceeds the child's current level of cognitive development. It represents the child's attempt to preserve his or her cognitive freedom by trying to perform the task on his or her own.

What are the major characteristics of inner speech, egocentric speech turned inward?

In inner speech, the role of syntax and phonetics is minimalized. The sentence-level subject (agent) and other syntactic expressions associated with it are deleted. This reduction may be explained by the fact that the agent of the action expressed in the subject of a sentence is well known to the speaker; therefore, there is no need, from the speaker's point of view, to mention it. According to Vygotsky, inner speech exhibits "abbreviations" on both the syntactic and the semantic level. As we may expect to hear a single "No" in place of a complete answer, "No, I do not want to go to the movies," for example, a similar syntactic phenomenon is observed in inner speech. Vygotsky calls this abbreviation of the syntax of inner speech "predicativity" because of its heavy reliance on a predicate and elimination of the sentence-level subject.

According to Wertsch (1991, 41), this predicativity should not be associated with the predicate of a sentence but with a psychological predicate. In psychological predicativity the elements that are recognized by the speaker are eliminated and those that are not recognized remain. As indicated above, inner speech is fragmented and incomprehensible to the outside world because of its contracted nature. The outside observer is unable to understand it without a specific reference to a particular situation, which may only be relevant to the speaker.

The reduced nature of phonetics is also typical of inner speech. That is, one basic characteristic of inner speech is the absence of its vocalization. There is no need to fully pronounce words in the mind of the speaker; they are understood completely by the speaker. "Inner speech works with semantics, not phonetics" (Vygotsky 1986, 244). The nature of the relation between the phonetics and the semantics of inner speech is a major source of controversy (Ushakova 1998). That is, the acoustic and "voiceless" interaction and the storage of the phonetic information are the subjects of an ongoing debate.

Vygotsky considers inner speech to be the main vehicle of higher mental functions such as planning and monitoring of activity. He also regards it as "a distinct plane of verbal thought" (1986, 248). As the term "verbal thought" seems to suggest, two basic components of inner speech are language (words) and thoughts. He writes: "But while in external speech thought is embodied in words, in inner speech words die as they bring forth thought. Inner speech is to a large extent thinking in pure meanings. It is a dynamic, shifting, unstable thing, fluttering between word and thought, the two more or less stable, more or less firmly delineated components of verbal thought" (249).

As this quotation indicates, words play a crucial role in inner speech. Any word carries two meanings, according to Vygotsky: one is stable, "fixed" across different contexts, just as one may find it in a dictionary; the other—sense—has less to do with its recognizable external meaning than with its many psychological associations, acquired during the process of internalizing the many words, utterances, and voices one has encountered in many different sociocultural contexts in the course of his or her life. The latter feature of inner speech is "the preponderance of the sense [*smysl*] of a word over its meaning [*znachenie*]" (Vygotsky 1986, 244). The notion of sense is closely connected with Vygotsky's unit of semiotic analysis: the word.

As indicated above, Vygotsky distinguishes between meaning (*znaczenie* and sense *(smysl)*. The former has a referential function and is constant across different contexts, like a dictionary definition, and the latter differs depending on a context. For example, the meaning of the word *green* indicates a color; its sense, however, may indicate either a color or the name of a political party (the Green Party), a personal trait (being gullible), or something else. There is no one-to-one correspondence between meaning and sense of a word. Inner speech consists of sense, which, in contrast to meaning, is highly abstract and decontextualized. Vygotsky writes: "The sense of a word . . . is the sum of all the psychological events aroused in our consciousness by the word. It is a dynamic, fluid, complex whole, which has several zones of unequal stability. Meaning is only one of the zones of sense, the more stable and precise zone. A word acquires its sense from the context in which it appears; in different contexts, it changes its sense" (1986, 244–45).

Another basic semantic quality of inner speech is speech called *agglutination*. The term derives from the process found in synthetic languages in which a given word meaning is formed by merging several words into one word. Vygotsky writes: "When several words are merged into one word, the new word not only expresses a rather complex idea, but designates all the separate elements contained in that idea" (1986, 246). The same phenomenon is observed in inner speech, in which new senses are created by merging several senses into one.

Thus, "influx of sense" (ibid.) represents another characteristic of inner speech in which "the senses of different words flow into one another—literally 'influence' one another—so that the earlier ones are contained in, and modify, the later ones" (246–47). As in agglutinating languages, the senses of a word are fused with one another, with the principal sense serving as a point of reference, evoking other associations (senses) that can be quickly identified by the speaker. Vygotsky illustrates this point by making an analogy to a title that carries the sense of the entire work of literature. For example, the title *Hamlet,* denoting a specific Shakespearean masterpiece, carries the maximum semantic load and serves as a point of departure for other senses of this word that the individual may have internalized in the course of his or her life. It may evoke the play the individual watched in London, the exam he or she failed at school on the topic of Shakespeare, or the role he or she played in a high school production of *Hamlet.* The title, thus, illustrates one of the characteristics of inner speech—agglutination—in which the meaning of the word consists of a series of interconnected, fused, senses that are comprehensible only to the speaker.

In developing his semiotic ideas, Vygotsky was influenced by the Russian formalist school (Wertsch 1985a), which dominated the literary criticism and

linguistics of his time, including the work of Jakobson and especially Yaku-
binskii, who distinguished between two functions of speech: one for social
communication among people, and the other more abstract. The first function of speech is more indicative (or referential) and is very contextualized,
and the other is more symbolic and decontextualized. Vygotsky applied these
ideas to his semiotic analysis of higher mental functions.

According to Vygotsky, the decontextualization of a word's meaning—the
development of sense—constitutes a prerequisite for the transition from the
interpersonal to the intrapersonal plane. This decontextualization is acquired
by means of a gradual movement across various stages. The first stage is
unorganized. In this stage, the child categorizes things based on his or her
subjective ground. For example, the word *dog* may refer to any object with
four legs. In the second stage, the child categorizes objects based on objective
categories inherent in objects. For example, the child is able to categorize
objects according to colors. The next stage, pseudoconcept, is a transition to
the conceptual stage. In the pseudoconcept stage, the child is able to exhibit
some characteristics of thinking in concepts, but not consistently. In the last
stage, the genuine concepts appear. The development of the sense of word
mediates the child's ability to develop higher mental functions that can only
be developed in educational settings, where learning in the zone of proximal
development is created and encouraged.

For Vygotsky, learning and development are not the same thing. His view
concerning the relation between learning and development stand in a sharp
contrast to Piaget's. Vygotsky made a revolutionary claim that social factor
can override biological or natural factors in the development of higher mental consciousness. The child's unfolding development is not shaped by
programmed cognitive code, as Piaget's cognitive psychology seems to suggest, but by other people in the community to which the child has been
exposed. The speech of this community affects the child's higher mental
development.

Thought, in Vygotsky's view, is basically inner speech. And since the root
of inner speech can be found on the social plane, in social speech, thought is
fundamentally a human activity in which learning plays a crucial role. Learning, especially learning in educational settings, provides a unique opportunity for the development of decontextualized meanings of words indispensable for the development of inner speech and thus higher levels of rational
thinking.

Vygotsky's semiotic theory—his theory of mediational functions of sign
systems—provides a crucial line between cultural and communicative form
of behavior among individuals (on the interpersonal plane) and psycholog-

cal processes within the individual (on the intrapersonal plane). He writes: "The internalization of cultural forms of behavior involves the reconstruction of psychological activity on the basis of sign operations" (1978, 57). We engage in many social activities, which are mediated by all kinds of signs including linguistic signs. With the assistance of these mediational means, "sign operations," the external interactions conducted in a variety of social contexts are appropriated and become inner speech—speech for oneself—verbal thinking.

Note that in SCT linguistic signs and cognitive processes do not precede their application in real-life social contexts: they are the results of the individual's participation in social activities. Social interaction constitutes the prerequisite for the emergence of higher forms of consciousness. From SCT's perspective, linguistic signs should not be viewed as arbitrary because their origin can be traced back to a variety of social interactions. Once they are internalized, they become objects of reflection that, in turn, affect their external application. Vygotsky's theory is about the dialectic interaction between the external (social) and internal (mental) planes, one transforming the other. This dialectic relation rejects the binary tradition of the hard sciences: it rejects separation of the human mind and body, mental and social processes, the individual and society, and language and context.

In sum, Vygotsky's theory points to the multileveled nature of inner speech and its connection to external speech. Connections between speech and thought originate on the interpersonal plane, where speech is used for communication among people. By means of the mediated power of semiotic sign systems in which language plays the most crucial role, the patterns and behaviors observed on the social plane are being internalized.

Activity Theory

The relation between sociocultural theory and activity theory is still the object of debate. In general, Russian psychologists see more discrepancies between these two theories than do Western psychologists. Contrary to their Russian counterparts, Western psychologists and scientists have a tendency to merge these two theories into one framework.

If we are to understand the connection between SCT and activity theory, some historical background is needed (Wertsch 1981, 1985a, 1985b, 1991; Wertsch et al. 1995). As mentioned in the section concerning Vygotsky's life, Leont'ev was one of Vygotsky's closest students and collaborators. He worked with Vygotsky in the Institute of Psychology in Moscow. He also made some major contributions to Vygotsky's sociocultural theory. In 1930, Leont'ev moved to Kharkov, in the Ukraine, where he began working on developin[new school of psychology: activity theory.

Those who claim that sociocultural theory and activity theory represe one framework point to the fact that Leont'ev himself acknowledged several occasions that these two theories are indeed closely related. Desp his assurance, there is one major difference between them. The main focus SCT is on the mediated function of sign systems, or the role of language a society in the development of higher consciousness. The main focus of ε tivity theory is on tools and objects of labor in the development of hum consciousness. This apparent difference may be explained, as Zinchen (1995) suggests, by the different political realities in which these two : searchers (Vygotsky and Leont'ev) had to work.

Recall that after Vygotsky's death, his writings were banned by Stali regime because of their divergence from the official Marxist philosopl Perhaps because of their fear of persecution, Leont'ev and his colleagι subordinated their research interests to the demands of the Soviet regin They diminished the role of more idealistic and symbolic forces (that is, t role of language and culture) in human mental functioning and concentra instead on tools, more materialistic forces. These changes in the focus of th scientific investigations, at least on the surface, gave an impression of bei more in line with the official political doctrine, which advocated the elimir tion of private property and creation of one secular, materialistic worke society.

As mentioned above, there is a tendency to merge these two theories ir one framework. For example, Wertsch in the introduction to *The Concep Activity in Soviet Psychology* describes the theory of activity in terms of sε eral features. Some of these features, such as genetic method, internalizatic and egocentric speech, replicate Vygotsky's ideas. A feature that does r appear in SCT but appears in activity theory is the structure of activity its (Wertsch 1981).

In activity theory, the structure of an activity consists of three lev motives, actions, and operations. An activity is not understood as an activ for the sake of doing something but as doing something that is motivated either biological or cultural needs. An example of the former could be t need for food or shelter, and an example of the latter could be the need become successful in one's professional career. Activity can be analyzed these three levels separately because each level utilizes a different unit analysis: *motive, goal,* and *operation.*

Motives can be realized only if specific actions are performed. These ₴ tions need to be goal-oriented and also need to be executed using spec operations (or under specific conditions). To use the previous example, in order to become successful, the individual may need to take actions such as taking classes or attending workshops. These goal-oriented actions need to be carried out under specific conditions. For example, in order to take a course in advanced computer programming, the individual may be required first to take less advanced courses.

Knowledge of the structure of an activity is important because what distinguishes one activity from the other is not their realization, but their *motives*. That is, two activities may be realized differently on the level of action, but because their motives are the same, these activities are viewed as identical. Or two activities may be the same on the level of action, but because they are associated with different motives, these activities are viewed differently. For example, if two individuals taking part in an experiment that aims at solving a puzzle follow directions in a similar fashion and the outcome of their actions is the same (the puzzle is solved), but the motives of these individuals are different—for example one is participating in the experiment because of personal interest, the other just to please the researcher or to get a better grade—these two individuals are participating in two different activities.

To summarize, the theory of activity was developed by Vygotsky's student and follower, Leont'ev. Although some disagreement as to the relation between these two theories still exists, the theory of activity is viewed as part of sociocultural theory (Wertsch 1981). Activity theory is described in terms of the following features: the structure of an activity (motives, actions or goals, and operations); mediation (activity is mediated by tools and sign systems); method (activity is investigated by applying a genetic method); interaction (activity is developed in social interactions); and internalization (activity is developed by the process of internalization of the patterns observed initially in the interpersonal plane).

As Wertsch (1990) points out, Vygotsky's early death prevented him from pursuing his interests in finding out the effects of various social and institutional settings on human mental development. At the end of his life, Vygotsky was especially interested in investigating the connection between speech characteristics of academic settings and certain types of mental development that exposure to these environments triggers. These relative "shortcomings" of Vygotsky's theory may be remedied by borrowing some of the ideas of his contemporary, Mikhail Bakhtin. In the next chapter I introduce the reader to the fundamental principles of Bakhtin's literary theory: dialogized heteroglossia.

7

Bakhtin's Dialogized Heteroglossia

Mikhail Bakhtin (1895–1975) was introduced to an American audienc in 1968 when his "Role of Games in Rabelais" was included in a volume of th Yale French Studies series on the topic of game, play, and literature. Althoug most of his works were written in the 1920s and 1930s, they were not availab to the Western public until the 1970s.

Bakhtin's contribution to the field of human sciences, in particular to theory of literature, has been compared to the works of Barthes (1972 Derrida (1981), and Lévi-Strauss (1972). Considering the fact that these ind viduals are regarded as the greatest thinkers of the twentieth century, it rather disappointing that Bakhtin's ideas have been given so little attention t researchers working in the fields of linguistics and SLA. His relative lack c popularity in the field of SLA could be explained or justified to a certai degree by his intricate style of writing.

Bakhtin had a tendency to jot down his thoughts and ideas. His writin and the translations of his works seem to reflect this particular style c writing, in which the same ideas are frequently repeated in the same wor His broad background in literature, however, may explain best why his ide: are rather unexplored by SLA researchers. In order to appreciate the dept and originality of his ideas, rather extensive knowledge of Russian literatu (in particular, Dostoevsky, Pushkin, Tolstoy, and Gogol), as well as Frenc

German, British, and classic Greek and Roman literature is necessary. His work also reflects his solid background in philosophy, in particular, that of Kant. Thus, in addition to being a literary critic and linguist, Bakhtin may also be regarded as a philosopher of language.

Although Bakhtin was very well acquainted with linguistics of his time, Russian Formalism and Structuralism, he rejected the major principles of these two schools. He objected to their insistence on the separation of sentence-level linguistics from utterance-level linguistics that was initiated by the work of de Saussure. As mentioned in Chapter 5, Saussure (1959) divided language into two domains: the domain of *la langue,* linguistic forms and structures, and the domain of *la parole,* the usage of language in real-life contexts. *La langue* could be viewed as sentence-level linguistics and *la parole* is utterance-level linguistics.

Bakhtin took issue with the Saussurian definition of an utterance as an "individual act" and as "a completely free combination of forms of language" (Bakhtin 1986, 81). He claimed that Saussure "ignores the fact that in addition to forms of language there are also forms of combinations of these forms, that is, he ignores speech genres" (ibid.).

This brings us to one of the greatest of Bakhtin's contributions to our understanding of what language is. This understanding is essential to our ability to explore the effects of language as the most powerful mediational sign system in the development of human consciousness: human cognition. In this respect, Bakhtin's work complements the work of Vygotsky.

Like Vygotsky, Bakhtin viewed language not as an abstract system of linguistic forms—lexicon, morphology, and syntax—but as speech. He contrasted the unit of speech with the unit of language as a form. The *utterance* is the unit of speech, and the *sentence* is the unit of language. The latter is the object of linguistic analysis, which he strongly criticized because of its frequent equation of sentence and utterance and its preoccupation with the creation of an abstraction (that is, an abstract and arbitrary system of signs), which then was analyzed as the "whole picture" of what knowledge of language entails.

Bakhtin provides a detailed description of the basic unit of speech: the utterance. The utterance, in contrast to the sentence, possesses the following three characteristics. First, any utterance has its boundaries delineated by "a change of speaking subjects" (1986, 71). The second feature is its completion, which assures that there will be a response to the utterance, some kind of reaction to it. This characteristic is associated with the notion of *addressivity,* which Bakhtin defines as follows: "Any utterance always has an addressee (of various sorts, with varying degrees of proximity, concreteness, awareness, and so forth), whose responsive understanding the author of the speech work seeks and surpasses. This is the second party (again not in the arithmetical sense). But in addition to this addressee (the second party), the author of the utterance, with a greater or lesser awareness, presupposes a higher *superad dressee* (third), whose absolutely just responsive understanding is presumed either in some metaphysical distance or in distant historical time (the loophole addressee)" (1986, 126).

This quotation indicates that the utterance, not the sentence (which is an abstraction of the utterance devoid of a context), presupposes, because of its second characteristic—responsiveness—a dialogic relation between the speaker and the addressor. Thus, each utterance evokes three entities: the speaker, the addressee for whom the utterance was intended (whether this addressee is present or "invisible" like the future generations for whom the utterance was intended), and the superaddressor, who, like God or absolute truth, fully understands the intention and the meaning of the utterance. It seems that we need a superaddressee, a third party, because our different experiences in speech genres and our different degrees of mastery of these speech genres can never be completely understood by the second party. Without Bakhtin's addressivity, defined as "the quality of turning to someone" (1986, 99), which is not assumed in a sentence but only in the utterance, the utterance cannot exist.

Note that the second characteristic of the utterance—addressivity and responsiveness—implies that the utterance may take on a variety of forms: anything that can be responded to, small or lengthy. An exclamation, a gesture, a question, a letter, a lengthy work of literature—each falls into the category of the utterance as the basic unit of speech communication. Bakhtin writes: "Any utterance—from a short (single-word) rejoinder in everyday dialogue to the large novel or scientific treatise—has, so to speak, an absolute beginning and an absolute end: its beginning is preceded by the utterances of others, and its end is followed by the responsive utterances of others (or although it may be silent, others' active responsive understanding, or, finally a responsive action based on this understanding)" (1986, 71).

According to Bakhtin, because of the existence of many realizations of the utterance—the heterogeneity of the utterance's forms—linguistics dispense with it and gave its full allegiance to the unit of language—the sentence—which is more uniform and limited in form. In spite of this heterogeneity of forms of utterances, however, Bakhtin states that utterances, so mistrusted and avoided by the followers of de Saussurian linguistics, can be studied because each utterance can be traced back to a particular speech genre. Bakhtin writes: "Each separate utterance is individual, of course, but each sphere in which language is used develops its own relatively stable types of these utterances. These we may call *speech genres*" (1986, 60). A speech genre is "not a form of language, but a typical form of utterance; as such the genre also includes a certain typical kind of expression that inheres in it. In the genre the word acquires a particular typical expression. Genres correspond to typical situations of speech communication, typical themes, and, consequently, also to particular contacts between the meanings of words and actual concrete reality under certain typical circumstances" (87).

Despite their diversity, speech genres can be divided into two major groups: primary and secondary. The former includes daily conversations, narrations, diaries, letters; the latter includes novels, dramas, all kinds of scientific research. They represent "more complex and comparatively highly developed and organized cultural communication (primarily written) that is artistic, scientific, sociopolitical and so on" (Bakhtin 1986, 62). Secondary, more complex genres arise from primary genres, which have been internalized and transformed into secondary genres.

Why is it necessary to study genres? Because, according to Bakhtin, we speak in genres; "speech genres organize our speech" (1986, 78). We do not learn language by learning its lexical, morphological, and syntactic representations but by exposure to a variety of speech genres. He writes: "If speech genres did not exist and we had not mastered them, if we had to originate them during the speech process and construct each utterance at will for the first time, speech communication would be almost impossible" (79). A close connection of the utterance to a stable speech genre of the type described in the quotation represents the third characteristic of the utterance. Recall that the first characteristic is the change of the speaker and its completion, the second its addressivity and responsiveness.

In producing an utterance, we are not generating the utterance for the first time. We are not "the first speaker, the one who disturbs the eternal silence of the universe" (69). We simply make a subjective choice of a particular speech genre, which typically hosts the type of utterance we wish to convey to others, whether we do it consciously or unconsciously. We, therefore, do not speak with one voice but with many voices. The utterance belongs not to us but to others before the utterance was appropriated (that is, internalized) by us. For Bakhtin, language is a *living* thing, and as a living thing, it reflects and defines at the same time the various contexts in which it has been used. Language always lies on "the borderline between oneself and the other. The word in language is half someone else's. It becomes 'one's own' only when the speaker populates it with his own intention, his own accent, when he appropriates the word, adapting it to his own semantic and expressive intention. Prior to this

moment of appropriation, the word does not exist in a neutral and impersonal language (it is not, after all, out of a dictionary that the speaker gets his
words!), but rather it exists in other people's mouths, in other people's contexts, serving other people's intentions: it is from there that one must take the
word, and make it one's own" (Bakhtin 1981, 293–94).

Thus, the utterance is always in a *dialogic* relation with other utterances
that precede it, with other voices that had uttered it before we appropriated it.
Although we speak with many voices, which Bakhtin calls *heteroglossia*, these
voices can be recognized and studied because they are associated with a given
type of speech genre. These speech genres have a "normative significance for
the speaking individuum, and they are not created by him but are given to
him" (1986, 80–81). This statement implies that there is a limit to the utterance's individuality. This limit is associated with the speaker's exposure to and
mastery of speech genres. The lack of exposure to and mastery of a particular
speech genre cannot be compensated by the individual's knowledge of lexicon
and morphosyntactic rules. This is evident in the native speaker's inability to
perform certain speech functions characteristic of a given speech genre although the native speaker can be considered well-educated. Bakhtin states:
"Frequently a person who has an excellent command of speech in some areas
of cultural communication, who is able to read a scholarly paper or engage in
scholarly discussion, who speaks well on social questions, is silent or very
awkward in social conversation" (1986, 80).

We need to dispense with the rigid demarcation of zones between the view
of language as a system of formal and abstract grammatical features and the
view of language as speech. Although the linguistic code provides some
fundamental bases for communication, it does not explain the full nature of
human speech communication, which according to Bakhtin is embedded in
speech genres: "Thus, a speaker is given not only mandatory forms of the
national language (lexical composition and grammatical structure), but also
forms of utterances that are mandatory, that is, speech genres" (1986, 80).

What defines each speech genre is its own "typical conception of addressee" (1986, 95). How the speaker perceives his or her addressee, what the
speaker's real or imaginary view of this addressee is, will affect the speaker's
choice of speech genres. It can also lead to the creation of a new genre, as is
evident in the development of email correspondence, which, because of its
imaginary "closeness" to the addressee, created the style and the form of
writing typical of Internet communication.

As discussed above, Bakhtin claims that we only speak in "definite speech
genres, that is, all our utterances have definite and relatively stable typical

forms of construction of the whole," and we may not be even aware of it: "Like Molière's Monsieur Jourdain, who, when speaking in prose, had no idea that was what he was doing, we speak in diverse genres without suspecting that they exist" (1986, 78).

In Bakhtin's view, not only do we speak in speech genres, but also we hear in terms of speech genres. Thus, without speech genres, human communication would not be possible. He writes: "We learn to cast our speech in generic forms and, when hearing others' speech, we guess its genre from the very first words; we predict a certain length (that is, its approximate length of the speech whole) and a certain compositional structure; we foresee the end; that is, from the very beginning we have a sense of the speech whole, which is only later differentiated during the speech process" (1986, 79).

Bakhtin's voices and speech genres are always in a dialogic relationship. In fact, a dialogic relationship is at the core of his literary theory. According to him, we only "speak" in the form of a dialogue; even if we speak to ourselves, as in a monologue, we speak in the form of a dialogue. Bakhtin's dialogue is not synonymous with the conventional meaning of dialogue, which presupposes the presence of two interlocutors who take turns at producing utterances. Every utterance, every voice, stands in multiple dialogic relations with other utterances, with other voices in a text, but since every utterance, every word, is "half someone else's," this dialogic relationship extends to the original owner of the utterance and to the social, cultural, and institutional context in which it was originally situated.

For Bakhtin, language (that is, speech) is dialogically, not monologically based. To be more precise, there are no monologues in speech communication because our utterances are always addressed to someone. Even when we talk to ourselves as in a monologue, we actually conduct a dialogue with the "imaginary" addressee, and we adjust our style of speech according to how we perceive the power, status, and prestige of the invisible addressee. We are immersed in many speech genres that we acquired throughout our lives. We are all heteroglots: "Thus an illiterate peasant, miles away from any urban center, naively immersed in an unmoving and for him unshakable everyday world, nevertheless lived in several language systems: he prayed to God in one language (Church Slavonic), sang songs in another, spoke to his family in a third and, when he began to dictate petitions to the local authorities through a scribe, he tried speaking yet a fourth language (the official-literate language, 'paper' language). All these are different languages, even from the point of view of abstract socio-dialectological markers" (1981, 295–96). Our utterances are never uttered in a void, an empty universe, but are always connected to other voices, which, in turn, evoke different sociocultural and institutional contexts where these voices were acquired. In this theory, all speech is heteroglossic.

According to Bakhtin, in speech there are two forces that work simultaneously: centripetal and centrifugal. *Centripetal* forces move toward unity and system; examples of this force are the native language's grammatical and phonological systems. Bakhtin describes these unifying forces as follows: "Unitary language constitutes the theoretical expression of the historical processes of linguistic unification and centralization, an expression of the centripetal forces of language. A unitary language is not something given [*dan*] but is always in essence posited [*zadan*]—and at every moment of its linguistic life it is opposed to the realities of heteroglossia. But at the same time it makes its real presence felt as a force overcoming this heteroglossia, imposing specific limits to it, guaranteeing a certain maximum of mutual understanding and crystalizing into a real, although still relative, unity—the unity of the reigning conversational (everyday) and literary language, 'correct language'" (1981, 270). Although centripetal forces point toward one unified system of linguistic norms, these norms "do not constitute an abstract imperative; they are rather the generative forces of linguistic life, forces that struggle to overcome the heteroglossia of language" (ibid.).

Centrifugal forces tend to move toward heterogeneity, opposition, and diversity. Bakhtin writes: "Alongside the centripetal forces, the centrifugal forces of language carry on their uninterrupted work; alongside verbal ideological centralization and unification, the uninterrupted processes of decentralization and disunification go forward" (1981, 272).

The operation of centrifugal forces may provide an explanation as to why communication between two native speakers operating within the same centripetal, unifying, and centralizing forces of language (that is, speaking the same linguistic code) may break down.

Of these two forces, centrifugal forces are more powerful. It is here where Bakhtin placed his *dialogized heteroglossia* (1981, 273), his theory of knowledge that attempts to account for human behavior by means of the dialogic concept of language. The theory of dialogized heteroglossia represents the cornerstone of Bakhtin's epistemology of human sciences; it breaks away from the well-established norms of the cognitive tradition by proclaiming dynamic relationship between the individual's inner and outer worlds. For Bakhtin, the self represents a dynamic process of merging of two forces—external and internal—mediated by the means of speech in a form of dialogue. In the sphere of dialogism, the individual self is always relative (Holquist 1990). It is relative because the individual self cannot be isolated an abstracted from other voices to which the individual has been exposed in his or her life. The discovery of the individual self is the discovery of the relationship that exists between the individual's inner and outer realities mediated through speech conceived as a dialogue.

Why is Bakhtin so important for our discussion of Vygotsky? Bakhtin's ideas complement Vygotsky's ideas by providing a detailed analysis of speech genre. Vygotsky stresses the importance of speech for human cognitive development, which is advanced within the boundaries of the zone of proximal development and created in the process of interaction between the learner and a more capable tutor in a real sociocultural or institutional setting. Although Vygotsky stresses the importance of speech for human cognitive growth, his SCT does not examine its characteristics, the characteristics of speech in a given sociocultural context. This gap is filled by Bakhtin's work.

Also, Bakhtin's work on speech genres directly supports Vygotsky's genetic law of cultural development, which, you may recall, states that every human mental function takes place twice, first among people and then within the individual. Bakhtin's ideas regarding speech genres, the dialogic relations of utterances, and heteroglossia validate Vygotsky's sociocultural theory. Neither Vygotsky nor Bakhtin advocated the separation of *la parole* from *la langue* that after Chomsky (1965) has been known as the separation of language performance from language competence. As discussed in Chapter 5 on the historical evolution of communicative competence models, this separation still exists in SLA and is rigidly adhered to by most mainstream SLA researchers.

Bakhtin, like Vygotsky before him, called not only for the eradication of this obsolete and unjustified demarcation line but also for shifting our attention from language competence to speech communication, where the roots of human language, communication, and cognition lie. He also encouraged research into the complex nature of the relation between language as a system of rules and language as a speech genre.

To summarize, Bakhtin, like Vygotsky, viewed language as speech and not as an abstract set of rules. For Bakhtin, higher mental functioning is not only inner *speech* in a Vygotskian sense but is inner *dialogue*. This inner dialogue represents the individual's conversation with himself or herself, but since the individual self is grounded in the voices of others, this inner dialogue represents the dialogue with oneself and with others simultaneously.

Bakhtin proposed a new epistemology—dialogized heteroglossia—which is a "pragmatically oriented theory of knowledge; more particularly, it is one of several modern epistemologies that seek to grasp human behavior through the use humans make of language. Bakhtin's distinctive place among these is specified by the dialogic concept of language he proposes as fundamental" (Holquist 1990, 15).

Bakhtin claimed that the fields of linguistics, stylistics, and the philosophy of language strongly favor the investigation of the centripetal—unifying and centralizing—forces of language, with almost total exclusion of the centrifugal forces, where he placed his dialogized heteroglossia. He called for a new approach to language that does not look for "unity in diversity" (1981, 274) but tries to understand and examine language from a centrifugal perspective, from a perspective of speech genres. He called for examination of human behavior from the perspective of dialogized heteroglossia, where human language as a system of many voices and human cognitive development originate and reside.

8

Vygotsky's Sociocultural Theory and Second Language Learning

In this chapter I describe and discuss some of the most important research studies that investigated the application of Vygotsky's SCT to second language acquisition. This chapter is divided into four sections. Each presents studies that focused on one particular principle of SCT such as the zone of proximal development (ZPD), the role of interaction, activity theory, and private and inner speech. Most of the studies discussed in this chapter are included in Lantolf and Appel (1998) and Lantolf (2000). At this point, I would like to express my appreciation for the work of Lantolf, who has been one of the strongest advocates of the application of sociocultural theory to SLA. He has been truly a voice calling in the wilderness when the mainstream SLA research community was mainly preoccupied with building information processing models. My own work and the work of other researchers owes a great deal to his pioneering efforts to introduce SCT to the field of SLA.

The Zone of Proximal Development

In "Collective Scaffolding in Second Language Learning," Richard Donato (1998) addresses the role of collective scaffolding in the acquisition of French. The findings of his study reveal that, contrary to the accepted view of scaffolded help, in which help is provided by a more capable individual such as an expert, parent, or an adult native speaker, learners at the same level of second or foreign language proficiency appear quite capable of providing guided support to one another. His findings reveal that learners themselves could be considered a good source of L2 knowledge. Collectively constructed support (scaffolding) provides not only the opportunity for input exchange among learners but also the opportunity to expand the learner's own knowledge.

Donato's findings are important because they encourage us to reevaluate the role of input, interaction, and negotiation of meaning. As Donato rightly points out, underlying the constructs of L2 input and output in modified interaction (for example, Long 1985; Swain 1985) is the outdated conduit metaphor model. In the conduit metaphor model, the main goal of the participants in the interaction is a successful sending and receiving of linguistic information. Although to some extent this outdated model of L2 interaction accepts the fact that during interaction the individual is socially situated, it basically views interaction as processing of the incoming input.

The development of interlanguage remains confined to the mental processes of the learner. The notion that knowledge can be coconstructed during the process of collaboration with other learners is totally ignored in such models. In sum, according to Donato, current perspectives on the role of input and interaction maintain that social interaction supplies linguistic input to the learner, who develops the L2 solely on the basis of his or her mental processing mechanism.

The findings of Donato's study undermine such a view of interaction. They illustrate how participants' knowledge of linguistic features such as the compound past tense formation of reflective verbs in French (for example, "you remembered") has been acquired through the process of social interaction, in which the collective scaffolding created by all the participants brings about the developmental changes in the participants' own L2 knowledge. That is, the study illustrates how the construction of knowledge results in a major linguistic change among and within the individual learners: this developmental change is not individual, but social in nature.

In this study, the data obtained from the protocols were analyzed using the guidelines developed by Wood, Bruner, and Ross (1976), who argue that scaffolded help is characterized by six features:

1. *recruiting* interest in the task,
2. *simplifying* the task,
3. *maintaining* pursuit of the goal,
4. *marking* critical features and discrepancies between what has been produced and the ideal solution,

5. *controlling* frustration during problem solving, and
6. *demonstrating* an idealized version of the act to be performed.

(Donato 1998, 41)

The metaphor also implies that scaffolded help is not fixed but continually revised by the expert to accommodate the emerging abilities of the novice. The scaffolding mechanism is used to promote the novice's internalization of knowledge that has been coconstructed in a social activity.

Donato's study also acknowledges the importance of microgenetic analysis, viewed as "the gradual course of skill acquisition during a training session, experiment, or interaction" (1998, 42). Such a microgenetic analysis allowed Donato to observe directly how students help each other during their process of searching for, building, and constructing L2 utterances. This type of observation allowed the author to document not only how the learners actively assisted one another but also how this assistance led to the individual learner's own L2 knowledge development. This knowledge development was evident in the use of private speech by the participants in the interaction. Recall that private speech is used within Vygotsky's paradigm as a discursive developmental mechanism that enables children to guide themselves in carrying out a problem-solving activity that is beyond their current level of development. In Donato's study, the same behavior is exhibited by the learners of French as second or foreign language.

In sum, Donato's findings validate the importance of collective scaffolding for the learner's L2 development. In contrast to previous research findings, this study draws our attention to the fact that scaffolded help does not need to be created by the experts; it can be provided by the learners themselves. It is also important to note that the knowledge acquired during the scaffolded interaction among the learners was retained long after the study took place. At a later time, the participants could produce individually the linguistic forms that they previously could only produce with the scaffolded assistance of their peers. These findings support one of Vygotsky's fundamental claims: that the individual's knowledge is socially and dialogically derived.

In "Linguistic Accommodation with LEP and LD Children," Linda Schinke-Llano (1998) reviewed two experimental studies, which were analyzed from a Vygotskian perspective. Linguistic accommodations and their effect on the participants' language development and cognitive development are the focus of the two studies. Although in both cases the students differed greatly as to their age, gender, and the type of task they were asked to solve, the similarities of the outcomes of the two studies are striking. A critical issue raised by their findings is that there is a need to distinguish between a legitimate call for assistance and our unjustified perceptions of the need of assistance. It is the author's belief that too much accommodation may impede the subject's progression from the other-regulated to self-regulated stage.

In the first study presented in Schinke-Llano (1998), fifth- and sixth-grade teachers were asked to participate in problem-solving activities with twenty-four students: twelve children were native speakers of English, and twelve were nonnative speakers of limited English proficiency (LEP). All LEP students were native speakers of Spanish. The problem-solving activity required that the teacher communicate with native and LEP students in order to fill out a catalogue order form. Each student had to order two items from the catalogue. All the activities were audiotaped and coded in order to capture the nature of the instructional interaction. In order to identify the nature of interactional characteristics, abbreviations were developed and operationalized as the degree to which subdirectives of a task such as nonverbal directives (for example, pointing), direct directives ("The number goes in this blank."), and indirect directives ("Where does that number go?") were explicitly mentioned by the teacher (1998, 60). Filling out the catalogue forms was conceived as a single task that included many subsets, or "directives having many subdirectives" (ibid.). The type of abbreviation was related to the question of self-regulation, that is, whether the subsets of a task were performed by the student alone or performed with the teacher's assistance.

In the second study reviewed by Schinke-Llano, the subjects were twelve mother-child dyads whose native language was English and who came from Anglo-American backgrounds. All children were males, age three to seven and age three to eleven. Based on the scores they obtained on the Peabody Picture Vocabulary Test—Revised, six of the children were categorized as significantly below average (LD) and six as normally achieving (NA). The two groups of six dyads were asked to perform the same task: to complete an incomplete airport scene model on the basis of a copy of it, which was complete. That is, mothers were asked to assist children with the task of completing the model of the airport.

Despite the differences in age, language background, gender, sociocultural background of the participants and the nature of the problem-solving task, the results of these two research studies are strikingly similar. Adults in LEP and LD dyads structured their interaction and assistance differently than did those in NS and NA dyads. The adults' interactions with LEP students and LD children were more other-regulated, speech directed at them was less abbreviated, and the subsets of the tasks were made more explicit than they were with the NS students and NA children. The question arises whether such other-regulated assistance was indeed necessary, considering the fact that LEP students as well as LD children completed the task regardless of the degree of other-regulation and abbreviation.

A critical issue is whether perceptions of a need for assistance are accurate. Although perceptions of differences between the LEP and NS students and between LD and NA children are accurate, the perception of the need for assistance may not be. Too much assistance may impede students' and children's linguistic and cognitive development. Too much other-regulation may impede their transition to the self-regulation stage necessary for the development of higher cognitive functions. The prolonged reliance on other-regulated assistance may result in fossilization—a process that is of a particular interest to SLA. The issue of fossilization in the ZPD is addressed in the study reported by Gay Washburn (1998) titled "Working in the ZPD: Fossilized and Nonfossilized Nonnative Speakers."

The definition of fossilization varies greatly in SLA. For example, Celce-Murcia defines fossilization as second language acquisition that has "prematurely plateaued" (Celce-Murcia 1991, 462, cited in Washburn 1998, 69). Selinker defines it as "a mechanism which is assumed also to exist in the latent psychological structure" (Selinker 1972, 215, cited in Washburn 1998, 69). As Washburn points out, most research studies of fossilization in SLA rely on case studies, which document a particular behavior of individual subjects. For example, Lennon's (1991) study, which is characteristic of most of the studies of fossilization, analyzes the subject's ability to use five structures over a period of several months. The findings reveal that Lennon's advanced learner of English as a second language did not develop a more targetlike acquisition of one particular structure, future time forms; thus the subject's acquisition of this particular structure is viewed as fossilized.

Washburn notes that most research studies of fossilization fail to distinguish truly fossilized learners from those who are still in the process of learning. He proposes that a better operational definition of *fossilized speaker* be developed, which should include nonlinguistic criteria such as length of residence and learning history. He suggests that the new definition distinguish fossilized from nonfossilized learners. Such a definition is necessary to help researchers and teachers understand and better assist learners to remedy their fossilization.

Because the notion of fossilization is not unique to SLA, Washburn recommends that in order to better understand it, we turn to different scientific fields for insights and guidance. He suggests Vygotsky's SCT as a new framework for SLA research on fossilization.

Vygotsky (1978) explains fossilization in terms of mental processes that undergo prolonged development. He acknowledges that these processes are difficult to study because "they have lost their original appearance, and their outer appearance tells us nothing about their internal nature" (64). He claims that in order to study fossilization one must "alter the automatic, mechanized fossilized character of the higher form of behavior and to turn it back to its source through experiment" (ibid.). Vygotsky also suggests that its source lies in the basic social nature of language learning contexts, or social interaction.

Although most SLA researchers acknowledge the role of interaction and, in particular, the role of negotiation of meaning that occurs in the course of interaction as the necessary condition of second language acquisition, little attention is paid to the fact that the same interaction may be the source of fossilization.

A Vygotskian perspective sheds a new light on our current understanding of the processes involved in fossilization. It offers new insights as to how to determine the difference between a fossilized behavior and nonfossilized behavior. Vygotsky's ZPD encourages the researchers to look more closely at potential than actual development because it may very well be the case that the difference between fossilized and nonfossilized speakers lies in their ability to perform tasks in the ZPD rather than at the actual level of development. Therefore, Washburn, following Vygotsky's ideas, suggests that SLA research studies of fossilization focus on the learner's ZPD rather than the actual level of development to determine whether the learner's behavior qualifies as fossilized.

In order to illustrate the usefulness of Vygotskian theory to the study of fossilization in SLA, Washburn (1998) reports on the findings of a research study aimed at determining the difference between fossilized and nonfossilized speakers based on SCT. The eighteen subjects were undergraduate students at a large public university. All subjects were enrolled in the highest-level ESL course, and they all came from a variety of linguistic backgrounds. In the absence of an operational definition of fossilization, a working definition was developed that identified fossilized speakers by length of residence in the United States and by a history of failure in prior ESL courses. In this study, fossilized speakers had lived in the United States for five or more years and failed at least one ESL course. Nonfossilized speakers did not have a history of failure in ESL courses and had lived from six months to four years in the United States.

The subjects were all placed in the same ESL writing course on the basis of their written exam scores. The subjects were asked to participate in three language sessions that lasted forty-five minutes. In the first meeting subjects participated in a structured interview designed to elicit certain grammatical features such as negation, present perfect, and present perfect continuous. These grammatical structures were selected because the pilot study results had suggested that these particular features were problematic for the subjects.

In subsequent meetings, the subjects were given a cloze test, a grammaticality judgment and imitation task, and a short-term learning task. In the short-term learning task, the interviewer-researcher attempted to teach the targetlike utterances that caused the most difficulty during the grammaticality judgment and imitation task. The findings of the data analysis for this task reveal that, in contrast to nonfossilized speakers, fossilized speakers need more turns to produce the model utterance in targetlike forms: approximately eight turns were needed for the fossilized speakers versus approximately two turns for the nonfossilized speakers.

The overall results of this study indicate that the difference between fossilized and nonfossilized speakers is not very obvious or direct. All differences found between these two groups of speakers were quantitative rather than qualitative. That is, the fossilized and nonfossilized speakers both produced nontargetlike forms such as *He go to school*. The distinction between these two groups' behavior is not in the number of errors, however, but in the pattern of errors across different tasks. The fossilized speakers produced nontargetlike forms less consistently in less structured situations than did the nonfossilized speakers, although both groups were able to produce the grammatical structures accurately in imitation tasks. The fossilized learners also needed more turns to produce an utterance accurately. They also seemed to be insensitive to the input available to them and needed more explicit assistance to notice the difference between the utterance produced by them and the model utterance. Although the fossilized speakers in Washburn's study were eventually able to produce the correct forms, they required different external assistance than did their nonfossilized counterparts to notice, process, and produce the targetlike grammatical forms. The findings of Washburn's study are important because they offer new possibilities for investigating fossilization within Vygotsky's ZPD framework.

The study described in Ali Aljaafreh and James Lantolf (1994) titled "Negative Feedback as Regulation and Second Language Learning in the Zone of Proximal Development" represents one of the first and most advanced studies attempting to apply Vygotsky's framework to SLA. The study generated some interest in applying the construct of the ZPD to providing error correction in teaching L2 writing skills.

Error correction, or negative feedback, has been a source of major debate in SLA. Beginning with contrastive analysis studies, learners' errors were viewed either as "sins" that needed to be avoided at all cost or as a significant source of insights into the workings of learners' interlanguage processes. Attitudes toward error correction and their impact on language learning have varied depending on a theoretical framework that was favored at a given point in the history of SLA.

Aljaafreh and Lantolf's study was conducted under the assumption that there is some positive connection between error correction (negative feedback) and second language learning. Negative feedback, however, whether explicit or implicit, needs to be negotiated between the novice and the expert. This collaborative negotiation of corrective feedback is essential for SLA. The authors applied Vygotsky's notion of the ZPD to their investigation of the effect of negotiated negative feedback on the learning process. The learning process was investigated during the microgenesis of the second language learner's appropriation of grammatical features of articles, tense markings, prepositions, and modal verbs during an eight-week tutorial session.

Based on previous research concerning the mechanisms of effective help in the ZPD, the authors concluded that in order for the assistance to be effective it needs to be (1) *graduated* and (2) *contingent*. The former refers to the need to estimate the minimum level of assistance required by the novice to successfully complete a given task. According to the authors, this assistance should begin at an implicit level and become progressively more explicit. The latter indicates that assistance should only be offered when it is required and should be withdrawn as soon as the novice reveals signs of self-regulation, or control over the task. Graduation and contingency are closely interrelated and need to be continuously assessed and reassessed. They cannot be determined a priori. They can only be determined during a jointly constructed interaction between the learner and the expert in the ZPD.

For the purposes of the Aljaafreh and Lantolf (1994) study, three female ESL students were selected. On the basis of their placement test scores, it was determined that they all were at the same level of "actual development." As the findings of this study reveal, however, they were at different levels of potential development.

The three students were asked to participate in one tutorial per week and to write one in-class essay on the topic of their choice; they wrote eight essays each for the duration of this study. Each essay-writing session lasted thirty to forty-five minutes. All sessions were audiotaped. The first composition served as a needs analysis, designed to elicit the participants' most urgent linguistic needs. Based on this needs analysis, four grammatical features were selected: articles, tense markings, the use of prepositions, and modal verbs. Note that the focus of this study was on improving writing skills, not speaking skills, by providing an appropriate level of corrective feedback in the ZPD during dialogic interactions.

At the beginning of each session, the learner was asked to read her essay and identify any errors she herself noticed in the essay. If the learner identified an error but failed to correct it herself, the learner and the tutor collabratively negotiated the level of assistance required by the learner to complete the task of correction. The tutor's intervention began from the most implicit level, at which the tutor directed the learner's attention to a particular sentence in which the error was present. If this strategy failed, the tutor brought the learner's attention to the phrase in which the error occurred; if this also failed, the tutor identified the error himself.

The researchers developed two criteria to determine the microgenetic development of these four grammatical features in the learner's interlanguage: one was a product-oriented criterion that tried to capture the learner's improvement in the usage of the four features in subsequent essays; the other included a general five-level scale that tried to capture the transition from the interpersonal to the intrapersonal plane, or from the other-regulated stage to self-regulated stage.

The transition from level 1 to level 5 was determined on the basis of the frequency and quality of assistance that was elicited by the learner during the dialogic interaction when negotiated corrective feedback was provided by the tutor. The five general levels are as follows:

> *Level 1.* The learner is not able to notice or correct the error, even with intervention from the tutor. At this level, the learner does not have a sufficient basis from which to interpret the tutor's moves to provide help, and probably has no awareness that there is even a problem. The tutor, therefore, must assume full responsibility for correcting the error. Thus, rather than providing corrective help, the tutor's task is to bring the target form into focus and, in so doing, begin the process of coconstructing the ZPD with the learner.
>
> *Level 2.* The learner is able to notice the error, but cannot correct it, even with intervention. This indicates some degree of development, but more importantly, even though the learner must rely heavily on the tutor, in contrast to level 1, an opening is provided for the tutor and the learner to begin negotiating the feedback process and for the learner to begin to progress toward self-regulation. The help required tends to be toward the lower, explicit end of the regulatory scale. . . .
>
> *Level 3.* The learner is able to notice and correct an error, but only under other-regulation. The learner understands the tutor's intervention and is able to react to the feedback offered. The levels of help needed to correct the error move toward the strategic, implicit end of the regulatory scale.
>
> *Level 4.* The learner notices and corrects an error with minimal or no obvious feedback from the tutor and begins to assume full responsibility

for error correction. However, development has not yet become fully intramental, since the learner often produces the target form incorrectly and may still need the tutor to confirm the adequacy of the correction. The learner may even reject feedback from the tutor when it is unsolicited (e.g., "Let me see if I can do it alone").

Level 5. The learner becomes more consistent in using the target structure correctly in all contexts. In most cases, the individual's use of the correct target form is automatized. Whenever aberrant performance does arise, however, noticing and correcting of errors do not require intervention from someone else. Thus, the individual is fully self-regulated.   (Aljaafreh and Lantolf 1994, 470)

The five levels of this scale represent three developmental levels: other regulation (levels 1 to 3), in which the learner relies on the tutor's help to notice and correct an error, partial regulation (level 4), in which the learner is capable of noticing the error but is not able to correct himself or herself, and self-regulation (level 5), in which corrective feedback is self-generated and automatic.

Aljaafreh and Lantolf (1994) also designed a regulatory scale arranged according to the type of feedback presented to the learner. According to this regulatory scale, the individual's microgenetic development is detected when the corrective feedback moves from the most explicit level (level 12) toward the least explicit level. The authors describe their regulatory scale as follows:

Regulatory Scale—Implicit (Strategic) to Explicit
0. Tutor asks the learner to read, find the errors, and correct them independently, prior to the tutorial.
1. Construction of a "collaborative frame" prompted by the presence of the tutor as a potential dialogic partner.
2. Prompted or focused reading of the sentence that contains the error by the learner or the tutor.
3. Tutor indicates that something may be wrong in a segment (e.g., sentence, clause, line)—"Is there anything wrong in this sentence?"
4. Tutor rejects unsuccessful attempts at recognizing the error.
5. Tutor narrows down the location of the error (e.g., tutor repeats or points to the specific segment which contains the error).
6. Tutor indicates the nature of the error, but does not identify the error (e.g., "There is something wrong with the tense marking here").
7. Tutor identifies the error ("You can't use an auxiliary here").
8. Tutor rejects learner's unsuccessful attempts at correcting the error.

9. Tutor provides clues to help the learner arrive at the correct forms (e.g., "It is not really past but something that is still going on").
0. Tutor provides the correct form.
1. Tutor provides some explanation for use of the correct form.
2. Tutor provides examples of the correct pattern when other forms of help fail to produce an appropriate responsive action. (1994, 471)

Note that in this scale, level 1 represents the level at which construction of "collaborative frames" begins. Recall that the methodology of this study requires the construction of a dialogic interaction during which the corrective feedback is negotiated by the learner and the tutor. Unlike level 1, level 0 is not collaborative. That is, the actions of the tutor and the learner do not require collaboration. While the tutor is engaged in a different activity, the learner is reading and correcting errors by herself. The activity changes, however, when their actions are intertwined in a collaborative dialogue, when they create a "collaborative frame." This collaborative frame, then, opens the possibility for the creation of the ZPD, which is essential for the learning process.

The findings of the study support Vygotsky's claim that different learners, although at the same actual level of development, exhibit different ZPDs; therefore, they require different levels of regulation or assistance. This particular point is illustrated by the learners' varying need for help in using the English article system. Two different learners in the tutorial sessions had difficulty with placing the definite article in front of *U.S.* One required all the levels of assistance captured in the regulatory scale (from the implicit to the most explicit); the other, however, only required assistance at levels 1 and 2 to correct the error.

The findings also reveal the importance of paying attention to the emergence of the learner's private speech during the transition from the other-regulated to the self-regulated stage. They seem to suggest that the emergence of private speech places the reader on level 3 or even level 4.

The importance of Aljaafreh and Lantolf's study lies in their ability to link negotiated corrective feedback with language learning by developing criteria to be used in analyzing the impact of negotiated assistance in the ZPD on the microgenetic development of the learner's interlanguage. Their regulatory scale, which describes the type of assistance elicited by the learner in jointly created collaborative frames, is linked with the three general stages of language development: other-regulation, partial regulation, and self-regulation, which are reflected in their five transitional levels.

The type of feedback provided to the learner signals the hierarchy of regulation; it determines the level of the learner's linguistic development. The study advocates that feedback be not only graduated but also contingent. I needs first to be distributed between the learner and the expert, with the expert having control over the learner's performance, and then, under the expert's guidance, control over the performance is gradually appropriated by the learner. When the learner shows signs of total control over his or her performance, the expert needs to relinquish control; otherwise, development will not be possible.

According to the authors of this study, interlanguage development is not only reflected in the learner's linguistic performance but "is also revealed through the kind of help that is jointly negotiated between experts and novices" (Aljaafreh and Lantolf 1994, 480). Therefore, the transition from the other-regulated to the self-regulated stage needs to be encouraged and promoted in all learning contexts, classroom contexts in particular. This could require that the teacher relinquish his or her power over the learning process. The teacher should encourage the learner's progression from the lower level of the regulatory scale to the top level. This does not mean, however, that the implicit type of assistance should be regarded as superior to the explicit type of feedback.

Recall that different learners have different levels of potential development. For some learners explicit feedback will be the most appropriate, and for others the implicit type will be the most appropriate. What is important is that independent of the learner's ZPD situation, movement from the more explicit to the less explicit type of assistance should be promoted. Implicit feedback is considered more self-regulatory than explicit feedback and therefore more significant for the learner's linguistic development. Recall that according to Vygotsky, the transition from other-regulation to self-regulation represents the necessary condition for human cognitive development.

In addition to its theoretical implications, Aljaafreh and Lantolf's (1994) study has some practical implications for classroom teaching and assessment. It offers language teachers new perspectives and techniques for providing assistance to the learner. It offers a new tool for promoting the learner's development using negotiated corrective feedback provided in collaborative dyadic interactions between the learner and the teacher, and it encourages teachers to search for the learner's potential level of development rather than the learner's actual level of development. This study has opened the door for research into second language learning processes from a Vygotskian perspective.

The role of interaction and its influence on the developmental processes of second language learning is the topic of the case study reported by Amy Ohta (2000) in "Rethinking Interaction in SLA: Developmentally Appropriate As istance in the Zone of Proximal Development and the Acquisition of L2 Grammar." In this study, two learners' collaborative interaction is documented and analyzed in order to demonstrate its influence on the acquisition of L2 grammar. The findings of this case study also offer some insights into the interactional mechanisms involved in obtaining and providing assistance within the ZPD.

The construct of Vygotsky's ZPD specifies that learning cannot occur if too much assistance is provided or if a problem-solving task is too easy. Helping too much or withdrawing help from the learner too soon impedes the process of development. The responsibility for providing the appropriate level of assistance to the learner is predicated on both the interlocutor's sensitivity to the learner's needs and the interlocutor's ability to withdraw assistance when it is not needed.

Ohta (2000) reports on the interactional clues to which the participants in the interaction in her study oriented themselves in order to ensure a developmentally appropriate level of collaborative assistance. Note that this assistance was not provided by a teacher or tutor but by the students themselves. Because more research is needed into the nature of effective assistance in peer learning situations, this study offers unique insights into the mechanism of such assistance among peers.

In Ohta's study, two students' collaborative interactions were recorded and analyzed within a Vygotskian framework with a special emphasis given to Vygotsky's general genetic law of cultural development within the ZPD. The role of collaborative interaction in L2 development was analyzed according to the three constructs described below (Ohta 2000, 60):

Construct	Focus of Analysis
Mechanisms of assistance	Analysis examines the sequential structure of episodes of assistance, examining what triggers suppliance of assistance.
Appropriate assistance	It is not assumed that all assistance is helpful. "Appropriate assistance" is defined as assistance which leads to language development, with language development defined as gains in learner performance on the sentence-construction task and maintained in the subsequent communicative task. Analysis focuses upon changes in performance and how these changes relate to the assistance provided.

Construct	Focus of Analysis
Internalization processes	These are examined through analysis of microgenesis (Wertsch 1985)—of how language structure is appropriated for individual use. Internalization of linguistic structure is visible through increasing independence of appropriate task performance.

The collaborative peer interaction that was recorded took place between two learners of Japanese. Both students were not native speakers of English. One was a thirty-three-year-old MBA student who had studied Japanese in his native country, Taiwan, before he came to the United States, and the other was a twenty-year-old Filipino American student. They were given the pseudonyms Hal and Becky, respectively. The two students participated in many problem-solving tasks; however, the task of translation that required a correct supplementation of Japanese particles was the main focus of the study.

The translation task was "a decontextualized grammar practice task that does not provide any communication practice in terms of information exchange" (Ohta 2000, 59). Also, as the author points out, the translation task did not meet the criteria for optimal communicative task design delineated in Skehan's (1996) framework. Within this framework, which stresses the importance of meaning rather than form, the translation task implemented in Ohta's study should not have produced much meaningful interaction. Despite these reservations, the translation task, although not particularly communicative in nature, produced a great deal of collaborative peer assistance that allowed the researcher to identify and examine sociocultural constructs presented above.

The results of the data analysis indicate that much was accomplished during this translation task. First of all, the detailed, narrow transcription of the data, which noted articulatory and supersegmental phonological features such as intonation, glottal stops, and vowel elongations, along with nonverbal commutation signs such as gestures and nodding, allowed Ohta to identify the mechanisms by means of which the assisted performance took place.

The findings of the data analysis indicate that the peer help, which led to the acquisition of the correct Japanese desiderative construction, was not offered in a haphazard manner but that both participants bid for help and provided assistance in a predictable and developmentally sensitive manner. Both participants bid for help in explicit and implicit ways by providing subtle clues that sent the signal that they were ready for the other partner assistance. The participants oriented themselves to these clues, and when the clues disappeared, they withdrew their assistance. As seen in the patterns outlined in Aljaafreh and Lantolf (1994), their negotiated assistance was graduated and contingent.

In general, the learners in the study did not interrupt each other to provide help when one of the speakers was clearly continuing his or her turn. In Hal and Becky's interaction, help was only offered when the speaker was not continuing his or her turn. The noncontinuation was signaled by falling intonation, an elongated vowel in the last syllable, and pauses. Hal, the more proficient learner of Japanese, oriented himself to these cues while providing assistance to his peer and partner in the translation task. His assistance was developmentally cued, contingent on Becky's bid for help. The form of his assistance went from being explicit to less explicit and was contingent on his assessment of Becky's developmental level as expressed by the number of the correct Japanese structures produced by Becky. At the end of the translation task, as a result of collaboration that produced the appropriated level of assistance, Becky was able to make the transition from the other-regulated to the self-regulated stage.

The analysis of collaborative interaction between Becky and Hal provides some evidence as to how interaction promotes L2 development in the ZPD. Because of their collaborative interaction, Becky, a less proficient learner of Japanese, was able to appropriate the linguistic forms and then produce the language that was required to accomplish the task that at first she had not been able to complete without assistance. Becky was able to progress from level 1 to level 4 on Aljaafreh and Lantolf's five-level scale for capturing the transition from the interpersonal to the intrapersonal plane. Her gains in performance remained long after the collaborative activity was completed, and they were documented in the follow-up interview and reports to her teacher.

As in Aljaafreh and Lantolf's (1994) study, Hal's assistance to his partner was graduated, but not necessarily in the form included in their regulatory scale. Recall that in Aljaafreh and Lantolf's study, assistance began in the form of implicit feedback provided by the tutor; the tutor was responsible for "noticing" the learners' errors first in a collaboratively constructed frame. The progression from implicit to explicit feedback is viewed by the authors as the most effective assistance in the ZPD.

Aware of this apparent discrepancy as to the form of the most effective assistance in the ZPD, Ohta suggests: "Other careful analyses of the collaborative interaction of language learners are needed to clarify how assisted performance in the ZPD is realized for a broader range of L2 learners. To understand how different tasks may have an impact on L2 development, analyses of various tasks as realized in learner-learner interaction is essential" (76). Thus, her study calls for expanding our investigation of the interaction in the ZPD from interaction between the learner and teacher to that between learner and learner. Despite variations in the forms of assistance provided in the ZPD, Ohta's study and Aljaafreh and Lantolf's study support the importance for L2 development of negotiated assistance in the ZPD during collaboratively constructed interaction.

Exploring the Role of Interaction from a Vygotskian Perspective

Merrill Swain (2000), in "The Output Hypothesis and Beyond: Mediating Acquisition Through Collaborative Dialogue," argues for the expansion of the existing focus on input and interaction to include output produced by the second language learner. Agreeing with van Lier (2000), she calls for broadening the well-established metaphor of output to include collaborative dialogues and to develop a new terminology that captures the new view of interaction promoted by Vygotsky's SCT. Swain agrees with critics of the term *output* that it is too closely attached to the view of SLA as the container, computer, or information processor, too cognitively oriented to allow the possibility of conceiving output as a jointly created social interaction dialogue.

She stresses the importance of these collaborative dialogues as tools for knowledge building. By being actively engaged in a collaborative dialogue learners have an opportunity to discover not only what they can do with language but also what they cannot do. This newly discovered inability promotes cognitive (that is, learning) growth by providing a context for learner to notice their linguistic shortcomings, which, in turn, require that learner pay attention to form while attending to meaning-making. The process of building linguistic knowledge by means of learners' participation in collaborative dialogues is illustrated by descriptions of several studies that examine the effect of "verbalization" during collaborative activities in L2 acquisition.

One of these studies describes the way two eighth-grade French immersion students working together resolved the problem of the phrase "des nouvelle menaces":

1. Rachel: Cher[chez] nou . . . des nouveaux menaces.
[Look up new (as in) new threats.]
2. Sophie: Good one!

3. Rachel: Yeah, nouveaux, des nouveaux, de nouveaux. Is it des nouveaux or de nouveaux?

4. Sophie: Des nouveaux or des nouvelles?

5. Rachel: Nou[veaux], des nou[veaux], de nou[veaux].

6. Sophie: It's menace, un menace, une menace, un menace, menace ay ay! [exasperated]

7. Rachel: Je vais le pauser.

[I am going to put it on pause (the tape-recorder).]

[They look up "menace" in the dictionary.]

8. Sophie: C'est des nouvelles! [triumphantly]

9. Rachel: C'est féminin . . . des nouvelles menaces.   (Swain 2000, 101)

As this excerpt illustrates, Rachel came up with the word *menaces,* which her partner enthusiastically approved. In using this word, they collaboratively resolved the grammatical problem of *des* as well as *nouvelles.* They also referred to a dictionary for assistance in solving their problem.

This excerpt also reveals very important insights as to the role of collaborative dialogues for language learning. These interactions produced output—an utterance—and the verbalization of this utterance served as a means of reflection for both participants and sent them on a "quest" for knowledge-building experiences. Linguistic knowledge was acquired because some verbalization took place in a social context. This verbalization, in turn, revealed some gaps in their linguistic knowledge. The problem was solved collaboratively with the assistance of a dictionary, which confirmed their final solution to the linguistic problem at hand.

As Swain (2000) points out, unlike the type of research studies of negotiation documented in the work of Pica (1994), for example, this search for linguistic knowledge was not triggered by misunderstanding—or the lack of comprehension of the message by one of the interlocutors—but simply by producing (verbalizing) the utterance in a social activity. This verbalization allowed the learners to identify a linguistic problem and solve the problem jointly and collaboratively in a dialogic interaction. Swain calls for the application of collaborative dialogues in the classroom as well as for conducting more research into the nature of collaborative dialogues and their effect on second language development. Swain considers collaborative dialogue an important tool for language learning because it performs two functions: social and cognitive.

Patricia Sullivan (2000), in a study described in "Playfulness as Mediation in Communicative Language Teaching in a Vietnamese Classroom," reminds us that the concept of collaborative work frequently associated in the second or foreign language classroom with pair work or group work ought not be disassociated from social, cultural, institutional, and political settings. The classroom and its activities should not be viewed as being neutral. The classroom is part of a larger sociocultural and political context, and classroom interaction reflects motives and beliefs concerning the external reality. They are closely related.

Sullivan (2000) criticizes the current push toward communicative language teaching (CLT) as the most communicatively oriented and thus most effective method of teaching English as a second or foreign language. In her historical overview of CLT, she points out three areas that unite different versions and interpretations of CLT: the promotion of an Anglo-Saxon value system of choice, freedom, and equality; the focus on the concept of work as opposed to play; and the focus on the information exchange function of language.

She claims that embedded in the notion of pair or group work is the idea of choice because students have a choice of partners or groups; the ideal of freedom because students in pairs or groups have a right to talk freely and are also free from the teacher's control; and the ideal of equality because students in groups are equal, and the power of the teacher within groups is also diminished or neutralized (that is, equalized).

The second focus of CLT pertains to the notion of the value of work, which the terms *group work* and *pair work* seem to project. Even the term *collaboration* seems to promote the notion of the value of work because it indicates co-labor. Therefore, various activities connected with these collaborative endeavors evoke the expectations commonly associated with the concept of work. Communicative language teaching also operates within the information processing view of language. This may explain why information gap tasks are so popular in CLT.

Sullivan takes issue with these three fundamental principles of CLT. She claims that the values inherent in CLT may be appropriate in North American contexts but may not be appropriate in other parts of the world. The values of choice, equality, and freedom may be confusing or even alien to students outside of North American sociocultural settings. In her study Sullivan describes language classroom activities in Vietnamese universities that differ from classroom activities in the United States. Vietnamese society adheres to and values Confucianism, which emphasizes the importance of dependence rather than independence, hierarchy rather than equality. Vietnamese culture also values "wordplay, one-upmanship and oral impromptu playfulness" (Sullivan 2000, 126), which stand in a drastic contrast to the information transmission view of language prevalent in Western cultures.

These ancient traditions are reflected in language teaching and learning practices. The author describes the findings of her classroom observations of Vietnamese university students. The L2 classrooms described by the author are primarily teacher-fronted, with students sitting in very close proximity on the benches. Students do their assigned tasks together as one big group. Their responses are frequently constructed not independently but dependently, with the whole class participating in jointly constructed playful narratives. The following illustrates such a playful narrative construction:

1. S1: My father himself try and [try to stop] smoking.
2. T: [( )   ]
3. S1: One time he uh he uh had some uh medical medical [( )]
4. T and Ss: [some medicine]
5. S1: Yeah and he tried to stop smoking but he can't because after he uh one time he got ill very serious and he ( ) and the doctor ( ) from his lungs
6. T: OK.
7. S1: So he had to stop smoking but
8. T: He can not
9. S1: Yeah he couldn't.
10. T: He couldn't. OK.
11. S2: After that he was more interested in [eating].
12. Ss: ((laugh))   [eating]
13. S2: in eating and uh he smoked more
14. Ss: ((laugh))
15. S3: He smoked more.
16. S4: He is more addicted to smoking.
17. T: He is more [addicted] to eating.
18. Ss: [addicted]
19. S1: But it can't it couldn't make him stop eating.
20. T: Yes. He doesn't lose (a problem) but he gains another.
21. Ss: ((laugh))   (Sullivan 2000, 127)

As this excerpt illustrates, although the student (S1) began her story, she did not complete it. She was interrupted by other students, who assisted her in the narration of her story. The whole class helped her turn a potentially tragic story of illness into a funny and playful story by laughing and repeating each other's words and by playing on each other's words. They all seem to enjoy participating in this verbal exchange not for the sake of providing the necessary information but to simply engage in "verbal pleasure" (128). This active engagement in playing with words and taking pleasure from it is linked to their traditions of dependence and nurturing, and above all of "hat doi" (126), which is an ancient Vietnamese oral tradition of using verse to make friends and establish relationships. The Vietnamese language classroom reflects all these outside sociocultural and institutional values, which, in turn, affect their discourse practices. Thus, Vietnamese students' view of communication in a small group or in pairs differs from the view of communication advocated by CLT.

Sociocultural theory attunes us to the fact that human cognitive development does not take place in a sociocultural vacuum; a universal value system does not exist no matter how well-packaged or how well-intentioned this system may be. In order to understand human behavior outside or inside the classroom, whether L1 or L2, one needs to examine the sociocultural contexts to which the individual has been exposed in the course of his or her life.

Sullivan's findings send a cautionary note to the advocates of group and pair work activities to pay attention to the sociocultural and personal experiences that guide students' behaviors in the classroom. Vygotsky's SCT offers a powerful tool for understanding complex student behavior that may not adhere to well-established Western norms.

Activity Theory and Second Language Acquisition

As described in Chapter 6, initial motives constitute the guiding force for engaging in a given activity and represent the major force for determining the outcomes of an activity.

Motives affect the goals and determine the conditions under which these goals are realized in a concrete, spatial, and temporal circumstance. Motives thus represent the driving force for the basic orientation to the activity at hand, which, in turn, affects the process of learning. This phenomenon is applicable to all learning situations including the learning of a second or foreign language, as illustrated by the findings of the two studies described below.

The effect of the power of a basic orientation that is strongly embedded in the learner's social and personal histories is described in Barbara Gillette (1998) study titled "The Role of Learner Goals in L2 Success." The participants in this study were six students of French as a second or foreign language. The students were enrolled in an intermediate French course at the University of Delaware. They were selected on the basis of their performance on a set of instruments including a cloze test, an oral imitation task, classroom observation, essays describing the participants' experiences, and writing samples. The selected students agreed to participate in a longitudinal study that aimed at investigating effective and ineffective language learners. Three of the participants fell into the category of ineffective learners and three into the category of effective learners. All six agreed to keep a diary and class notes for the duration of the study in which they documented their learning habits in and outside of class.

As indicated above, the framework used to investigate the learning processes of effective and ineffective learners was based on activity theory, which claims that although the outcomes of an activity may look the same, if the motives behind these outcomes are different, then the activities in which the participants engaged are different and the total outcome of the learning process will be different as well.

The study illustrates the point that the participants, whether effective or ineffective, have different personal orientations towards learning French, and their orientations affect their strategic approaches to language learning.

A thorough examination of the participants' social background revealed whether they considered acquiring a second language to be a "worthwhile pursuit or not" (Gillette 1998, 197). This social background, combined with their personal histories, formed the basis for their orientation, which affects their attitude toward classroom learning of French. Those who saw value in studying foreign languages approached the task of learning French in a way that was diametrically different from the approach of those who did not value the importance of speaking other languages. This initial orientation to studying foreign languages seems to be closely associated with the participants' exposure to the world at large: those who had traveled and lived abroad seem to be positively predisposed to learning French. This basic predisposition separated the effective learners from the ineffective learners and visibly affected the way they approached all the classroom assignments. The effective group was genuinely interested in learning the language. They drew personal satisfaction from acquiring a new language, as the following excerpt illustrates: "Learning French, or any other language, makes me feel a greater scope of things in this world that I can appreciate. With each increment of language ability I feel a growth in my self. At times, after a period of quantitative accumulation, there is a qualitative shift, a pleasure akin to discovering harmony on fourth hearing where there seemed dissonance, as with a Bartók quartet. This artificial stammering of pronoun order, gender agreement, and inflection becomes the faculty of speech and finally the act of thinking and feeling in new ways" (199).

The learning of a new language is viewed by the effective learners as personal growth, or as the ability to acquire other "voices," that, in turn, allows these learners to expand their notion of self; it increases their potential for self-discovery and expansion of their cognitive and emotional spheres. In contrast, the ineffective group viewed learning French as a requirement. They needed to pass the course in order to fulfill the college requirement. This point is illustrated in the following excerpt: "I am not a big fan of learning French, or other foreign languages. The reason why I am in this class is to fulfill the language requirement for Arts and Science majors" (Gillette 1998, 198).

Thus, students' basic orientation (that is, whether they value or do not value learning foreign languages) affects their learning behavior. The effective learners approached all the classroom assignments differently than did the ineffective learners. They went out of their way to learn the language. They did more than what was required of them. In contrast to the ineffective learners, they exhibited a functional, communicative approach to language learning. They did not try to memorize or translate the new grammatical rules and vocabulary. They interacted with the text and made inferences. They also disliked relying too much on dictionaries and straightforward translations because this encouraged "abstract," out of context, and mechanical repetitions of lexical items. They seemed to resent the fact that they were being, in Vygotsky's term, object-regulated (here dictionary-regulated), and their aim was to become self-regulated by the process of internalization of words from different sociocultural and historical contexts on their own. The following illustrates their frustration at being other-regulated: "Working on my essay on Haiti, I became discouraged. . . . I depended on the dictionary too much for my liking. I felt kind of dumb, and a little uncomfortable about writing the essay in words that didn't come from me. I felt I was not doing anything productive by copying words out of the dictionary" (Gillette 1998, 206).

The ineffective learners, because of their different value system and motives, persisted "in their goal to do only the minimum required" (200). They seemed to insist on staying within the other-regulated domain almost exclusively. They seemed to spend all of their energies on preventing the transition from the other- to the self-regulated stage, which would require a greater personal involvement in the classroom assignments. They relied heavily on dictionaries. They approached the assignments from an analytical point of view; they memorized vocabulary and rules only to complete the assignment. They also did not make an attempt to integrate their knowledge. That is, each task was viewed as a closed and independent unit; once the elements of the unit were memorized and arranged in the way that allowed them to complete the task, the elements—whether words or grammatical rules—were forgotten. They equated reading with the ability to memorize a list of words.

Note that the participants' original motives concerning learning a foreign language and the value they place on learning a new language do not change with their actual positive or negative learning experiences. That is, effective learners do not seem to be discouraged by their negative classroom experiences. Their basic orientation toward learning a new language is not affected. They persevere in their desire to learn the foreign language. Ineffective learners seem to be immune to positive learning experiences, and negative experiences only reinforce their basic negative orientation to the whole situation. Thus, according to Gillette (1998), the effort to teach ineffective learners "good language strategies" advocated by such researchers as O'Malley et al. (1985), strategies that are believed to positively affect L2 acquisition, remains ineffective. These strategies are utilized by ineffective learners for the purpose of doing even less work.

Gillette cautions us against heavy reliance on applying learning strategies to SLA without taking into consideration students' initial motives and goals for learning and without investigating students' personal and social histories. Training programs geared toward learning strategies may be viewed as attempts to cure a symptom without investigating its causes. Activity theory draws our attention to the fundamental force behind any activity: its initial motive. Only if the motives are changed will the outcomes of the learning process be permanently and profoundly changed.

The difference between a task and an activity, and the relation between the task and the activity and its implications for SLA research and practice, are investigated in Coughlan and Duff (1998) and Roebuck (2000).

Peter Coughlan and Patricia Duff's study, reported in "Same Task, Different Activities: Analysis of a SLA Task from an Activity Theory Perspective," laid the foundation for the subsequent investigation of the same issue by Roebuck; therefore, Coughlan and Duff's study will be discussed first.

Coughlan and Duff make an important distinction between a task and an activity. Their distinction is even more important nowadays, when interest in a task-based approach to ESL teaching seems to be on the rise because of the popularity of the work of Skehan (1996) and Nunan (1989).

It was insightful of Coughlan and Duff to recognize this problem of equating a task with an activity and to present some evidence for the need to approach these two structures differently. They also called for investigation of the relation between tasks and activities. In their study, Coughlan and Duff provide a working definition of *task:* "A task, we propose, is a kind of 'behavioral blueprint' provided to subjects in order to elicit linguistic data . . . these blueprints, or research tasks, are motivated by a set of research objectives . . . and their selection is usually constrained by several practical considerations (including time; availability, number and proficiency of sub jects; and transcription requirements)" (1998, 175).

This definition indicates that in designing the task, the researcher has th ultimate power; subjects who are expected to perform under certain condi tions and according to the researcher's predetermined expectations have litt to say. They are treated like objects in an experiment that are controlled an manipulated by the researcher. The task needs to elicit a predictable behavic that later can be generalized to a different context or to a different popula tion. The purpose of the task is to elicit certain linguistic behaviors from th subjects that later can be compared over time and across different subject "Since many facets of the research task's implementation are subject to th control of the researcher, tasks earn the status of *constants* in the researc design" (1998, 174).

The authors set out to question these assumptions by applying Vygotsky fundamental principles of SCT, in particular activity theory. Activity theor forces us to look at the dynamic nature of the activity as it emerges i response to the subject's engagement in a problem-solving task. Thus, a activity, for Coughlan and Duff, in contrast to a task, consists of "the b havior that is actually produced when an individual (or group) performs task. It is the process, as well as the outcome, of a task, examined in i sociocultural context" (175).

The activity represents a dynamic and unpredictable process that emerg as a result of the subject's participation in the task, which is placed in a giv sociocultural setting. Unlike the task, the activity does not exhibit any obje tives; the participants have objectives that may or may not interact or conc with the researcher's objectives and that are negotiated during interactic while performing a problem-solving task.

All these different characteristics of tasks and activities need to be tak into consideration while investigating the relationship between the two. order to illustrate the point that a task does *not* equal an activity, the r searchers described the findings of the study in which five different subjec one Cambodian and four Hungarian, were asked to perform the same tas They were asked to describe a picture that depicted a beach scene. T findings of their data analysis indicate that the description of the same pi ture produced five different activities. They were not the result of looking different pictures but the result of different orientations, objectives, a collaboration frames developed by the researcher and the subject. Also, t findings reveal that even the same subject's behavior, his linguistic outp differs from one session to another in response to the same task.

Thus, the same task produced different activities, ranging from descri

ions to personal narratives, across different subjects and within the same
ubject. For example, during the first interview with a Cambodian immi-
grant to Canada who was enrolled in an intensive government-sponsored
ESL program, the subject produced a detailed description of the picture. That
first interview took place in the researcher's home and lasted almost an hour.
It is interesting to note that in the introduction to the picture description
task, the researcher gave the subject three options: to describe the picture, to
tell the story, or "anything." The subject decided to select the first option; he
described the picture as if the researcher, who sat next to him and had access
to the same picture, was not able to see it.

Another learner, in contrast, produced personal narratives with a clear
intention to engage the researcher in the activity. At one point in her description of the picture, the subject made evaluative comments about the significance of the beach picture. It reminded her of a scene from the movie *Jaws*,
an assessment that can be viewed as an attempt to create an alignment—a
"footing," to use Goffman's term (1974)—with her American researcher.

A similar attempt on the part of a different subject is illustrated in excerpt
of Coughlan and Duff's transcribed data, in which the subject associated
the scene with California, which is the researcher's home. The subject even
presented a personal revelation as to why he or she associated this picture with California: "I don't know I like that place and ((@)) and because
Michael Jackson lives there—somewhere there" (1998, 182). Yet another subject associated the beach scene with Lake Balaton in Hungary.

The analysis of the data clearly illustrates that the same task, description of
beach scene, produced different outcomes. The reasons for that may be
explained by the fact that the researcher's involvement in the same task with
different subjects varied. The time constraints could also influence the outcomes. In the first interview, the researcher was not pressed for time; recall
that the researcher spent almost an hour interviewing the Cambodian subject at home. In other interviews, conducted in a secondary school in Hungary, the researcher was pressed for time and did not probe the subjects
enough to elicit descriptions from them. The researcher accepted any language in response to his or her initial question.

Of some interest is a second interview with the Cambodian subject, which
was supposed to serve as a "posttest" to determine the subject's gain in
language acquisition. A year after the first interview, the Cambodian subject
was asked to describe the same picture. The subject recognized the picture,
but the language he produced was drastically different from that used in his
first interview. Considering that he had already seen the picture and that he
had already completed several ESL courses, his second performance on the

same task was very poor and incomplete, providing evidence that the same task produces different outcomes not only among different subjects but also within the same individual. This apparent difference in this subject performance could be due to many factors such as the subject's orientation to the task itself. This orientation, which was different from the researcher's may differ from context to context; even though the blueprint stays the same the individual's orientation may differ.

We may never know what caused this subject's poor performance on th same task the second time. Perhaps he did not give the same importance tha he gave it the first time; perhaps he resented being treated as a subject in study rather than as a human being engaged in a real-life conversation. Th impersonal and artificial nature of the task at this point in his persona social, and cultural development in the second language could have als prompted his negative reaction. Whatever the reason, the same task did no produce the same outcomes.

The findings of this study suggest that the data collected on presumably th same task cannot be viewed in isolation, removed from the sociocultura context in which the data were created. The findings also suggest that th activity, not the task, is born of dynamic interaction among different facto such as participants' motives and objectives, their ever-evolving person histories, their personalities, and the setting. Therefore, the created ever cannot be replicated. We need to stop deluding ourselves that the same tas will create the same linguistic event across different subjects and across di ferent points in time. Although tasks (blueprints) may be the same, activiti they produce will never be the same. The insistence that the task and th activity are the same could be compared to an attempt to equate a model of house with a home. The building may be the same, but the atmosphere insic the building will be different, even with the same occupants, on a differe occasion.

The same line of reasoning is presented in Regina Roebuck's (2000) stuc "Subjects Speak Out: How Learners Position Themselves in a Psycholingui tic Task." Like Coughlan and Duff (1998), Roebuck claims, in accordan with Vygotsky's theory, that human activity is a complex and dynamic pr cess that is determined by individuals' personal goals, their sociocultur history, and the context in which the activity takes place. She also makes clear distinction between a task and an activity and calls for more researc into the nature of the relation between tasks and activities and what types activities are likely to be promoted by a given set of tasks.

In her study, written protocols produced by twenty-seven elementary a five intermediate students of Spanish at the university level were analyze

The subjects read and immediately recalled three experimental texts: Two were newspaper reports, one each in the L1 and the L2, on the topics of political issues in Latin America, and the third text was in English, the subjects' native language, and dealt with the very complex topic of physics.

The findings seem to reinforce the claim that task (in Roebuck's study, a request to produce a written protocol after having read the text) does not equal activity. In fact, the same task produced many different activities that reflected different subjects' orientations to the task at hand.

Note that, contrary to a common practice in quantitative, experimental studies, the subject in Roebuck's study who had not performed the task according to the researcher's instructions was not eliminated. Despite the fact that the subject's behavior deviated from the group's behavior, his data were included in the study. Because Roebuck worked within Vygotsky's framework, in which the activity is determined by the individual's perception of a task, past experiences, and orientations toward the task itself, this subject's data were carefully examined to determine the reasons for this particular subject's "deviation" from the group's behavior.

On reading the first text, the subject admitted that he had misunderstood the instructions and therefore had produced a shorter recall of the text. He had interpreted the task as a literal translation of a much shorter text. His orientation to the task was thus much different from that of the rest of the group. He did not, however, change his orientation to the remaining texts, though he knew by now that the task required a recall of the entire text. He produced a short, literal translation of the second text. It is not clear why the subject insisted on interpreting the recall of the reading texts in such a fashion. Perhaps a combination of his initial orientation, his assessment of the task itself, his past experiences, and his lack of ability to complete the task prompted him to produce the short literal translations of the selected reading texts.

Many subjects in Roebuck's study oriented themselves to recalling a fairly complete and accurate representation of the Spanish article. Some, however, tried to focus on "documenting" their own processes of reading comprehension. Their recalls seem to take on private speech functions: They were trying to help themselves to understand the task by producing their own private speech, which guided them in the process of reading comprehension.

Some subjects interrupted the activity in order to conduct lexical search, which was documented in the margin of the page. For example, one subject attempted to figure out the meaning of the Spanish word *viernes*. Thus, for this particular subject, the recall task produced two activities: that of producing a recall protocol and that of teaching herself the meaning of *viernes*.

Another subject began the activity with recall information but later abandoned the goal of producing a coherent text and instead produced a list of ideas. This particular subject was not able to go back to her initial activity. Her protocol ends not with a coherent summary of the recalled information but with a list of fragments generated for herself as a potential reminder to connect them into a coherent text later. Thus, from these examples, it is evident that the subjects responded to their initial task in individual ways, employing different cognitive and linguistic tools, transforming the same task into different activities.

The data also reveal some interesting insights about the subjects' protection of "self." This phenomenon was observed during the recall of the English physics text. As the author suggests, some subjects tried to "reposition" themselves "from being a student asked to perform under normal conditions, to the one asked to perform under unfair conditions" (Roebuck 2000, 92). At the end of an unsuccessful attempt to recall the English text, one subject commented that he was out of time and therefore was not able to complete the task. This repositioning seems to indicate the need on the part of the subject to save face. Recall that the text was in English, in the subject's native language. Instead of overtly admitting that he did not fully understand the main ideas in the physics text, the subject opted for a different solution: His ability to explain his comprehension of the text was prevented "unfairly" by circumstances beyond his control.

Yet another subject "attempted to reposition himself and to reframe the task entirely by putting himself on par with the researcher" (ibid.). He provided some evaluative remarks concerning the value of the "experiment" itself (that is, on the value of the article on the topic of physics). By doing so, he was sending a message that he viewed his role in the activity different from the one assigned to him by the researcher. This new repositioning allowed him to step out of his assigned position and critique not only the article but also the researcher herself. He commented on the whole activity: "I think that this was the last sentence. [space of about four inches] A cruel thing to make students read" (93). This subject, by putting himself on a par with the researcher, created for himself a different activity that allowed him to be excluded from performing the assigned task and to become a commentator on the article. He created a new activity that allowed him to save face, allowing him to protect his cognitive ability: he did not wish to be viewed by the outside expert as someone who was not able to comprehend his native language. The task of recalling these two different texts, one in the L2 and one in the L1, was perceived by this subject as a linguistic task. He excluded the possibility that there are different levels of difficulty associated with reading that go beyond linguistic ability.

These findings, like Coughlan and Duff's (1998), illustrate the need to reconceptualize our current understanding of what a task represents and its effect on the learner's performance. Roebuck concurs with Coughlan and Duff that the task should be viewed as different from the activity and that the same task produces different activities across subjects and within the same subject. Different levels of difficulty evoke different reactions in subjects, whose interaction with the assigned task often introduces "repositioning" of the self and thus produces a different activity in which the subject creates a "safe zone" for himself or herself. Not only does the same task produce different activities because of the participants' different orientations to the task and their different sociocultural and personal histories, but also the same task produces a multileveled activity: one subsumes the other. This could be visually presented as an onion being peeled, one layer revealing and subsuming another, each closely related to the others.

An activity is a dynamic and individual process that cannot be easily generalized from one context to another. Roebuck, Coughlan, and Duff call for "reconditioning" our way of current thinking about generalizability, or uniformity of the learner's behavior from one study context to another where supposedly the same task is employed. We need to get accustomed to the fact that if activity theory were to be applied to SLA, particularities, unpredictability, and "fuzzy" findings should not be viewed as "unscientific." Such findings should not be disregarded because in this seeming chaos insights about human learning wait to be discovered.

The Role of Private Speech and Inner Speech in SLA

As described in Chapter 7, private speech (egocentric speech) plays a crucial role in human cognitive development; it represents, according to Vygotsky, a clear illustration of the interconnectedness of language and thought. Private speech also signals the learner's attempt to self-regulate, to take control of his or her cognitive growth.

Despite its importance for human cognitive development, little attention has been given to the phenomenon of private speech in the field of SLA. In order to remedy this situation, Steven McCafferty (1998) conducted an empirical study to examine the relation between the use of private speech and L2 proficiency level. The assumption was that with increased L2 proficiency, the use of private speech would diminish in a similar fashion to the child's diminishing use of private speech when the child's cognitive development increases.

The researcher expected that ESL learners at the low proficiency level would employ private speech more often than ESL students at the higher

level of L2 proficiency because of their greater difficulty in expressing them
selves in English as a second language. As opposed to advanced learners, low
proficiency students in his study were expected to produce more privat
speech, which was categorized into three levels: object-, other-, and self
regulation. In addition, McCafferty investigated another issue, the use of th
simple past tense, which according to a previous study conducted by Frawle
and Lantolf (1985), served as a means of object-regulation.

Thirty-nine subjects in McCafferty's study were divided into two group:
learners of low-intermediate proficiency and learners of high-intermediate t
advanced proficiency. These ESL students were attending the University (
New Mexico. Their proficiency level was based on the rater's evaluatio
of their spoken performance on the picture narration task. To control fo
possible cross-cultural differences in the use of private speech, the two group
were relatively balanced in regard to their gender and cultural background
the more advanced group consisted of nine students of Asian backgroun
and six students of Hispanic background, and the lower-proficiency grou
consisted of seven Hispanics and eight Asians. Both groups were also simil
in terms of their distribution of female and male subjects. The researcher als
controlled for the language learning backgrounds, since an earlier stud
revealed differences in the use of private speech as a result of exposure t
different language learning contexts. The participants in both groups ha
received approximately the same amount of exposure to English instructio
in their native countries, although the amount of exposure to English in th
United States differed. The advanced group had on average three years
exposure, and the lower proficiency group had one year of exposure t
English in the United States.

The subjects in both groups were asked to provide a narration based on
series of six pictures, which were shown one by one. Although the researche
was present during the narration, interaction between the subject and th
researcher was not permitted. The narratives were tape-recorded, then tran
scribed and coded in order to examine the use of private speech by th
subjects in both groups. The sequence of pictures used in the study did n
require any specialized knowledge. The following illustrates the sequence
the pictures:

1. A hat seller sits beneath a tree in which there are five playful monkeys.
2. As the hat seller sleeps, the monkeys each take a hat from one of tv
   baskets next to the tree.
3. The hat seller awakens and is startled to see his hats on the heads of th
   monkeys—now back up in the tree.

4. The hat seller shakes his fist at the monkeys and they imitate him.
5. The hat seller holds his hat in his hand and scratches his head—the monkeys imitate him.
6. The hat seller smiles and throws his hat downward; the monkeys do the same. (McCafferty 1998, 125)

A data analysis was performed on the coded data. The criteria developed for the coding of the narratives were based on the Frawley and Lantolf (1985) study, which included the categories of object-regulation, other-regulation, and self-regulation.

The *object-regulation* category was divided into three subcategories: subcategory 1 consisted of "attempts to impose inappropriate schemata on the task" (McCafferty 1998, 126); subcategory 2 consisted of "labeling, counting, or commenting on some aspect of the narrative" (ibid.); and subcategory 3 consisted of "sigh, laughter, exclamations when indicating that the learner felt he or she did not have a complete grasp of some element of the task"(127).

The *other-regulation* category consisted of questions posed either to the researcher (recall that interaction between the researcher and the subjects was not permitted) or to himself or herself. The *self-regulation* category included utterances produced by the subjects that indicated their control over any source of confusion on their part regarding the pictures.

The findings indicated that the low intermediates produced twice as many private speech forms (236) as the advanced subjects (115). In fact, the low-intermediate learners produced a significantly higher incidence of object-regulation (185), especially of subcategories 2 and 3, as well as other-regulation (38) and self-regulation (13), than the advanced learners. The following represents the difference in the use of private speech between the advanced and the low-intermediate learners (McCafferty 1998, 129):

Proficiency Level	Object	Other	Self
Low Intermediate	185	38	13
Advanced	92	17	6
Total	277	55	19

The study results provide evidence for the appropriateness of applying Vygotsky's ideas regarding the mediational function of egocentric speech to the L2 learning context. The author warns, however, that there could be other factors that override the proficiency aspect in connection with the use of private speech, such as the nature of the task, subjects' motivational predispositions, and subjects' cultural backgrounds.

The findings of McCafferty's study regarding the use of past-tense forms seem to contradict the findings obtained by Frawley and Lantolf (1985). In contrast to those in the latter study, the advanced students in McCafferty's study used this tense significantly more often than did the low-intermediate students. Frawley and Lantolf claim that the past tense represents a form of object-regulation; therefore, this tense should not have been used that often by the advanced learners. McCafferty (1998) suggests that his contradictory findings regarding the use of past tense may be the result of discourse continuity. Recall that the pictures were shown one at a time.

In sum, McCafferty's study findings seem to validate the importance of the role of Vygotsky's egocentric speech (private speech) not only for a child's cognitive development but also for second language learning.

The nature of L2 inner speech and its functions are investigated in Maria C. M. de Guerrero's (1998) study, described in "Form and Functions of Inner Speech in Adult Second Language Learning." Inner speech was operationalized in her study as "the linguistic characteristics of inner speech related to sound, structure, meaning, and vocabulary, as well as the functional role, or roles, of inner speech in learning the L2" (85). The study was executed in two phases. In phase I, 426 participants responded to a thirty-five-item questionnaire. The data were analyzed quantitatively. In phase II, a qualitative analysis was performed on the data obtained from interview protocols generated by nine participants.

The results obtained from the analysis of the questionnaire data revealed that a significant majority of the participants experienced inner speech in the L2. With regard to sound, the participants admitted to hearing inner speech in English and to hearing the voices of other people in English. In sum, L2 inner speech seems to be vocalized. With regard to structure, inner speech may take on the form of words, phrases, sentences, or even conversations; however, the complexity of L2 inner speech was associated with the participants' level of language proficiency.

With regard to vocabulary, inner speech consisted of words the subjects repeated in order to learn their pronunciation and words with unfamiliar meanings that they tried to use in the construction of sentences. In addition, inner speech was associated with functions such as mnemonics used, for example, to store language in memory; evaluative functions used, for example, in self-correction; interpersonal functions used in imagining conversations with other people; and intrapersonal functions employed in conversations with oneself.

The analyzed data concerning the differences in inner speech among the three groups (low, intermediate, and advanced proficiency) revealed that a

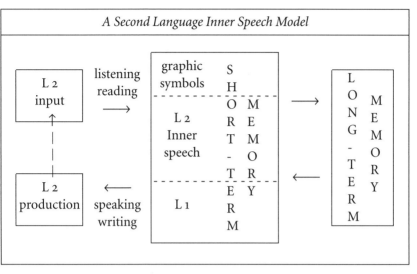

Fig. 8.1. A Second Language Inner Speech Model (Source: Maria C. M. de Guerrero, "Form and Functions of Inner Speech in Adult Second Language Learning." In *Vygotskian Approaches to Second Language Research,* edited by James P. Lantolf and Gabriela Appel, 3d ed. Norwood, N.J.: Ablex Publishing Corporation, 1998: 103. An imprint of Greenwood Publishing Group, Inc., Westport, Conn. Reproduced with permission.)

L2 proficiency increased so did the length and the complexity of L2 inner speech. The advanced students were more likely to use more complex structures such as conversations in their inner speech. All groups, however, regardless of their level of L2 proficiency, indicated that their inner speech was abbreviated, with a heavy reliance placed on word structure. The high-proficiency students seemed to rely less on their L1 in planning, monitoring, and evaluating their mental rehearsing of the activities to be performed externally. The differences among the three proficiency level groups seem to confirm the developmental nature of L2 inner speech.

The combined findings of this study have led to the development of a second language inner speech model, illustrated in figure 8.1.

As shown in this model, L2 input is processed and transformed into inner speech, and from inner speech it is transferred to long-term memory, where L2 knowledge is permanently stored, then retrieved from long-term memory for the purpose of speaking and writing. Thus, according to this model, inner speech serves as a conduit for L2 thoughts and L2 external realizations of these thoughts. Note that according to this model, inner speech involves the integration of L1 knowledge and *graphic* symbols. The identified components of the model seem to indicate that the growth of inner speech, so indispensable for L2 learning, is dependent not only on the initial verbal means but also on nonverbal means. This leads us to a study conducted by Steven McCafferty and Muhammed Ahmed (2000) and discussed in "The Appropriation of Gestures of the Abstract by L2 Learners," which examines the role of gestures in second language acquisition.

Gestures were given an important role in Vygotsky's theory of mind: "The word, at first, is a conventional substitute for the gesture: it appears long before the child's crucial 'discovery of language' and before he is capable of logical operations" (Vygotsky 1986, 65). Since gestures are for the most part synchronized with external speech, the researchers conducted the study in order to determine whether gestures are appropriated in the same fashion by learners acquiring the L2 under two different conditions: the naturalistic condition and instruction-only condition.

The *naturalistic* condition in the study was defined as "residing in a country where the L2 is the everyday language of use" (McCafferty and Ahmed 2000, 206), and the *instruction-only* condition was defined as the acquisition of a second language as a foreign language primarily through instruction.

On the basis of the subjects' backgrounds, four different types of gestures were selected: bounded container (a), potential (b), unbounded container (c), splitting the gesture space (d), and beats (e, f). Figure 8.2 illustrates the types of gestures selected for the study. The study included thirty-six participants from four different language contexts who were placed in the following four groups:

1. eight advanced Japanese speakers of English as a second language who were learning English in naturalistic contexts and who had been living in the United States and Canada for at least 3 years;
2. ten Japanese advanced speakers of English who learned English in instruction-only contexts;
3. twelve monolingual native speakers of American English; and
4. eight monolingual speakers of Japanese.

The participants in each group were paired and asked to express their opinions on the topic of marriage. They were given a list of questions that pertained to the topic of marriage. Their discussions, which lasted up to ten minutes, were videotaped. Each gesture was identified and coded to determine the type and frequency of occurrence. The results of the study validated the authors' initial contention that the naturalistic learners would appropriate not only the linguistic code but also American gestures. In contrast to the naturalistic learners and despite their advanced English proficiency, the Japa-

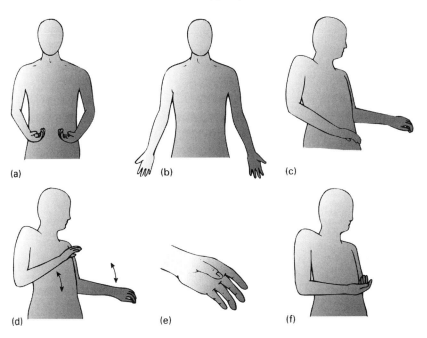

Fig. 8.2. Illustration of Gestures *(Source: Reproduced by permission of Oxford University Press from "The Appropriation of Gestures of the Abstract by L2 Learners," by S. G. McCafferty and M. K. Ahmed, in Sociocultural Theory and Second Language Learning, James P. Lantolf, ed. © Oxford University Press, 2000.)*

nese subjects in the "instruction-only" condition had not acquired American gestures. Their gestures were similar to those of the monolingual Japanese subjects.

The Japanese naturalistic learners of English seemed to have acquired the type of gestures that traditionally tend to be associated with Western cultures (bounded container gestures). Note that unbounded container gestures are part of their metaphoric nonverbal cultural heritage; however, on being exposed to American culture they appropriated the Western types of gestures, which they employed in conversations with their Japanese interlocutors. Recall that the participants were paired within each group; for example, the naturalistic Japanese learners were conversing in English with other naturalistic Japanese learners.

The findings of the study seem to indicate that naturalistic contexts provide ample opportunities to appropriate not only verbal but also nonverbal sign systems. Nonverbal clues such as gestures should be viewed as important vehicles for conveying meaning. The inability to appropriate nonverbal signs may lead to a breakdown in communication. The findings reveal that great care should be given to introducing activities in the L2 classroom that provide the learner with opportunities to be exposed to nonverbal signs. Development of the L2 within a Vygotskian perspective requires that all the necessary mediational signs be appropriated. The L2 should be viewed as a system of both linguistic and nonlinguistic signs that are closely related to a variety of sociocultural and institutional contexts.

The individual's full participation in the target language culture and the complex issue of the (re)construction of the individual's identity (self) are addressed in a very insightful and provocative study by Aneta Pavlenko and James Lantolf (2000) titled "Second Language Learning as Participation and the (Re)construction of Selves," with which I conclude this chapter.

Pavlenko and Lantolf propose a new metaphor for second language learning—the *participation metaphor* (PM)—not as a replacement for but as a complement to the prevailing *acquisition metaphor* (AM). This participation metaphor is introduced as a necessary framework for the analysis of the unique type of data presented in their study: personal narratives.

The authors describe the major characteristics of these two metaphors and compare and contrast them. Thus, AM is viewed as the mainstream metaphor for conducting SLA research; it assumes that language acquisition entails learning linguistic rules and vocabulary. The acquisition metaphor focuses on the individual's cognitive processes, processes that lead to the accumulation of linguistic knowledge. This metaphor is commonly associated with the computer, the container, and the information processor metaphors.

The participation metaphor, which is not yet well accepted by the mainstream SLA community, entails viewing language acquisition "as a process of becoming a member of a certain community" (Sfard 1998, 6, cited in Pavlenko and Lantolf 2000, 155). Becoming a member of the community requires that the individual communicate "in the language of this community and act according to its particular norms" (ibid.). This metaphor focuses on the individual's ability to integrate himself or herself into a new culture; it focuses on the individual's ability to actively engage in the target culture.

As indicated above, the creation of the participation metaphor was indispensable for the authors' ability to analyze first-person narratives produced by biculturals and bilinguals, who shared their personal stories of becoming active participants in a new L2 society.

As the authors point out, first-person narratives, although employed by some SLA researchers such as Schmidt and Frota (1986), have not been well accepted by members of the SLA community, who typically favor quantitative and experimental types of methodologies. Despite their "unscientific" nature, these personal narratives, nevertheless, adhere to the acquisition metaphor because their main purpose is to document learning of a linguistic code rather than to document (re-)constructing of a new identity during the process of becoming a member of the target language culture. And this is precisely what the personal narratives used by Pavlenko and Lantolf try to document: the process of participation and (re)construction of a new self rather than the process of acquiring the linguistic code.

Pavlenko and Lantolf (2000) examine the autobiographical work of several American and French authors of eastern European backgrounds in the context of the participation metaphor in order to obtain insights as to the learning processes the subjects underwent during their "cultural border crossings."

The selected authors included the Polish-English bilinguals Eva Hoffman (the author of *Lost in Translation*) and Anna Wierzbicka, the Romanian-English bilingual Andrei Codrescu, and the Czech-English bilingual Jan Novak, all of whom learned their second language as adults. The selection of their stories was based on (1) their atypical learning experience of becoming "native" speakers of their second language and (2) the relation of their native language to the target language (English or French). This relation reflects the asymmetrical power that exists between their L1, a Slavic language in most cases, and the target language. Slavic languages do not exert the same power and prestige as English or French; therefore, becoming an active participant in the dominant language adds to the power and prestige of these successful bilinguals.

The analysis of their personal stories led to identifying two major phases in second language learning viewed from the perspective of PM: the initial phase of loss and the phase of recovery and (re)construction. Each phase consists of many stages. The following summarizes the processes that lead to the (re)construction of selves according to Pavlenko and Lantolf.

> The initial phase of loss can be segmented into five stages:
> —loss of one's linguistic identity ("careless baptism," according to Hoffman 1989)
> —loss of all subjectivities
> —loss of the frame of reference and the link between the signifier and the signified
> —loss of the inner voice
> —first language attrition.

The phase of recovery and (re)construction encompasses four critical stages:
—appropriation of others' voices
—emergence of one's own new voice, often in writing first
—translation therapy: reconstruction of one's past
—continuous growth "into" new positions and subjectivities.

(Pavlenko and Lantolf 2000, 162–63)

In the loss phase, the first step that occurs is "careless baptism," or the name change. This renaming initiates the process of self-translation, of crossing the cultural borders. The most revealing account of careless baptism is Hoffman's change of her name from the Polish Ewa to Eva and her sister's name from Alina to Elaine. She writes: "Nothing much has happened, except a small, seismic mental shift. The twist in our names takes them a tiny distance from us—but it's a gap into which the infinite hobgoblin of abstraction enters. Our Polish names didn't refer to us; they were as surely us as our eyes and hands. These new appellations, which we ourselves can't yet pronounce, are not us. They are identification tags, disembodied signs pointing to objects that happen to be my sister and myself. . . . [They] make us strangers to ourselves" (Hoffman 1989, 105, cited in Pavlenko and Lantolf 2000, 164).

By changing her name, Hoffman lost her Polish identity, her own sense of "agency in the world—an agency in large part, constructed through linguistic means" (Pavlenko and Lantolf 2000, 164). Hoffman's personal connection "I-Ewa" with the external world, which had been already established in the Polish sociocultural context, had to be lost in order to create a space for a new agency, a new relationship between "I-Eva" and the new North American culture.

This loss of agency, necessary for the process of "self-translation," is also associated with another process, that of reevaluating, reorganizing, and (re)creating one's inner speech. This reorganizing of inner speech can be painful and confusing because the established system of inner speech in the L1 does not fulfill the requirements of the newly created relationship between Eva and the external world of American culture. "Her inner speech in Polish has ceased to function, while the inner speech sparked by English, her new language, has yet to emerge" (Pavlenko and Lantolf 2000, 165).

This is illustrated in the following excerpt from Hoffman's (1989) autobiographical story: "I wait for that spontaneous flow of inner language which used to be my nighttime talk with myself. . . . Nothing comes. Polish, in a short time, has atrophied, shriveled from sheer uselessness. Its words don't apply to my new experiences, they're not coeval with any of the objects, or faces, or the very air I breathe in the daytime. In English, the words have not penetrated to those layers of my psyche from which a private connection could proceed" (Hoffman 1989, 107, cited in Pavlenko and Lantolf 2000, 165). The phase of recovery and (re)construction of selves begins with the process of appropriation of other "voices": "All around me, the Babel of American voices, hardy midwestern voices, sassy New York voices, quick youthful voices, voices arching under the pressure of various crosscurrents. . . . Since I lack a voice of my own, the voices of others invade me as if I were a silent ventriloquist. They ricochet within me, carrying on conversations, lending me their modulations, intonations, rhythms" (Hoffman 1989, 219–20, cited in Pavlenko and Lantolf 2000, 167).

In the beginning, these voices do not need to be fully appropriated as the individual's own, but by repeating them, by using them as his or her own, just to get by, the individual gradually appropriates these voices. They eventually become the individual's own: "I do not yet possess them; they possess me. But some of them satisfy a need; some of them stick to my ribs. . . . Eventually, the voices enter me; by assuming them, I gradually make them mine" (Hoffman 1989, 219–20, cited in Pavlenko and Lantolf 2000, 167).

With the appropriation of new voices a (re)construction of self emerges. Very frequently these new voices are first captured in writing; writing is a crucial stepping stone for a total recovery of one's self and one's inner speech. Writing in a new voice—a second language—plays a crucial role in one's own reflection on a gradually emerging self. "Because this self exists primarily in writing, it is experienced not as a fully agentive self, but as an 'impersonal' and 'objective' self" (Pavlenko and Lantolf 2000, 168). Slowly, then, this objective self becomes a complete "agentive self" when, step by step, the individual discovers and fully appropriates new cultural and linguistic norms and their nuances. The individual finally feels at home in his or her newly discovered and inhabited space: "This godddamn place is my home now. . . . I know all the issues and all the codes here. I am as alert as a bat to all subliminal signals sent by word, look, gesture. I know who is likely to think what about feminism and Nicaragua and psychoanalysis and Woody Allen. . . . When I think of myself in cultural categories—which I do perhaps too often—I know that I'm a recognizable example of a species: a professional New York woman. . . . I fit, and my surroundings fit me" (Hoffman 1989, 169–70, cited in Pavlenko and Lantolf 2000, 168–69). As Hoffman describes it in the excerpt above, the new cultural space with its intricate tapestry of social and cultural norms has been fully internalized. The painful process of uniting one's self with the new external world—the recovery of the lost self—has been completed. The individual has become a full participant in the target language community.

Viewed from the perspective of the participation metaphor, second language learning is no longer about acquiring the target language code; progress in the L2 should no longer be assessed by comparing the learner's mastery of phonetics, phonology, and morphosyntactic rules with an idealized, homogeneous, and imaginary native speaker. Second language acquisition is no longer about acquiring linguistic knowledge but about the individual's willingness and persistence in becoming a full-fledged participant in the discursive practices of the target language culture.

In this new view of SLA, ultimate success or failure does not equal the failure to master the target language's linguistic code but the emergence of the lost self and new agency as well as the individual's conscious, goal oriented efforts to become an active participant in the new cultural community. "It is ultimately through their own intentions and agency that people decide to undergo or not undergo the frequently agonizing process of linguistic, cultural, and personal transformation" (Pavlenko and Lantolf 2000, 171). In order to gain a better understanding of these agonizing processes of rising out of the ashes like a phoenix, it is necessary to legitimize different types of data and different types of methodologies such as personal narratives.

It is also important to note that Pavlenko and Lantolf recognize the complexity of becoming a true participant in a new L2 society. They caution against equating their model with Schumann's model of acculturation. "This is because the integration process is much more complex than the [Schumann] model assumes" (Pavlenko and Lantolf 2000, 170). In order to make this distinction clear as well as to illustrate the complexity of the processes of becoming an active participant in an L2 culture, they cite Kozulin and Venger's (1994) report on the Russian Jews who immigrated to Israel from what once was the Soviet Union. According to this report, the Russian Jews showed a strong tendency to integrate themselves into the institutional life of their new country; however, they resisted cultural integration. They expressed their strong positive attitude toward the new country, yet they insisted on preserving their Russian cultural identity.

In the end, Pavlenko and Lantolf (2000, 175) also raise interesting questions for future theoretical and practical considerations, for example: "Do all those who attempt border crossings experience the intense personal reconstruction?" and "How and to what extent is the participation metaphor implicated in classroom second language learning . . . and how does this relate to participation outside of the classroom?"

In this chapter I have reviewed several studies that investigated second language learning within Vygotsky's sociocultural theory. In each section of this chapter I have discussed the studies that are most relevant to the application of one fundamental principle of SCT to second language learning. Most of the studies presented in this chapter may be categorized as falling within the third scientific tradition—the dialogical tradition—described in Chapter 2, although their authors do not attempt to classify their studies that way. Even the most dialogically oriented authors, Pavlenko and Lantolf, do not wish to propose the replacement of the acquisition metaphor with the participation metaphor: "We want to make it clear, however, that neither we nor Sfard are prepared to propose the new metaphor as a replacement for the acquisition metaphor. Rather it is intended as a complement to the older metaphor" (2000, 156).

In the next chapter I propose a new approach to SLA—a dialogic approach. I call for the *replacement* of the existing cognitive approach to SLA with a new dialogic approach, which is based on Vygotsky's SCT and Bakhtin's literary theory. I contend that this new approach is broad enough to unify within its borders both cognitive and social perspectives. Therefore, I do not see any need to divide the field of SLA into so many competing and diverse branches in which the same phenomena are investigated and interpreted in different ways. This new framework provides a unified basis for all SLA theories, models, and practices, including teaching and testing. This new paradigm also promotes true cooperation among all parties involved in investigating and understanding the complex processes of second language acquisition: researchers, teachers, students, and language testers. I strongly believe that this new approach provides the ultimate answer to our attempts to understand language learning; it empowers at the same time all who are involved in second language acquisition processes by acknowledging the importance of all different voices and by promoting local independence, active participation, and self-reliance.

9

Building a New Model of
Second Language Acquisition

In this chapter I describe a new model of SLA that is based on Lev Vygotsky's sociocultural theory and Mikhail Bakhtin's dialogized heteroglossia, and I discuss its implications for SLA theory and practice. This chapter is divided into three sections: in the first I discuss some implications of this new model for SLA theory and research; in the second I address its implications for teaching; and in the third I discuss its implications for second language testing.

A Dialogically Based Model of SLA and
Its Implications for SLA Theory and Research

As the findings of the studies described in Chapter 8 indicate, Vygotsky's theory holds great promise for the field of second language theory and practice. Vygotsky's SCT, combined with Bakhtin's dialogism, as an epistemology for human sciences offers the field of second language acquisition unique opportunity to "heal" the schism that currently separates the learner social environment from his or her mental functioning.

Vygotsky's and Bakhtin's theories provide a bridge between the learner external and internal realities. They allow us to examine learning process from a holistic perspective in which the two seemingly opposite parts o human existence, mental and social, merge together in a dialectical relation. That is, the external world affects and transforms the individual's mental functioning, which, in turn, affects and transforms social, cultural, and institutional settings.

The Vygotsky framework forces us to examine the learner's second language social environment in a different light than the currently accepted one. Within this new framework, social environment is regarded not only as the source of the learner's language input but also as the source of the learner's cognitive growth. This is illustrated in figure 9.1.

Note that within this theoretical framework our current insistence on separating language ability from cognitive ability would be viewed as inappropriate. Such a separation would undermine the basic tenet of SCT, which dictates that language represents an indispensable tool for human cognitive growth. Therefore, exposure to a variety of potentially new sociocultural and institutional settings, and discursive practices associated with these settings, are viewed as having a major impact on the learner's consciousness, on his or her cognitive growth. The assertion that an invisible line separates the learner's cognitive development from the learner's language development may be acceptable within the cognitive scientific tradition, but this position would not be acceptable within this new dialogic approach, in which cognition and language (whether first, second, or third) are closely intertwined.

The application of Vygotsky's and Bakhtin's theories to SLA theory and research would also require that the well-accepted distinction between language competence and language performance be erased. Please recall that most of the communicative competence models discussed in Chapter 5 separate language competence from language performance (language use in real-life contexts). Communicative competence models focus on the investigation and explanation of language competence—human mental processes devoid of social contexts. Communicative competence models give an impression that their creators are in denial of their human existence in the real world or of human communication with all its imperfections, ambiguities, and unpredictability. Vygotsky's and Bakhtin's theories restore the "dignity" and value to the neglected part of human language—language performance.

Thus, if we were to redesign some of the communicative competence models according to Vygotsky's and Bakhtin's theories, there would not be any separation between language competence and language performance; the arrow (see figure 9.2) would not lead unidirectionally from the human mind (competence) to the external world (performance) but, if anything, would be reversed. Figure 9.2 illustrates the relation between language performance and language competence in the new dialogically based SLA approach.

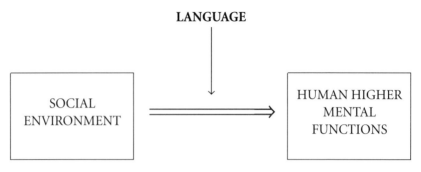

Fig. 9.1. The Origin of Human Higher Mental Functions

A dialectical interaction between the interpersonal and the intrapersonal planes leads to the merging of language performance and language competence: they represent two sides of the same coin. The outcome of this process is illustrated in figure 9.3.

In this new model of SLA, the origin of second language competence lies not in the language acquisition device or any other mechanism, such as Bley-Vroman's (1989) general problem-solving system, but in social reality—in language use. This language use does not take place in a vacuum or in an imaginary social context but in a real and discernible social context. Social contexts create language, and language creates social contexts: one constitutes the other. These contexts are *not* universal. They are highly localized and therefore language ability is also locally bound: it reflects all the characteristics of a well-defined sociocultural and institutional context. Second language ability is not situated in the learner's mind but in a multitude of sociocultural and institutional settings and in a variety of discursive practices to which the learner has been exposed throughout his or her life. This is illustrated in figure 9.4 (please note that the term *ability* refers to the merged language performance and competence).

The application of Vygotsky's SCT to SLA theory and research would require that we abandon theories that proclaim the existence of a general language ability. Also, we would need to eradicate the assertion that SLA progresses along a predetermined mental path that cannot be altered no matter how much exposure to the target language the learner has experienced in naturalistic or instruction-only contexts.

In addition to erasing the distinction between language performance and competence and the abandonment of the idea of the existence of a general language ability, the application of Vygotsky's and Bakhtin's theories to SLA would require that we view language not as an abstract system of morphemes

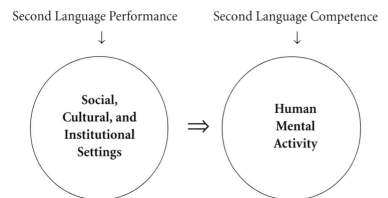

Fig. 9.2. The Merging of L2 Performance with L2 Competence

yntactic rules and structures but as *speech*. In this new paradigm, the heterogeneous nature of speech is "normalized" and homogenized in the term
peech genres. That is, the many different voices captured in Bakhtin's heteroglossia are united within speech genres (discursive practices) that reflect a
ariety of sociocultural and institutional settings.

Within this new paradigm, SLA research would focus on identifying, de-
cribing, and explaining all the possible speech genres one may encounter
1 a given sociocultural and institutional context. Here, current advances
1 corpus linguistics as well as in discourse analysis should provide essen-
tal tools for conducting authentic discourse analyses of a variety of speech
enres.

In addition, SLA research would focus on investigating the effects of vari-
us speech genres on the learner's second language ability. For example, how
o discursive practices typical of a university context, such as lectures or
cademic discussions, affect the learner's language ability? What kind of
anguage ability does this type of environment evoke in the learner? And how
asily is the language ability acquired in one sociocultural setting transferable
) other contexts?

Note that discourse analyses of speech genres typical of a given socio-
ultural and institutional context would be conducted not in terms of lin-
uistic code but in terms of utterances, speech acts, turn-taking mechanisms,
pair mechanisms, topic patterns, and nonverbal signs such as gestures and
cial expressions. These thorough discourse analyses are necessary because,
. you will recall from the discussion of Bakhtin's ideas (Chapter 7), we are
l products of the appropriation of the many voices we encountered in a
ariety of contexts such as educational, family, political, economic, justice,

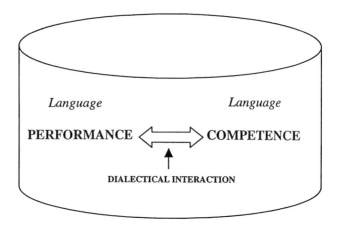

Fig. 9.3. A Dialectical Interaction Between L2 Performance and L2
Competence

healthcare, and religious institutions. New voices of the target language'
sociocultural and institutional settings need to be experienced, absorbed, an
appropriated by L2 learners not for the sake of appropriation but to help L
learners become active participants in the target language culture.

The appropriation of new voices needs to take place in real-life context:
which may be similar to L2 learners' native language contexts, but becaus
these contexts are now filled with different people, with different voices, the
need to be reappropriated. Second language learners should not be presente
with a false sense of security regarding the existence of one shared reality suc
as the post office, the bank, or the doctor's office or with a false sense that
they master the grammatical rules and structures of the target language, the
will automatically achieve mutual understanding with members of the targe
language culture.

The theory and research based on Vygotsky's and Bakhtin's ideas woul
require that we all be "reconditioned" regarding our current expectations ;
to the existence of one universal voice, one linguistic code, and one reali‹
that can be conquered and completely understood by all the participant
The complex processes that lead to the establishment of *intersubjectivity,* th
mutual understanding of a shared reality by participants in a given soci‹
cultural context, need to be carefully examined.

The recognition of many realities and many voices assumes that the lear
er's "old" voices, the voices of his or her native-language culture, be a‹
knowledged and respected. Note that within this new model of SLA, whe
we talk about "old voices," voices that evoke the learner's native cultural ar

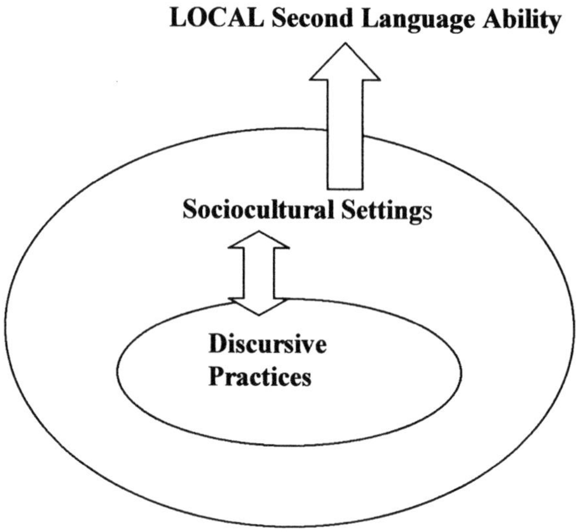

LOCAL Second Language Ability

Fig. 9.4. Local Second Language Ability

nstitutional settings, or their native speech genres, we are not referring to he learner's native language as an object or an abstraction that can be extracted from the learner's mind but to the learner's consciousness, the learner's self.

This merging of the old and new selves, which Pavlenko and Lantolf (2000) called the (re)construction but which I would like to call *coconstruction* or cocreation of self, needs to be examined, nurtured, and encouraged. More esearch studies, similar in nature to Pavlenko and Lantolf's (2000) study, are urgently needed if the dialogic approach based on SCT and dialogized hetroglossia were to be applied to SLA.

We need to gain more understanding of the processes of the appropriation f new voices by investigating both successful and unsuccessful second lanuage learners. This, in turn, would require that we conduct more qualitative esearch studies such as longitudinal case studies, personal narratives, obserations of the learner's participation in different target language contexts, nd interviews with native speakers who either allowed nonnative speakers to ctively participate in a variety of contexts by offering them, for example, cademic or business positions, or those who denied them various such ositions.

We need to better understand the processes associated with Pavlenko and antolf's (2000) participation metaphor, which I consider the fundamental netaphor of a dialogically based approach to SLA. I would like to expand on this metaphor, however. In my opinion, it needs to be applied not only to L2 learners but also to native speakers. Not only does the L2 learner need to be educated and encouraged to appropriate new voices and thus become an active participant in the target language culture, but the native speaker also needs to be educated and encouraged to provide appropriate assistance to the L2 learner to become an active participant. Active involvement on the part of native speakers should not be viewed as an exception to the rule but as the norm. This revised participation metaphor should be viewed as the new domain of SLA theory and research.

The ultimate goal of SLA theory and practice would be to investigate interactive processes that pertain to the learner's journey toward becoming an active participant in the target language culture. The new paradigm also requires examination of what it means to become a successful business owner, computer programmer, or university professor. To be considered successful in these sociocultural settings and discursive practices obviously requires more than achieving a perfect mastery of grammatical or phonological systems, as the successes of a former security advisor, Zbigniew Brzezinski, or a former secretary of state, Henry Kissinger, seem to indicate. It means being able to acquire new voices without forgetting old voices, to be able to merge past experiences with new ones. Active, engaged, and successful participants in the process of transforming and coconstructing their own selves have a unique potential and a unique opportunity to transform the target language culture as well. Their voices may serve as catalysts for the progress and growth of the target language culture. Becoming an active participant in second language sociocultural life should therefore be regarded as beneficial for both the native speaker and the nonnative speaker, since becoming an active participant may contribute to the native speaker's and the nonnative speaker's cognitive growth and to the coconstruction of the native speaker's self and nonnative speaker's self.

In sum, the ultimate purpose of this dialogically based model of SLA is to discover the processes that allow the L2 learner to become an active participant in the target language culture, or to investigate how participation in a variety of *local* sociocultural contexts affects the learner's second language ability and how participation in one sociocultural context affects the learner's participation in another. This idea is illustrated in figure 9.5.

A dialogically based SLA requires that we utilize research methodologies that may not be regarded as "scientific" from the hard sciences' perspective. As Vygotsky pointed out, however, "for each discipline and each student the interacting curves of learning and development need to be plotted individually" (Kozulin 1990, 171, cited in van Lier 1996, 191). Second language acquis-

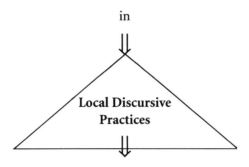

Active Participation

in

**Local Discursive
Practices**

LOCAL Second Language Ability

Fig. 9.5. Local Second Language Ability Acquired in
the Process of Active Participation in Local Discursive Practices

ion, as a scientific discipline, has a right to develop "the interacting curves of
earning and development" that satisfy its own scientific needs. Since the field
of SLA, in my opinion, has already passed the stages of infancy and adoles-
ence, it no longer requires the approval of the other scientific fields to feel
good" about its scientific endeavors or progress. The age of adulthood re-
uires an honest self-examination, taking responsibility for one's own ac-
ions, and finding one's unique voice. Although I do not mean to suggest
utting off all connections with other sciences, I strongly believe that these
onnections need to be reexamined and reevaluated. Establishing appropri-
te interdisciplinary connections is important; however, following scientific
rends only in order to be accepted as a member of the "club," so to speak,
nay sound attractive in the short run but may prove to be destructive in the
ong run.

Researchers of SLA should not be afraid to explore uncharted territories or
onduct studies that are regarded as "unscientific" such as personal narra-
ves or diary studies. Ironically, most experimentally oriented researchers
working within the information processing paradigm tend to rely on the
ndings obtained from diary studies (a qualitative research method). Recall
at the concept of "noticing the gap" was originally introduced to the field of
LA by Schmidt and Frota (1986) on the basis of their diary study, which
ocumented their personal experiences of studying Portuguese as a second
nguage.

Research studies should also be conducted to investigate the relation between a task and an activity. Currently the popularity of the task-based approach is on the rise. But I see a problem with placing so much trust in the power of this approach to second language learning. The difficulty with such an approach, as advocated by Skehan (1996), for example, is that it confuses tasks with activities, that is, it confuses tasks with the learning process itself. This confusion may be illustrated by the example of building the most efficient car for someone who does not know how to drive, and the process of building a car and the process of learning how to drive are viewed as being the same. Thus, it is falsely assumed that possessing an efficient car equals being able to drive. The learner is viewed as a passive observer, who is expected to be able to drive as soon as he or she enters the car. As our daily experience teaches us, however, being inside a car does not automatically mean that the learner will be able to drive successfully. Simply stated, a task based approach to SLA is like building a car (a task) without consulting a potential driver (learner) as to whether he or she will be willing to drive the car. The point is that, although there is nothing wrong with building and designing efficient tasks, these tasks need to be accepted for what they are and nothing else. Tasks in themselves do not represent a magic bullet; the learner has the ultimate say about their usefulness.

Contrary to what the advocates of a task-based approach to classroom learning claim, tasks in themselves do not determine the nature of an activity; the participants in the task ultimately produce the activity. Recall Ohta's (2000) study, which discusses the impact of task design on classroom learning. Because of the participants' predisposition or orientation toward the task, the so-called uncommunicative translation task was turned into a very productive and communicative activity. The fallacy of a task-based approach lies in the fact that it associates the communicativeness of a task with the task itself rather than with the learner and the learner's motives. The learner is ultimately responsible for determining the degree of the communicativeness of a task. Also, we should not assume that the same task produces the same activity every time it is used in a given context.

Understanding of the nature of the interaction between tasks and activities is essential for our ability to assist learners in their language development. What we need are careful analyses of what learners actually do with a task and how their involvement in an activity initiated by a task affects their language development. The time has come to examine the role of a task-based approach not from the researcher's perspective but from the learner's perspective, regardless of the researcher's expectations as to what kind of behavior a given task should elicit. The complexity, fluidity, and unpredictability of the interaction between tasks and activities should be acknowledged and investigated.

The new dialogical model of SLA based on Vygotsky's SCT and Bakhtin's heteroglossia can be summarized as follows:

1. Language learning is not universal or linear but localized and dialectical.
2. Language performance and language competence cannot be separated because they are in a dialectical relationship.
3. Language is not viewed as a linguistic code but as speech embedded in a variety of local sociocultural contexts.
4. The learner is not viewed as a limited processor that cannot attend to both form and meaning at the same time. Therefore, information-gap tasks such as structured input activities or spot-the-difference-in-pictures tasks are not considered to be useful for the appropriation of new voices or for the appropriation of language viewed as speech.
5. To acquire the target language is to acquire discursive practices (speech genres) characteristic of a given sociocultural and institutional setting.
6. Discursive practices typical of a given sociocultural setting are not limited to verbal signs. They also include nonverbal signs such as gestures, facial expressions, and other semiotic signs such as graphs and maps.
7. Cognitive and second language development are not separated in this model. They are in a dialectical relationship; one transforms the other.
8. Interaction between new voices and old voices is essential for the learner's language and cognitive development.
9. The development of second language ability is viewed as the process of becoming an active participant in the target language culture. The participation metaphor should replace, not complement, the existing acquisition metaphor.
10. The responsibility of researchers within this new approach is to investigate the processes that lead to becoming an active participant in locally bound social contexts. Such investigation requires that qualitative research methods be acknowledged as appropriate research methods for the field of SLA.
11. New research methods need to be developed to capture the fundamental processes of the participation metaphor. These methods need to investigate L2 learners who were successful or unsuccessful in their border-crossing endeavors. The ultimate goal of this investigation is to develop a prototype of an active participant in the target language culture.

Teaching

What would the practical implications of such a new theoretical model entail?

First of all, we would need to view the classroom as a sociocultural setting where an active participation in the target language culture is taught, promoted, and cultivated. The classroom would need to reflect as closely as possible outside sociocultural and institutional realities. That is, we would not be allowed to create artificial social contexts that do not resemble the external world. Also, in such a classroom, we would be expected to create for each student the ZPD in which, through dialogized interactions, not only are many different voices and different speech genres appropriated but also the learner's self and cognitive development are coconstructed.

Interaction within these individually created ZPDs may take on many forms. For example, it may be expressed in the format of a collaborative dialogue, a "knowledge-building dialogue" in which "language use and language learning can co-occur. It is language use mediating language learning. It is cognitive activity and it is social activity" (Swain 2000, 97). Or it may be realized in the format of an everyday conversation (van Lier 1996; Johnson 2000).

Van Lier advocates the use of the latter form of interaction in the second language classroom because symmetry of power is one of the basic characteristics of a conversation. In contrast to more asymmetrically oriented forms of interaction such as an interview or a lecture, in a conversation, each participant has equal rights and duties. That is, each participant has a right to decide what to talk about, for how long, who is to talk, and when to terminate the talk.

The works of Schegloff and Sacks (1973), Sacks, Schegloff, and Jefferson (1974), and Schegloff, Jefferson, and Sacks (1977) advanced our understanding of the nature of conversational discourse. Sacks, Schegloff, and Jefferson (1974) applied Garfinkel's (1967) ethnomethodology to the analysis of conversation (Schiffrin 1994; Brown and Yule 1983; Johnson 2001), and in the process they discovered certain fundamental characteristics of everyday conversation. According to these authors, conversation is locally managed and produced on a turn-by-turn basis. The turn size, turn order, and turn distribution are not specified in advance; they vary greatly on a case-by-case basis. What participants say is also not specified in advance. "The unplanned nature of conversation and the unpredictability of outcomes constitute two general characteristics of conversation" (Johnson 2001, 50).

Because of these characteristics, van Lier (1996) considers conversation the ideal form of interaction for developing the learner's autonomy, or his or her transition from the other-regulated stage to the self-regulated stage. Recall that within Vygotsky's SCT, the individual's autonomy is essential for the development of the individual's higher mental functioning.

I agree with van Lier that conversational interaction should not be limited to collaborative interaction with more capable peers or tutors; it should include interactions with learners who are at the same level of actual development. Van Lier (1996, 193) points out that "conversational interaction among language learners of roughly equal ability might be particularly useful, perhaps more so, in certain circumstances, than interaction with more capable peers or with native speakers." It "encourages the creation of different kinds of contingencies and discourse management strategies" (ibid.). Van Lier defines a *contingency* as "a web of connecting threads between an utterance and other utterances, and between utterances and the world" (174). Recall that the usefulness of conversational interactions among learners of equal ability was addressed in Ohta's (2000) study, in which two learners of Japanese as a second language successfully assisted themselves in their language development.

According to Newman, Griffin, and Cole, "the zone of proximal development is something more than social support that some today call scaffolding; it is not just a set of devices used by one person to support high-level activity by another. The ZPD is the locus of social negotiations about meanings, and it is, in the context of schools, a place where teachers and pupils may appropriate one another's understandings" (1989, xii). Thus, the ZPD is a place where cognitive change occurs. Since this cognitive change takes place "when people with different goals, roles, and resources interact" (2), second language teachers should not be afraid to create a variety of interactive possibilities in the ZPD. They should be assured that "the differences in interpretation provide occasions for the construction of new knowledge" (ibid.).

Second language teachers should not be afraid to experiment with creating as many interactive activities as possible with learners of the same L1 backgrounds or different backgrounds or with L2 learners who are at the same or different levels of language proficiency. This "experimentation," however, should not be conducted for the sake of experimentation. It should be conducted with a goal in mind: to help expose L2 learners to different interpretations of the same reality, to create an awareness of the existence of a multitude of shared realities, or to help L2 learners develop different levels of intersubjectivity. Also, the knowledge and skills acquired in interactive classroom activities within individualized ZPDs should be relevant to the L2 learner's particular needs and goals outside the classroom.

Since, according to this new approach, only a local language ability exists, the teacher and the learner should be given absolute freedom to decide collaboratively how the locally bound language ability is to be acquired and how to create for the learner the best ZPD, one that adheres to the learner's individual motives, goals, and cognitive needs.

I also support van Lier's call for the replacement of the term *input* with the ecological notion of *affordance,* which he defines as "the relationship between properties of the environment and the active learner" (2000, 257). If we were to accept van Lier's notion of affordance, then the learner's classroom environment should be viewed as an integral part of a broader sociocultural and institutional context. In the classroom, the learner should be exposed to a variety of speech genres that, in turn, should guide the learner in the appropriation of many new voices characteristic of different sociocultural settings. The classroom should provide a context for drawing the learner's attention to different discursive practices. It should reflect the social reality that exists outside the classroom.

Such a new approach to teaching a second language would inevitably require the development of many different videotapes and Internet programs that describe a variety of speech genres. Advances in technology should enable us to videotape many different discourse patterns typical of a given speech genre. These videotapes would assist the learner in the appropriation of new voices, new meanings, and new understandings. Also, new textbooks should be written that will promote the view of language as speech and the view of second language ability as the process of becoming an active participant in the target language culture.

As I indicated in my introduction, close cooperation among teachers, learners, and researchers is needed if we are to understand the complex processes of acquiring local second language ability, and becoming an active participant in the target language culture. This new approach to SLA would require that teachers, learners, researchers, and native speakers be involved in the theory building process and that their voices be given the same status and prestige.

Testing

In my book *The Art of Nonconversation: A Reexamination of the Validity of the Oral Proficiency Interview,* I developed a model for testing second language speaking ability that I called practical oral language ability (POLA). This model was developed as an attempt to provide some answers to the question "What is speaking ability?" After a thorough investigation of current tests such as the Oral Proficiency Interview and the Test of Spoken English, I came to the conclusion that there is an urgent need to develop a new test of spoken language proficiency.

Vygotsky's SCT and Bakhtin's literary theory provided me with the necessary theoretical and practical background for the development of a new
instrument for assessing speaking ability in a second language. Since the
OLA model falls under the dialogically based approach to language testing,
will first summarize its main principles, and then I will elaborate on
some issues that are relevant to my discussion of the application of the
dialogical approach to language testing such as assessing potential development, the difference between aptitude and Vygotsky's potential development,
and the relation between the traditional and the new testing method of
assessment.

The following summary of the guidelines for the development of a practi-
al oral language ability test is based on a more extensive description of the
guidelines included in Johnson (2001, 199–205).

. Major interactive oral events typical for a given sociocultural or institutional setting should be clearly identified and described. For example, in a
hypothetical university context with the international teaching assistant
(ITA) as a targeted audience, the following interactive oral events could
be identified: office hours, group discussions, lectures, and so on.

. Each selected interactive oral event ought to be carefully analyzed in
terms of its functions, tasks, abilities, and skills. Not all selected functions
and tasks need to be linguistic in nature. For example, the task of advising
during office hours may require additional abilities such as the ability to
listen.

. Once the selection of major functions and tasks for each oral event is
completed, its format should be decided. The format of each interactive
oral event should resemble as closely as possible its real-life format. For
example, we may ask the ITA to give a lecture in front of a real audience
and have the rater grade the candidate's performance. Note that within
this new framework, the format of each interactive oral event would be
different.

. Each interactive oral event should be rated separately. The evaluation of
each oral event could be as simple as "pass or fail," or the event could
be measured on a scale that describes in detail the strengths and weak-
nesses of the candidate's language ability in each identified function or
task. Criterial levels for judging performance within each interactive oral
event should be based on local sociocultural and institutional needs. This
would imply that a test taker would receive an array of scores for different
local activities.

If possible, there should be a group of evaluators who would be responsible for rating the candidate's performance within each interactive oral

event. These evaluators should not be participants. These interactive ora events should be videotaped for the purpose of being rated later b evaluators.

6. Not only should the candidate's performance be rated, but the tester performance should also be evaluated. Recall that within this new frame work, interaction is viewed as a social, not a cognitive, issue and therefor the candidate's speaking ability in each interactive event is dependent o the tester's performance.

7. The feedback provided to the candidate within this new system could b very practical and informative. For example, if the candidate happened t demonstrate problems with advising students during his or her offic hours, the candidate could be asked to observe office hours in a real-li context.

8. Within this system, language competence is locally situated. In our hypc thetical situation, we could say, for instance, that the ITA has a speakir ability to participate in all selected interactive events except for offi hours. We would not be able, however, to make general comments as the candidate's overall second language speaking ability. This could l illustrated as shown in figure 9.6. Note that each shape in figure 9 represents a different interactive oral event with its own format. The oral events are independent of one another, and the speaking abili required to participate in one may not be the same as the ability require to participate in another.

9. Although language competence is viewed as being locally situated in wel defined sociocultural and institutional settings, some local competenci are more universal than others. For example, the language competen needed to conduct a conversation in a cafeteria is much the same as th required for a conversation in a bar or a restaurant. These similariti cannot be assumed automatically, however. After all, participating in conversation with students during office hours is not the same as pa ticipating in a conversation with the president of the university.

10. Although we would not be able to make general statements regarding t candidate's speaking ability independent of a given context, we woul nevertheless, be able to make practical decisions regarding the cand date's ability to fulfill second language speaking requirements within t confines of institutional or sociocultural settings. For example, if the I1 is not able to perform certain functions during lectures, such as explanation but is able to provide some explanation during office hou the ITA may still be offered a position based on the fact that he or she h some potential ability.

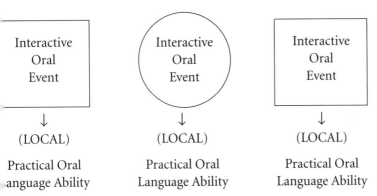

g. 9.6. (Local) Practical Oral Language Ability. (Source: Marysia Johnson, *The Art of Non-nversation: A Reexamination of the Validity of the Oral Proficiency Interview*. New Haven: le University Press 2001, 204.)

The issue of assessing the learner's potential development is at the core of ygotsky's theory, and if this idea were to be applied to language testing, it ould revolutionize everything we do in language testing. In traditional sting, the focus is on measuring the learner's actual level of development as recisely as possible. In order to do this, usually a series of tests is adinistered to the student at different points in time. These tests consist of a ries of tasks that are arranged in a linear and sequential fashion (Newman, riffin, and Cole 1989). For example, a task of subtraction precedes a task of ultiplication. The learner's actual development is inferred from his or her ility to perform certain tasks included in the tests. For example, if at one oint the learner was not able to perform a task but later was able to perform e same task, then it may be inferred that the learner's actual competence s improved. If the learner has failed to perform successfully the same task a different occasion, it would indicate a lack of competence.

As Newman and colleagues (1989) point out, "the ZPD provides a strikgly different approach. . . . Instead of giving the children a task and measurg how well they do or how badly they fail, one can give the children the task d observe how much and what kind of help they need in order to complete e task successfully" (77). Recall that this idea was utilized in Aljaafreh and ntolf's (1994) study, in which the five-level scale measuring the transition om the other-regulated to the self-regulated stage was developed on the sis of how much help and what kind of help was provided to the learner by e more capable peer during their interaction in the ZPD (see Chapter 8 for ore details).

According to Newman and colleagues (1989), this new type of assessment

in the ZPD has "a feature in common with the traditional testing method o
assessment in that it requires putting the child 'on her own.' Support has to b
removed until the child begins to falter. One difference between the tw
approaches lies in the fact that dynamic assessment achieves a finer-graine
idea of the child's level of 'independent ability' " (79). I disagree with th
authors' claim that there is one difference between the traditional testin
method and the new type of testing method. There are many difference
between these two approaches. For example, the former aims at measurin
the learner's actual development, and the latter aims at measuring the learr
er's potential development. Built into the concept of the ZPD, on which th
new testing method is based, are self-empowerment, self-regulation, an
encouragement to gain control of one's learning process, which is not alway
the case in the traditional method of assessment. In contrast to the trad
tional testing method, which is typically exemplified by a paper-and-penc
test, the new type of testing requires a *face-to-face interaction* with the mo
competent tester.

Since it is difficult to assess the learner's potential level of development ar
actively participate in the interaction at the same time, I suggested in tl
POLA model that the tester be responsible only for the interaction at han
and that another person or a group of people be responsible for assessing tl
learner's language ability. Recall that I also recommended that the tester
performance be rated, since the learner's ability to perform a task is deper
dent on the tester's performance in the same activity. Finally, in the trad
tional testing method, interaction is viewed as a cognitive issue. The learne
is solely responsible for his or her performance. In the new approach t
testing, interaction is a social issue. The learner's performance is jointly co
constructed during his or her interaction with the tester.

Now the question of how the learner's potential level of developme
would be measured arises. I recommend that a scale be developed utilizir
the two principles of Aljaafreh and Lantolf's (1994) study: how much assi
tance and what type of assistance is required on the part of the tester. Base
on these two principles a regulatory scale similar to Aljaafreh and Lantolf
(1994, 470) would need to be locally developed. The main theoretical a
sumption behind such a scale is that the more explicit assistance the cand
date requires, the less advanced the candidate is in his or her potential d
velopment within the ZPD. For example, let's imagine that the candidate w
given the task of providing some explanation of a certain scientific ter
during a lecture. Initially, the candidate was not able to perform this tas
however, once the tester pointed to a graph on the table, the candidate w
able to complete the task successfully. Thus, with a minimum of assistanc

he candidate was able to perform the task successfully. This candidate's
potential level of development should be rated higher than that of another
candidate who required more explicit assistance from the same tester in
order to be able to complete the task successfully.

One may ask whether this new testing method would replace the traditional method. The answer is no. What would be required of the traditional
testing system, however, is that it openly admit what it measures. The traditional method measures the learner's *actual* level of language development,
what the learner can do without any assistance at a particular moment in
time. If we are to assess the learner's *potential* ability, a new type of test needs
to be implemented. Such a test would have to be administered in the format
of a *face-to-face* interaction.

Also, the traditional testing method should focus on assessing the learner's
mastery of the linguistic code—the centripetal forces of language. Recall that
according to Bakhtin, the centrifugal forces override the centripetal forces,
and they need to be assessed in a localized environment—in a face-to-face
interaction. I recommend that a new testing method be developed to assess
the learner's potential development within the confines of the *centrifugal
forces* of the target language.

Within this new approach to language testing, each institution would
be solely responsible for developing its own instruments to measure the
learner's *local* second language ability. These local tests would provide individual institutions with some pertinent information regarding the candidate's local second language ability. Since each institution would directly
participate in the process of selecting tasks and activities and discursive practices typical of its sociocultural and institutional settings, the interpretation
of the candidate's score on the locally developed scale would be very informative and meaningful to the local institution. I also envision institutions of the
same type such as universities combining their resources and developing a
system for designing testing instruments that could be shared by many local
academic institutions in order to spread costs.

The new approach to language testing would empower local institutions
and would free them from their dependence on one source of testing knowledge—the Educational Testing Service (ETS). The role of the ETS in this new
testing system, however, would not diminish. Quite to the contrary, the ETS,
with its expertise in language testing, would provide guidance to the institutions that may be interested in developing their own local tests. This new
system also would encourage the ETS to develop more "localized" tests, for
example, tests for the medical profession, the legal profession, or the business
community.

Finally, I would like to address the issue of the difference between languag aptitude and potential ability since some researchers working in the field o language testing seem to equate aptitude with Vygotsky's potential develop ment. There are many differences between these two concepts. Aptitude part of the cognitive tradition and is viewed as an innate cognitive predispo sition to learn a language that unfolds independent of the outside world. typical aptitude test aims at assessing the candidate's logical and analytic abilities, and it adheres to the transactional view of language, according t which the test taker is solely responsible for his or her performance.

Potential ability is part of the dialogic paradigm, in which interaction viewed as a social, not a cognitive, issue. Potential development, althoug dependent on the learner's actual development, is predicated on the inte active skills of the tester. Potential ability cannot be assessed by a paper-an pencil test or a computerized version of such a test, a method that is typical aptitude tests. The learner's potential development needs to be assessed in face-to-face interaction. Also, this interaction needs to take place in a real-li context where *speech,* not the linguistic system, is being assessed. Potenti ability cannot be assessed by asking the test taker to solve a linguistic proble by himself or herself. Potential ability needs to be assessed in a jointly creat activity in which the learner's potential ability is negotiated during a face-t face interaction with the tester.

Parting Thoughts

The power of this new dialogically based approach to SLA lies in i ability to unite the two divergent traditions: the cognitive and the soci This framework reconciles a long-standing philosophical dispute regardi the superiority of one approach to the other. It offers a unique opportuni for "joining" scientific forces in our efforts to understand and explain tl complex processes of second language acquisition. It empowers researche teachers, L2 learners, and native speakers. They are all invited to contribu to our understanding of what it means to become an active participant the target language culture. It acknowledges the importance of viewing t learner as a whole being who, in the process of becoming an active partic pant in L2 culture, not only coconstructs a new notion of self but al matures cognitively. The learner should be encouraged to share acquir experiences connected with his or her border-crossing endeavors with oth L2 learners and native speakers.

Second language acquisition, viewed as the appropriation of many voic reflecting different discursive practices, allows us to examine the most powe ul forces of language: the centrifugal forces. Current SLA theories focus too exclusively on the centripetal forces of the target language—language as a system of linguistic rules—and in the process neglect to recognize the centrifugal forces of language.

Acknowledgment of the centrifugal forces of language would require that we dispense with the demarcation line between language competence and language performance. It would also raise our awareness of the role of social contexts in human higher mental development. This dialogic approach to SLA encourages the development of new research methodologies that shed light on the processes that lead to becoming an active participant in the target culture. It also reexamines the value of qualitative methods for second language acquisition theory and practice.

Furthermore, the model has practical implications. That is, it can be applied to second language classroom teaching and language testing. In the context of classroom teaching and testing, it stresses the importance of interaction as a social, not as a cognitive, issue and the creation of the ZPDs that are unique to each L2 learner's needs and goals.

The time has come to enter a new era, to make a major shift in our understanding of what the domain of SLA as a field should be and what kind of theory should be developed to explain such a new domain. The time has come to relinquish our absolute trust in the power of normal distribution, statistical logic, and probability and acknowledge the voices that for too long have been considered as skewed and therefore obliterated from our research investigations. We have stayed for too long in the mind of the learner, and in the process we have neglected to recognize the forces that interact with the individual mind. We have created an illusion of the reality and promoted a false sense of security by claiming that the knowledge of a linguistic system, the mastery of the centripetal forces of language, will allow us to create one global community, one shared reality, one level of intersubjectivity. As world events continually remind us, speaking the same language does not guarantee mutual understanding. In order for better mutual understanding to take place, we need to begin the process of real communication and engage in a true dialogue in which language is viewed not as an abstract object but as a living entity. The time has come to give new voices a chance. The time has come to give a dialogically based approach to SLA serious consideration.

Bibliography

Aljaafreh, Ali, and James P. Lantolf. 1994. "Negative Feedback as Regulation and Second Language Learning in the Zone of Proximal Development." *Modern Language Journal* 78: 465–83.

Bachman, Lyle F. 1990. *Fundamental Considerations in Language Testing*. Oxford: Oxford University Press.

Bachman, Lyle F., and Adrian S. Palmer. 1982. "The Construct Validation of Some Components of Communicative Proficiency." *TESOL Quarterly* 16: 449–95.

———. 1996. *Language Testing in Practice*. Oxford: Oxford University Press.

Bailey, Nathalie, Carolyn Madden, and Stephen D. Krashen. 1974. "Is There a 'Natural Sequence' in Adult Second Language Learning?" *Language Learning* 24, no. 2: 235–43.

Bakhtin, Mikhail M. 1968. "Role of Games in Rabelais." Yale French Studies no. 41: 24–32.

———. 1981. *The Dialogic Imagination*. Edited by Michael Holquist. Austin: University of Texas Press.

———. 1986. *Speech Genres and Other Late Essays*. Translated by Vern McGee. Austin: University of Texas Press.

———. 1990. *Art and Answerability*. Edited by Michael Holquist and Vadim Liapunov. Austin: University of Texas Press.

Barthes, Roland. 1972. "To Write: An Intransitive Verb." In *The Structuralists: From Marx to Lévi-Strauss*, edited by Richard D. de George and Fernande M. de George, 155–67. Garden City, N.Y.: Doubleday.

Bates, Elizabeth, and Brian MacWhinney. 1989. "Functionalism and the Competition Model." In *The Crosslinguistic Study of Sentence Processing,* edited by Brian MacWhinney and Elizabeth Bates, 3–73. Cambridge: Cambridge University Press.

Birdsong, David. 1989. *Metalinguistic Performance and Interlinguistic Competence.* New York: Springer-Verlag.

Bley-Vroman, Robert. 1989. "What Is the Logical Problem of Foreign Language Learning?" In *Linguistic Perspectives on Second Language Acquisition,* edited by Susan M. Gass and Jacquelyn Schachter, 41–68. Cambridge: Cambridge University Press.

Bloomfield, Leonard. 1933. *Language.* New York: Holt, Rinehart and Winston.

Bourdieu, Pierre. 1991. *Language and Symbolic Power.* Edited by John B. Thompson. Cambridge: Polity.

Brooks, Nelson. 1964. *Language and Language Learning: Theory and Practice.* New York: Harcourt, Brace and World.

Brown, Douglas. 2000. *Principles of Language Learning and Teaching.* White Plains, N.Y.: Addison Wesley Longman.

Brown, Gillian, and George Yule. 1983. *Discourse Analysis.* Cambridge: Cambridge University Press.

Brown, Penelope, and Stephan Levinson. 1987. *Politeness: Some Universals in Language Usage.* Cambridge: Cambridge University Press.

Brown, Roger. 1973. *A First Language: The Early Stages.* Cambridge: Harvard University Press.

Bruner, Jerome. 1990. *Acts of Meaning.* Cambridge: Harvard University Press.

———. 1996. *The Culture of Education.* Cambridge: Harvard University Press.

Cadierno, Teresa. 1995. "Formal Instruction from a Processing Perspective: An Investigation into the Spanish Past Tense." *Modern Language Journal* 79: 179–93.

Canale, Michael. 1983. "From Communicative Competence to Communicative Language Pedagogy." In *Language and Communication,* edited by Jack Richards and Richard Schmidt, 2–27. London: Longman.

Canale, Michael, and Merrill Swain. 1980. "Theoretical Bases of Communicative Approaches to Second Language Teaching and Testing." *Applied Linguistics* 1: 1–47.

Celce-Murcia, Marianne. 1991. "Grammar Pedagogy in Second and Foreign Language Teaching." *TESOL Quarterly* 25: 459–80.

Chierchia, Gennaro, and Sally McConnell-Ginet. 1992. *Meaning and Grammar: An Introduction to Semantics.* Cambridge: MIT Press.

Chomsky, Noam. 1959. "Review of 'Verbal Behavior' by B. F. Skinner." *Language* 35: 26–58.

———. 1965. *Aspects of the Theory of Syntax.* Cambridge: MIT Press.

———. 1975. *Reflections on Language.* New York: Pantheon.

———. 1980. *Rules and Representations.* New York: Columbia University Press.

———. 1981a. *Lectures on Government and Binding.* Dordrecht, Holland: Foris.

——. 1981b. "Principles and Parameters in Syntactic Theory." In *Explanation in Linguistics: The Logical Problem of Language Acquisition,* edited by Norbert Hornstein and David Lightfoot, 32–75. London: Longman.

——. 1988. *Language and Problems of Knowledge.* Cambridge: MIT Press.

——. 1995. *The Minimalist Program.* Cambridge: MIT Press.

Clahsen, Harald, and Pieter Muysken. 1986. "The Availability of Universal Grammar to Adult and Children: The Study of the Acquisition of German Word Order." *Second Language Research* 2: 93–119.

Clarke, Mark A. 1994. "The Dysfunctions of the Theory/Practice Discourse." *TESOL Quarterly* 28, no. 1: 9–26.

Cook, Vivian J. 1985. "Chomsky's Universal Grammar and Second Language Learning." *Applied Linguistics* 6, no. 1: 2–18.

——. 1988. *Chomsky's Universal Grammar.* Oxford: Basil Blackwell.

——. 1993. *Linguistics and Second Language Acquisition.* New York: St. Martin's.

——. 1994. "Universal Grammar and the Learning and Teaching of Second Languages." In *Perspectives on Pedagogical Grammar,* edited by Terence Odlin, 25–48. Cambridge: Cambridge University Press.

——. 1997. *Inside Language.* London: Arnold.

——. 2001. *Second Language Learning and Language Teaching.* London: Arnold.

Corder, Stephen P. 1967. "The Significance of Learners' Errors." *International Review of Applied Linguistics* 5, no. 4: 161–70.

Coughlan, Peter, and Patricia A. Duff. 1998. "Same Task, Different Activities: Analysis of a SLA Task from an Activity Theory Perspective." In *Vygotskian Approaches to Second Language Research,* edited by James P. Lantolf and Gabriela Appel, 173–93. Norwood, N.J.: Ablex.

Danziger, Kurt. 1990. *Constructing the Subject: Historical Origins of Psychological Research.* Cambridge: Cambridge University Press.

Derrida, Jacques. 1981. *Dissemination.* Translated by Barbara Johnson. Chicago: University of Chicago Press.

de Saussure, Ferdinand. 1959. *Course in General Linguistics.* New York: Philosophical Library.

Donato, Richard. 1998. "Collective Scaffolding in Second Language Learning." In *Vygotskian Approaches to Second Language Research,* edited by James P. Lantolf and Gabriela Appel, 33–56. Norwood, N.J.: Ablex.

Doughty, Catherine. 1991. "Second Language Instruction Does Make a Difference: Evidence from an Empirical Study of SL Relativization." *Studies in Second Language Acquisition* 13, no. 4: 431–69.

Dulay, Heidi C., and Marina K. Burt. 1974. "Natural Sequences in Child Second Language Acquisition." *Language Learning* 24: 37–53.

Edghill, E. M., trans. 1928. *The Works of Aristotle,* vol. 1, *Categoriae and De Interpretatione.* London: Oxford University Press.

Ellis, Rod. 1985. *Understanding Second Language Acquisition.* Oxford: Oxford University Press.

———. 1990. *Instructed Second Language Acquisition*. Oxford: Basil Blackwell.

———. 1994. *The Study of Second Language Acquisition*. Oxford: Oxford University Press.

Færch, Claus, and Gabriele Kasper. 1980. "Processes in Foreign Language Learning and Communication." *Interlanguage Studies Bulletin* 5: 47–118.

Felix, Sascha W. 1984. "Maturational Aspects of Universal Grammar." In *Interlanguage,* edited by Alan Davies, Clive Criper, and A. P. R. Howatt, 133–61. Edinburgh: Edinburgh University Press.

———. 1985. "More Evidence on Competing Cognitive Systems." *Second Language Research* 1: 47–72.

Fisiak, Jacek, ed. 1981. *Contrastive Linguistics and the Language Teacher*. Oxford: Pergamon.

Flynn, Susan. 1987. *A Parameter-Setting Model of L2 Acquisition: Experimental Studies in Anaphora*. Dordrecht: Reidel.

Frawley, William, and James P. Lantolf. 1985. "Second Language Discourse: A Vygotskian Perspective." *Applied Linguistics* 6: 19–44.

Frege, Gottlob. 1960. *Translations from the Philosophical Writings of Gottlob Frege*. Edited by Peter Geach and Max Black. Oxford: Basil Blackwell.

Fries, Charles C. 1945. *Teaching and Learning English as a Foreign Language*. Ann Arbor: University of Michigan Press.

Garfinkel, Harold. 1967. *Studies in Ethnomethodology*. Englewood, N.J.: Prentice-Hall.

Gass, Susan M. 1980. "An Investigation of Syntactic Transfer in Adult Second Language Learners." In *Research in Second Language Acquisition,* edited by Robin C. Scarcella and Stephen D. Krashen, 132–41. Rowley, Mass.: Newbury House.

———. 1988. "Integrating Research Areas: A Framework for Second Language Acquisition Studies." *Applied Linguistics* 9: 198–217.

———. 1997. *Input, Interaction, and the Second Language Learner*. Mahwah, N.J.: Lawrence Erlbaum.

Gass, Susan M., and Larry Selinker. 2001. *Second Language Acquisition: An Introductory Course*. Mahwah, N.J.: Lawrence Erlbaum.

Gibson, James J. 1979. *The Ecological Approach to Visual Perception*. Boston: Houghton Mifflin.

Gillette, Barbara. 1998. "The Role of Learner Goals in L2 Success." In *Vygotskian Approaches to Second Language Research,* edited by James P. Lantolf and Gabriela Appel, 195–213. Norwood, N.J.: Ablex.

Goffman, Erving. 1967. *Interaction Ritual: Essays on Face-to-Face Behavior*. New York: Anchor.

———. 1974. *Frame Analysis*. New York: Harper and Row.

———. 1976. "Replies and Responses." *Language in Society* 5: 254–313.

———. 1981. *Forms of Talk*. Philadelphia: University of Pennsylvania Press.

Goodwin, Charles, and Alessandro Duranti. 1992. "Rethinking Context: An Introduction." In *Rethinking Context: Language as an Interactive Phenomenon,* edited by Alessandro Duranti and Charles Goodwin, 1–42. Cambridge: Cambridge University Press.

Goodwin, Charles, and Marjorie H. Goodman. 1992. "Assessments and Construction of Context." In *Rethinking Context: Language as an Interactive Phenomenon,* edited by Alessandro Duranti and Charles Goodwin, 147–90. Cambridge: Cambridge University Press.

Gregg, Kevin R. 1989. "Second Language Acquisition Theory: The Case for a Generative Perspective." In *Linguistic Perspectives on Second Language Acquisition,* edited by Susan M. Gass and Jacquelyn Schachter, 15–40. Cambridge: Cambridge University Press.

Grice, H. Paul. 1975. "Logic and Conversation." In *Syntax and Semantic,* edited by Peter Cole and Jerry L. Morgan, 41–58. New York: Academia.

Guerrero, Maria C. M. de. 1998. "Form and Functions of Inner Speech in Adult Second Language Learning." In *Vygotskian Approaches to Second Language Research,* edited by James P. Lantolf and Gabriela Appel, 83–115. Norwood, N.J.: Ablex.

Gumperz, John J. 1982. *Discourse Strategies.* Cambridge: Cambridge University Press.

Habermas, Jürgen. 1987. *The Theory of Communicative Action,* vol. 2, *Lifeword and System: A Critique of Functionalist Reason.* Translated by Thomas McCarthy. Boston: Beacon.

Haegeman, Liliane. 1991. *Introduction to Government and Binding Theory.* Oxford: Basil Blackwell.

Hall, Joan K. 1993. "The Role of Oral Practices in the Accomplishment of Our Everyday Lives: The Sociocultural Dimension of Interaction with Implications for the Learning of Another Language." *Applied Linguistics* 14: 145–66.

——. 1995. "(Re)creating Our Worlds with Words: A Sociohistorical Perspective on Face-to-Face Interaction." *Applied Linguistics* 16, no. 2: 206–32.

Halliday, Michael A. K. 1973. *Explorations in the Functions of Language.* New York: Elsevier North-Holland.

——. 1976. *Halliday: System and Function in Language,* edited by Gunther R. Kress. London: Oxford University Press.

Halliday, Michael A. K., and Ruqaiya Hasan. 1976. *Cohesion in English.* Cambridge: Cambridge University Press.

Harré, Rom, and Grant Gillett. 1994. *The Discursive Mind.* Thousand Oaks: Sage.

Hatch, Evelyn. 1978. "Acquisition of Syntax in a Second Language." In *Understanding Second and Foreign Language Learning,* edited by Jack Richards, 34–70. Rowley, Mass.: Newbury House.

He, Agnes, and Richard Young. 1998. "Language Proficiency Interviews: A Discourse Approach." In *Talking and Testing: Discourse Approaches to the Assessment of Oral Proficiency,* edited by Richard Young and Agnes He, 1–24. Amsterdam: John Benjamins.

Hoffman, Eva. 1989. *Lost in Translation: A Life in a New Language.* New York: Dutton.

Holquist, Michael. 1990. *Dialogism: Bakhtin and His World*. London: Routledge.

Hymes, Dell. 1972. "On Communicative Competence." In *Sociolinguistics*, edited by John B. Pride and Janet Holems, 269–93. Harmondsworth, U.K.: Penguin.

———. 1974. *Foundations in Sociolinguistics: An Ethnographic Approach*. Philadelphia: Pennsylvania University Press.

Jacoby, Sally, and Elinor Ochs. 1995. "Co-construction: An Introduction." *Research on Language and Social Interaction* 28: 171–83.

Jakobson, Roman. 1972. "Linguistics and Poetics." In *The Structuralists: From Marx to Lévi-Strauss*, edited by Richard de George and Fernande de George, 85–122. Garden City, N.Y.: Anchor.

Johnson, Marysia. 1997. "What Kind of Speech Event Is the Oral Proficiency Interview? Problems of Construct Validity." Ph.D. diss., Georgetown University. Abstract in Dissertation Abstracts International 58–09A (1998), 3492.

———. 2000. "Interaction in Oral Proficiency Interview: Problems of Validity." *Pragmatics* 10, no. 2: 215–31.

———. 2001. *The Art of Nonconversation: A Reexamination of the Oral Proficiency Interview*. New Haven: Yale University Press.

Johnson, Marysia, and Andrea Tyler. 1998. "Re-analyzing the OPI: How Much Does It Look Like Natural Conversation?" In *Taking and Testing: Discourse Approaches to the Assessment of Oral Proficiency*, edited by Richard Young and Agnes He, 27–51. Amsterdam: John Benjamins.

Kozulin, Alex. 1990. *Vygotsky's Psychology: A Biography of Ideas*. New York: Harvester Wheatsheaf.

Kozulin, Alex, and Alexander Venger. 1994. "Immigration Without Adaptation: The Psychological World of Russian Immigrants in Israel." *Mind, Culture, and Activity* 4: 230–38.

Krashen, Stephen D. 1985. *The Input Hypothesis: Issues and Implications*. London: Longman.

———. 1989. "We Acquire Vocabulary and Spelling by Reading: Additional Evidence for the Input Hypothesis." *Modern Language Journal* 73: 440–64.

Krashen, Stephen D., and Tracy D. Terrell. 1983. *The Natural Approach: Language Acquisition in the Classroom*. Oxford: Pergamon.

Lado, Robert. 1957. *Linguistics Across Cultures: Applied Linguistics for Language Teachers*. Ann Arbor: University of Michigan Press.

Lantolf, James P., ed. 2000. *Sociocultural Theory and Second Language Learning*. Oxford: Oxford University Press.

Lantolf, James P., and Gabriela Appel, eds. 1998. *Vygotskian Approaches to Second Language Research*. Norwood, N.J.: Ablex.

Larsen-Freeman, Diane, and Michael H. Long. 1993. *An Introduction to Second Language Acquisition Research*. London: Longman.

Lennon, Paul. 1991. "Error Elimination and Error Fossilization: A Case Study of an Advanced Learner in the L2 Community." *ILT Review of Applied Linguistics* 93–94: 129–51.

Leont'ev, A. A. 1970. "Social and Natural in Semiotics." In *Biological and Social Factors in Psycholinguistics,* edited by John Morton, 122–30. Urbana: University of Illinois Press.

Levinson, Stephen C. 1983. *Pragmatics.* Cambridge: Cambridge University Press.

Lévi-Strauss, Claude. 1972. "History and Dialect." In *The Structuralists: From Marx to Lévi-Strauss,* edited by Richard D. de George and Fernande M. de George, 209–37. Garden City, N.Y.: Doubleday.

Long, Michael H. 1983a. "Linguistic and Conversational Adjustments to Non-Native Speakers." *Studies in Second Language Acquisition* 5, no. 2: 177–93.

———. 1983b. "Native Speaker/Non-Native Speaker Conversation and the Negotiation of Comprehensible Input." *Applied Linguistics* 4, no. 2: 126–41.

———. 1985. "Input and Second Language Acquisition Theory." In *Input in Second Language Acquisition,* edited by Susan M. Gass and Carolyn G. Madden, 337–93. Rowley, Mass.: Newbury House.

———. 1996. "The Role of the Linguistic Environment in Second Language Acquisition." In *Handbook of Language Acquisition,* edited by William C. Ritchie and Tej K. Bhatia, 413–68. San Diego: Academic.

———. 1997. "Construct Validity in SLA Research: A Response to Firth and Wagner." *Modern Language Journal* 81: 318–23.

Long, Michael H., Shunji Inagaki, and Lourdes Ortega. 1998. "The Role of Implicit Negative Feedback in SLA: Models and Recasts in Japanese and Spanish." *Modern Language Journal* 82: 357–71.

Long, Michael H., and Peter Robinson. 1998. "Focus on Form: Theory, Research, and Practice." In *Focus on Form in Classroom Second Language Acquisition,* edited by Catherine Doughty and Jessica Williams, 15–41. Cambridge: Cambridge University Press.

Luria, Alexander, and James V. Wertsch, eds. 1981. *Language and Cognition.* New York: John Wiley.

Mackey, Alison. 1999. "Input, Interaction, and Second Language Development: An Empirical Study of Question Formation in ESL." *Studies in Second Language Acquisition* 21: 557–87.

Mackey, Alison, Susan Gass, and Kim McDonough. 2000. "How Do Learners Perceive Interactional Feedback?" *Studies in Second Language Acquisition* 22: 471–97.

Mackey, Alison, and Jenefer Philp. 1998. "Conversational Interaction and Second Language Development: Recasts, Responses, and Red Herrings?" *Modern Language Journal* 82: 338–56.

Mangubhai, Francis. 1991. "The Processing Behaviors of Adult Second Language Learners and Their Relationship to Second Language Proficiency." *Applied Linguistics* 12: 268–97.

Markee, Numa P. 1994. "Toward an Ethnomethodological Respecification of Second-Language Acquisition Studies." In *Research Methodology in Second-Language Acquisition,* edited by Elaine E. Tarone, Susan M. Gass, and Andrew D. Cohen, 89–116. Hillsdale, N.J.: Lawrence Erlbaum.

McCafferty, Steven G. 1998. "The Use of Private Speech by Adult ESL Learners at Different Levels of Proficiency." In *Vygotskian Approaches to Second Language Research*, edited by James P. Lantolf and Gabriela Appel, 117–34. Norwood, N.J.: Ablex.

McCafferty, Steven G., and Muhammed K. Ahmed. 2000."The Appropriation of Gestures of the Abstract by L2 Learners." In *Sociocultural Theory and Second Language Learning*, edited by James. P. Lantolf, 199–218. Oxford: Oxford University Press.

McLaughlin, Barry. 1990. "Restructuring." *Applied Linguistics* 11, no. 2: 114–28.

McNamara, Tim. 1996. *Measuring Second Language Performance*. London: Addison Wesley Longman.

Newman, Denis, Peg Griffin, and Michael Cole. 1989. *The Construction Zone: Working for Cognitive Change in School*. Cambridge: Cambridge University Press.

Nunan, David. 1989. *Designing Tasks for the Communicative Classroom*. Cambridge: Cambridge University Press.

Ochsner, Robert. 1979. "A Poetics of Second-Language Acquisition." *Language Learning* 29, no. 1: 53–80.

Ohta, Amy Snyder. 2000. "Rethinking Interaction in SLA: Developmentally Appropriate Assistance in the Zone of Proximal Development and the Acquisition of L2 Grammar." In *Sociocultural Theory and Second Language Learning*, edited by James P. Lantolf, 51–78. Oxford: Oxford University Press.

O'Malley, Michael J., Anna Uhl Chamot, Gloria Stewner-Manzanares, Rocco P. Russo, and Lisa Küpper. 1985. "Learning Strategy Applications with Students of English as a Second Language." *TESOL Quarterly* 19: 557–84.

Pavlenko, Aneta, and James P. Lantolf. 2000. "Second Language Learning as Participation and the (Re)construction of Selves." In *Sociocultural Theory and Second Language Learning*, edited by James P. Lantolf, 155–77. Oxford: Oxford University Press.

Pica, Teresa. 1994. "Research on Negotiation: What Does It Reveal About Second-Language Learning Conditions, Processes, and Outcomes?" *Language Learning* 44: 493–527.

Pienemann, Manfred, and Malcolm Johnston. 1987. "Factors Influencing the Development of Language Proficiency." In *Applying Second Language Acquisition Research*, edited by David Nunan, 45–141. Adelaide, Australia: National Curriculum Resource Center.

Pylyshyn, Zenon W. 1973. "The Role of Competence Theories in Cognitive Psychology." *Journal of Psycholinguistic Research* 2: 21–50.

Radford, Andrew. 1988. *Transformational Grammar: A First Course*. Cambridge: Cambridge University Press.

Reddy, Michael J. 1979. "The Conduit Metaphor: A Case of Frame Conflict in Our Language About Language." In *Metaphor and Thought*, edited by Andrew Ortony, 284–324. Cambridge: Cambridge University Press.

Richards, Jack C., and Theodore S. Rodgers. 2001. *Approaches and Methods in Language Teaching.* Cambridge: Cambridge University Press.

Roebuck, Regina. 2000. "Subjects Speak Out: How Learners Position Themselves in a Psycholinguistic Task." In *Sociocultural Theory and Second Language Learning,* edited by James P. Lantolf, 79–95. Oxford: Oxford University Press.

Rommetveit, Ragnar. 1968. *Words, Meanings, and Messages: Theory and Experiments in Psycholinguistics.* New York: Academic.

——. 1974. *On Message Structure: A Framework for the Study of Language and Communication.* London: John Wiley.

——. 1987. "Meaning, Context, and Control: Convergent Trends and Controversial Issues in Current Social-Scientific Research on Human Cognition and Communication." *Inquiry* 30: 79–99.

——. 1992. "Outlines of a Dialogically Based Social-Cognitive Approach to Human Cognition and Communication." In *The Dialogical Alternative: Towards a Theory of Language and Mind,* edited by Astri Heen Wold, 19–44. Oslo: Scandinavian University Press.

Sacks, Harvey, Emanuel A. Schegloff, and Gail Jefferson. 1974. "A Simplest Systematics for the Organization of Turn Taking in Conversation." *Language* 50, no. 4: 696–735.

Schegloff, Emanuel A., Gail Jefferson, and Harvey Sacks. 1977. "The Preference for Self-Correction in the Organization of Repair in Conversation." *Language* 53: 361–82.

Schegloff, Emanuel A., and Harvey Sacks. 1973. "Opening up Closings." *Semiotics* 8: 287–327.

Schiffrin, Deborah. 1990. "Conversational Analysis." *Annual Review of Applied Linguistics* 11: 3–16.

——. 1994. *Approaches to Discourse.* Oxford: Blackwell.

Schinke-Llano, Linda. 1998. "Linguistic Accommodation with LEP and LD Children." In *Vygotskian Approaches to Second Language Research,* edited by James P. Lantol and Gabriela Appel, 57–68. Norwood, N.J.: Ablex.

Schmidt, Richard W. 1983. "Interaction, Acculturation, and the Acquisition of Communicative Competence: A Case Study of an Adult." In *Sociolinguistics and Language Acquisition,* edited by Nessa Wolfson and Elliot Judd, 137–75. Rowley, Mass.: Newbury House.

——. 1990. "The Role of Consciousness in Second Language Learning." *Applied Linguistics* 11, no. 2: 129–58.

——. 1993. "Awareness and Second Language Acquisition." *Annual Review of Applied Linguistics* 13: 206–26.

——. 1994. "Deconstructing Consciousness in Search of Useful Definitions for Applied Linguistics." *AILA Review* 11: 11–26.

Schmidt, Richard W., and Sylvia Nagem Frota. 1986. "Developing Basic Conversational Ability in a Second Language: A Case Study of an Adult Learner of Portuguese." In *Talking to Learn: Conversation in Second Language Acquisition*, edited by Richard R. Day, 237–326. Rowley, Mass.: Newbury House.

Schumann, John H. 1980. "The Acquisition of English Relative Clauses by Second Language Learners." In *Research in Second Language Acquisition*, edited by Robin C. Scarcella and Stephen D. Krashen, 118–31. Rowley, Mass.: Newbury House.

Selinker, Larry. 1972. "Interlanguage." *International Review of Applied Linguistics* 10: 209–31.

Sfard, Ann. 1998. "On Two Metaphors for Learning and the Danger of Choosing Just One." *Educational Researcher* 27: 4–13.

Sharwood Smith, Michael. 1994. *Second Language Learning: Theoretical Foundations*. London: Longman.

Skehan, Peter. 1996. "A Framework for the Implementation of Task-Based Instruction." *Applied Linguistics* 17: 38–62.

Stubbs, Michael. 1983. *Discourse Analysis: The Sociolinguistic Analysis of Natural Language*. Chicago: University of Chicago Press.

Sullivan, Patricia. 2000. "Playfulness as Mediation in Communicative Language Teaching in a Vietnamese Classroom." In *Sociocultural Theory and Second Language Learning*, edited by James P. Lantolf, 115–31. Oxford: Oxford University Press.

Swain, Merrill. 1985. "Communicative Competence: Some Roles of Comprehensible Input and Comprehensible Output in Its Development." In *Input in Second Language Acquisition*, edited by Susan M. Gass and Carolyn G. Madden, 235–53. Rowley, Mass.: Newbury House.

——. 1993. "The Output Hypothesis: Just Speaking and Writing Aren't Enough." *Canadian Modern Language Review* 50: 158–64.

——. 1995. "Three Functions of Output in Second Language Learning." In *Principle and Practice in Applied Linguistics: Studies in Honour of H. G. Widdowson*, edited by Guy Cook and Barbara Seidlhofer, 125–44. Oxford: Oxford University Press.

——. 2000. "The Output Hypothesis and Beyond: Mediating Acquisition Through Collaborative Dialogue." In *Sociocultural Theory and Second Language Learning*, edited by James P. Lantolf, 97–114. Oxford: Oxford University Press.

Tarone, Elaine. 1984. "On the Variability of Interlanguage Systems." In *Universals of Second Language Acquisition*, edited by Fred R. Eckman, Lawrence H. Bell, and Diane Nelson, 3–23. Rowley, Mass.: Newbury House.

Tomlin, Russell S., and Victor Villa. 1994. "Attention in Cognitive Science and Second Language Acquisition." *Studies in Second Language Acquisition* 16: 183–203.

Ushakova, Tatiana N. 1998. "Inner Speech and Second Language Acquisition: An Experimental-Theoretical Approach." In *Vygotskian Approaches to Second Language Research*, edited by James P. Lantolf and Gabriela Appel, 135–56. Norwood, N.J.: Ablex.

van Lier, Leo. 1996. *Interaction in the Language Curriculum: Awareness, Autonomy, and Authenticity*. London: Longman.

——. 2000. "From Input to Affordance: Socio-Interactive Learning from an Ecological Perspective." In *Sociocultural Theory and Second Language Learning,* edited by James P. Lantolf, 245–59. Oxford: Oxford University Press.

VanPatten, Bill. 1996. *Input Processing and Grammar Instruction: Theory and Research.* Norwood, N.J.: Ablex.

VanPatten, Bill, and Teresa Cadierno. 1993. "Explicit Instruction and Input Processing." *Studies in Second Language Acquisition* 15: 225–43.

VanPatten, Bill, and Soile Oikkenon. 1996. "Explanation Versus Structured Input in Processing Instruction." *Studies in Second Language Acquisition* 18: 495–510.

VanPatten, Bill, and Cristina Sanz. 1995. "From Input to Output: Processing Instruction and Communicative Tasks." In *Second Language Acquisition: Theory and Pedagogy,* edited by Fred R. Eckman, Diane Highland, Peter W. Lee, Jean Mileham, and Rita Rutkowsky Weber, 169–85. Mahwah, N.J.: Lawrence Erlbaum.

Vygotsky, Lev S. 1978. *Mind in Society: The Development of Higher Psychological Processes.* Edited by Michael Cole, Vera John-Steiner, Sylvia Scribner, and Ellen Souberman. Cambridge: Harvard University Press.

——. 1981. "The Genesis of Higher Mental Functions." In *The Concept of Activity in Soviet Psychology,* edited by James V. Wertsch, 144–88. Armonk, N.Y.: Sharpe.

——. 1986. *Thought and Language.* Translated by Alex Kozulin. Cambridge: MIT Press.

Wardhaugh, Ronald. 1970. "The Contrastive Analysis Hypothesis." *TESOL Quarterly* 4, no. 2: 123–30.

Washburn, Gay N. 1998. "Working in the ZPD: Fossilized and Nonfossilized Nonnative Speakers." In *Vygotskian Approaches to Second Language Research,* edited by James P. Lantolf and Gabriela Appel, 69–80. Norwood, N.J.: Ablex.

Wertsch, James V. 1985a. *Vygotsky and the Social Formation of Mind.* Cambridge: Harvard University Press.

——. 1985b. *Culture, Communication, and Cognition: Vygotskian Perspectives.* Cambridge: Cambridge University Press.

——. 1990. "The Voice of Rationality in a Sociocultural Approach to Mind." In *Vygotsky and Education: Instructional Implications and Applications of Sociocultural Psychology,* edited by Lois C. Mall, 111–26. Cambridge: Cambridge University Press.

——. 1991. *Voices of the Mind: A Sociocultural Approach to Mediated Action.* Cambridge: Harvard University Press.

——, ed. 1981. *The Concept of Activity in Soviet Psychology.* Armonk, N.Y.: Sharpe.

Wertsch, James V., Pablo del Rio, and Amelia Alvarez, eds. 1995. *Sociocultural Studies of Mind.* Cambridge: Cambridge University Press.

White, Lydia. 1981. "The Responsibility of Grammatical Theory to Acquisitional Data." In *Explanation in Linguistics: The Logical Problem of Language Acquisition,* edited by Norbert Hornstein and David Lightfoot, 241–71. London: Longman.

——. 1989. *Universal Grammar and Second Language Acquisition.* Amsterdam: John Benjamins.

Widdowson, Henry G. 1998. "Context, Community, and Authentic Language." *TESOL Quarterly* 32, no. 4: 705–16.

Wilkins, David A. 1976. *Notional Syllabuses*. Oxford: Oxford University Press.

Wittgenstein, Ludwig. 1958. *Philosophical Investigations*. Translated by G. E. M. Anscombe. New York: Macmillan.

——. 1980. *Culture and Value*. Translated by Peter Winch. Oxford: Basil Blackwell.

Wood, David S., Jerome S. Bruner, and Gail Ross. 1976. "The Role of Tutoring in Problem Solving." *Journal of Child Psychology and Psychiatry* 17: 89–100.

Young, Richard. 1999. "Sociolinguistic Approaches to SLA." *Annual Review of Applied Linguistics* 19: 105–32.

Zinchenko, Vladimir P. 1995. "Cultural-Historical Psychology and the Psychological Theory of Activity: Retrospect and Prospect." In *Sociocultural Studies of Mind*, edited by James V. Wertsch, Pablo del Rio, and Amelia Alvarez, 37–55. Cambridge: Cambridge University Press.

Index